A Brief Commentary on the Apocalypse

by Sylvester Bliss

CONTENTS

PREFACE.

The Apocalypse should be regarded as a peculiarly interesting portion of scripture: a blessing being promised those who read, hear, and keep the things which are written therein. It has been subjected to so many contradictory interpretations, that any attempt to comprehend its meaning is often regarded with distrust; and the impression has become very prevalent, that it is a "sealed book,"--that its meaning is so hidden in unintelligible symbols, that very little can be known respecting it; and that to attempt to unfold its meaning, is to tread presumptuously on forbidden ground.

The attention of the Christian community has been called more of late to its study, by the publication of several elaborate Expositions. One in two large volumes, 8vo., by Prof. Stuart, was published at Andover, Mass., in 1845. A large 8vo. volume, by David N. Lord, was issued from the press of the Harpers, in New York, in 1847; and a smaller work, by Rev. Thomas Wickes, appeared in that city in 1851. These are the more important works on the subject which have been published in this country. In England, the "Hor?Apocalyptic?" by the Rev. E. B. Elliott, A.M., late Vicar of Tuxford, and fellow of Trinity College, Cambridge, has passed through several editions,--the fourth of which, in four large vols. 8vo., was published in London, in 1851. These works, with the writings of Habershon, Cunningham, Croly, Bickersteth, Birks, Brooks, Keith, and other distinguished English writers, have caused the study of the Apocalypse to be regarded with more favor of late than heretofore.

The Expositions of MR. LORD have thrown much light on the nature and laws of symbols, by unfolding the principles in accordance with which they are used. The evolving of these has removed from many passages the obscurity which had before caused them to be regarded as enigmatical. There are, doubtless, many portions of the Apocalypse, the meaning of which is as yet only dimly perceived, and which will be more clearly unfolded by the transpiring of future events; and it would be arrogant to claim that its interpretation had been freed from all perplexities. But it is believed that it may be as profitably and as satisfactorily studied as other portions of Scripture; and that the reader may feel an assurance of approximating to a knowledge of the true meaning of its symbolic teachings.

The Bible is its own interpreter; and when practicable, scripture should be explained by scripture. The meaning imputed to any passage must never contradict, but must harmonize with that of parallel texts. In illustrating the several references in the Apocalypse to the same events and epochs, a repetition of scripture is somewhat unavoidable.

These pages have resulted from notes prepared in a familiar course of Bible-class instruction, where the study of brevity was necessary. Without designing to speak dogmatically, the didactic was found the more direct and simple mode of expression. In presenting this exposition, merely as the opinion of the writer, it is with the hope that it will give, in a small compass, a common-sense view of the intricacies of this book, and be acceptable to those interested in the study of prophecy.

ELEMENTS OF PROPHETIC INTERPRETATION.

1. THE GRAMMAR of any science is a development of the principles by which it is governed. As the science of interpretation must be founded on some fixed and uniform laws, the unfolding of these is the first step in the study of prophecy.

2. BIBLICAL EXEGESIS and SACRED HERMENEUTICS, are terms applied to the science of interpretation, or of learning the meaning of Biblical words and phrases.

3. THE USUS LOQUENDI, is the usual mode of speaking. When applied to the Scriptures, it denotes the general scriptural use of words.

4. To learn the meaning of scriptural terms, their general use must be ascertained, by comparing their contexts in the several places of their occurrence.

5. PROPHECY is the prediction of a future event. The term sometimes denotes a book of prophecies (Rev. 22:18); and sometimes a history.--2 Chron. 9:29.

6. CONSECUTIVE Prophecy gives the succession of future events in the order in which they will transpire. Examples.--See Dan. 2d, 7th, 8th, 11th, and Rev. 6th and 7th, 9th to the 11th; 12th and 15th, &c.

7. DISCURSIVE Prophecy presents future events, irrespective of the order of their occurrence. Examples.--ISAIAH and the minor prophets.

8. CONDITIONAL Prophecy is when the fulfilment is dependent on the compliance of those to whom the promise is made, with the conditions on which it is given. Examples.--"If ye walk in my statutes and keep my commandments, and do them: then I will give you rain in due season, and the land shall yield her increase, and the trees of the field shall yield their fruit." Lev. 26:3, 4. "But if ye will not hearken unto me, and will not do all these commandments; and if ye shall despise my statutes, or if your soul abhor my judgments, so that ye will not do all my commandments, but that ye break my covenant: I also will do this unto you, I will even appoint over you terror, consumption, and the burning ague, that shall consume the eyes, and cause sorrow of heart: and ye shall sow your seed in vain; for your enemies shall eat it." Ib. 14-16.

"And it shall come to pass, if thou shalt hearken diligently unto the voice of the Lord thy God, to observe and to do all his commandments which I command thee this day: that the Lord thy God will set thee on high above all nations of the earth: and all these blessings shall come on thee, and overtake thee, if thou shalt hearken unto the voice of the Lord thy God." Deut. 28:1, 2. "But it shall come to pass, if thou wilt not hearken unto the voice of the Lord thy God, to observe to do all his commandments and his statutes which I command thee this day: that all these curses shall come upon thee, and overtake thee," &c. Ib. 15.

Predictions of mere national prosperity, or adversity, are usually conditional. When the condition is not expressed, it is implied. Example.-- The Lord said unto Jonah, "Arise, go unto Nineveh, that great city, and preach unto it the preaching that I bid thee.... And Jonah began to enter into the city a day's journey, and he cried, and said, Yet forty days, and Nineveh shall be overthrown. So the people of Nineveh believed God, and proclaimed a fast, and put on sackcloth, from the greatest of them even to the least of them.... And God saw their works, that they turned from their evil way; and God repented of the evil that he had said that he would do unto them: and he did it not."

For all cases of this kind, the Lord has given the following general RULE: "At what instant I shall speak concerning a nation, and concerning a kingdom, to pluck up, and to pull down, and to destroy it: if that nation against whom I have pronounced turn from their evil, I will repent of the evil that I thought to do unto them. And at what instant I shall speak concerning a nation, and concerning a kingdom, to build and to plant it; if it do evil in my sight, that it obey not my voice, then I will repent of the good wherewith I said I would benefit them." Jer. 18:7-10.

9. UNCONDITIONAL Prophecy includes all predictions which are absolute in their nature. Examples.--"But as truly as I live, all the earth shall be filled with the glory of the Lord." Num. 14:21.

"For behold, the darkness shall cover the earth, and gross darkness the people: but the Lord shall arise upon thee, and his glory shall be seen upon thee. And the Gentiles shall come to thy light, and kings to the brightness of thy rising.... For the nation and kingdom that will not serve thee shall perish; yea, those nations shall be utterly wasted.... Thy people also shall be all righteous: they shall inherit the land for ever, the branch of my planting, the work of my hands, that I may be glorified." Isa. 60:2, 3, 12, 21.

"But in the last days it shall come to pass, that the mountain of the house of the Lord shall be established in the top of the mountains, and it shall be exalted above the hills; and people shall flow unto it." Micah 4:1.

10. A VISION is a revelation from GOD, supernaturally presented. Future events are made to pass before the mind of the seer, as if actually transpiring. Examples.--See the prophecies of ISAIAH, AMOS, OBADIAH, &c.

11. A SYMBOLIC VISION is where the future events, instead of being presented to the mind of the prophet, are represented by analogous objects. Examples.--The prophecies of EZEKIEL, DANIEL, ZECHARIAH, and JOHN, are of this kind.

12. A LITERAL Prophecy is where the prediction is given in words used according to their primary and natural import. Examples.--Num. 14:21-35; Jer. 25:1-33.

13. Prophecy is figurative when it abounds in tropes, as in much of ISAIAH and the minor prophets; and it is symbolic, when symbols instead of the objects themselves are presented--as in DANIEL and JOHN.

14. POETRY is writing thus constituted by the metrical or rhythmical structure of its sentences; and is not necessarily any more figurative or obscure than prose writing. It is, also, a term sometimes applied to the language of excited imagination and feeling.

The Poetry of the Bible consists in Hebrew parallelisms, where the idea of the preceding line is repeated, or contrasted, in the succeeding one. Examples.--The Psalms, ISAIAH, and other prophets.

15. HIGHLY FIGURATIVE, or SYMBOLIC Prophecies--the laws and use of Tropes and Symbols being understood are not necessarily more equivocal, enigmatical or obscure, than those which are literal.

16. LITERAL FULFILMENT of prophecy is prophecy fulfilled in accordance with the grammatical interpretation of its language.

17. LITERAL INTERPRETATION, when technically applied to the interpretation of prophecy, is not opposed to tropes or figures of speech, but to spiritual interpretation. It interprets the language of the Scriptures, as similar language would be interpreted in all other writings.

18. SPIRITUAL INTERPRETATION (mystical) seeks, in the language of Scripture, a meaning that is not expressed by any of the ordinary rules of language. It sets at defiance all the laws of language, and makes fancy the interpreter of prophecy. "It subjects clear predictions to an exegetical alembic that effectually subtilizes and evaporates their meaning."--Bush.

19. ULTRA LITERAL INTERPRETATION is a disregard of the peculiarities of symbols and of the several kinds of tropes--understanding them as if they were literally expressed.

20. SYMBOLS and TROPES are literally explained, when interpreted in accordance with the grammatical laws which respectively govern their use.

21. PROPHETIC SYMBOLS are objects, real or imaginary, representative of agents or objects possessing analogous characteristics. All agents or objects seen in symbolic visions are symbols. The inspired explanations of symbols are always literal, except when they are affirmed to be the same as some other symbol which represents the same object, as in Rev. 17:9.

22. LAWS OF SYMBOLS.

I. "The Symbol and that which it represents resemble each other in the station they fill, the relation they sustain, and the agencies they exert in their respective spheres."--Lord.

II. The Symbol and that which it represents are of the same, or they are of different species, kinds, or rank, according to the nature and use of the symbol.

III. "When the Symbol is of such nature, or is used in such a relation that it can properly symbolise something different from itself, the representative and that which it represents, while the counterpart of each other, are of different species, kinds, or rank."--Lord.

Example.--Dan. 7:3, beasts; v. 17, governments.

IV. "Symbols that are of such a nature, station or relation, that there is nothing of an analogous kind that they can represent, symbolize agents, objects, acts, or events of their own kind."--Ib. Example.--Dan. 7:9.

V. "When the Symbol and that which it symbolizes differ from each other, the correspondence between the representative and that which it represents, still extends to their chief parts; and the elements or parts of the symbols denote corresponding parts in that which is symbolized."--Ib.

VI. "The Names of Symbols are their literal and proper names, not metaphorical titles."--Ib.

VII. "A single agent, in many instances, symbolizes a body and succession of agents."--Ib.

VIII. Symbols of the same kind, and used in the same relations, always represent one class of objects; and when the office of a symbol has been once shown, the same symbol, similarly used, always fills a like office. They are never used arbitrarily.

IX. While like symbols represent like objects, the same agents are often indicated by different symbols.

Thus, a church may be symbolized by a city and a woman; and government, by a beast and a mountain, &c.

23. INSPIRED EXPLANATIONS OF SYMBOLIC REPRESENTATIONS:--

Ancient of Days--The Most High.--Dan. 7:9, 22. Candlesticks--Churches.--Rev. 1:20. Carpenters--Destroyers of governments.--Zech. 1:21. Days--

Years.--Num. 14:34. Ezek. 4:4-6. Horns, of a wild beast--Kings or kingdoms succeeding to a divided empire.--Dan. 8:22 and 7:24. Heads, of a wild beast--Kings or forms of government.--Rev. 17:9, 10. Image, of different metals--A succession of governments.--Dan. 2:37-42. Incense, or odors--Prayers.--Rev. 5:8 and 8:4. Lamb, the--Christ.--Rev. 5:6, 9, 10. Lamb's wife--Risen saints.--Rev. 19:7, 8. Lake of fire and brimstone--The place of the second death.--Rev. 20:15. Likeness of a man--The Lord.-- Ezek. 1:26, 28, and 8:2, 4. Linen, fine and clean--Righteousness of saints-- Rev. 19:8. Mountains--Kings, or forms of government.--Rev. 17:9, 10. New Jerusalem--The redeemed Church, or the Bride, the Lamb's wife.--Rev. 21:9, 10. Revivification of dry bones--Resurrection of the dead.--Ezek. 37:11, 12. Stars--Angels, i.e., messengers of the churches.--Rev. 1:20. Souls of martyrs living again--The first resurrection.--Rev. 20:4, 5. Stone, becoming a mountain--Kingdom of God.--Dan. 2:45. Waters--Peoples.-- Rev. 17:15. Wild Beasts--Governments.--Dan. 7:17. Woman--A city.--Rev. 17:18. Explained to be a church.--21:9, 10.

24. TROPES are figures of various kinds, used to illustrate the subjects to which they are applied.--They embrace the Simile, Metaphor, Prosopopoeia, Apostrophe, Synecdoche, Allegory, &c.

25. LAWS OF FIGURES--(a.) "The terms in which they are expressed are used in their ordinary and literal sense."--Lord.

(b.) "The agents or objects to which figures are applied are always expressly mentioned. Figures, in that respect, differ wholly from symbols, which never formally indicate, unless an interpretation is given, who the agents, or what the objects are which they represent."--Ib.

(c.) "The figurative terms are always predicates, or are employed in affirming something of some other agent or object; and are therefore either nouns, verbs, adjectives or adverbs."--Ib.

(d.) "As their terms are used literally, the figure lies, when they are employed in an unusual manner, simply in their being applied to objects to which they do not properly belong."--Ib.

(e.) "They are used accordingly in all such cases for the purpose of illustration, and their explication is accomplished, not by assigning to them some new and extraordinary meaning, but simply by conjoining with them the terms of a comparison which expresses the relation in which they are employed."--Ib.

(f.) "It is in metaphors and personification only that acts and qualities are ascribed to agents and objects that are incompatible with their nature; or do not properly belong to them."--Ib. Theo. & Lit. Jour., vol. 1, p. 354.

26. A SIMILE, or comparison, is an affirmation that one agent, object, or act, is like, or as, another,--there being a real or imaginary resemblance. Sometimes only the mere fact of a resemblance is affirmed. At others, the nature of the resemblance is indicated.

Examples.--"As for man, his days are as grass." Psa. 103:15. "Whose garment was white as snow." Dan. 7:9.

27. ANTITHESIS is a contrast, or placing in opposite lights things dissimilar.

Example.--"The wicked are overthrown and are not; but the house of the righteous shall stand." Prov. 12:7.

28. A METAPHOR is a simile comprised in a word, without the sign of comparison. It is an affirmation of an object, incompatible with its nature-- i.e., it affirms that an object is, what literally it is only like; or attributes to it acts, to which its acts only bear a resemblance.

Examples.--"He is the Rock." Deut. 32:4. "Her gates shall lament and mourn." Isa. 3:25.

A metaphor may be a simple affirmation of what an object is, or it may embrace "the agent, the act, the object, and the effect of an action."--Lord.

(a.) When an object is affirmed to be what it only resembles, that of which the affirmation is made is always literally expressed.

(b.) "When a nature is ascribed to an object that does not belong to it, the acts or results affirmed to it are proper to that imputed nature, not to its own."--Lord.

(c.) "The meaning of a metaphorical passage is precisely what it would be if a comparison only were affirmed."--Ib.

29. AN ELLIPTICAL METAPHOR is where the figure is incomplete. An object, instead of being affirmed to be what it only resembles, is introduced by the name proper only to that resemblance. The literal name of the object and the affirmation to complete the figure are to be supplied.

To find the meaning of an elliptical metaphor, trace the word through the Bible, and find to what object such metaphorical term is applied. Example.--"And in that day there shall be a Root of JESSE, which shall stand for an ensign of the people." Isa. 11:10. Explanation.--"I [JESUS] am the Root and the offspring of DAVID." Rev. 22:16.

30. PROSOPOEIA, or PERSONIFICATION, is an address to an inanimate object, as if it were a person, and had intelligence.--Lord. Example.--"Give ear, O ye heavens, and I will speak; and hear, O earth, the words of my mouth." Deut. 32:1.

31. AN APOSTROPHE is a digression from the order of any discourse, and a direct address to the persons of whom it treats, or to those who are to form a judgment respecting the subject of which it treats.--Lord. Example.--"Hear the word of the LORD, ye rulers of Sodom: give ear unto the law of our GOD, ye people of Gomorrah." Isa. 1:10.

32. AN ALLEGORY is a narrative in which the subject of the discourse is described by an analogous subject, resembling it in its characteristics and circumstances--the subject of which it is descriptive being indicated in its connection. Examples.--See Ezek. 31:3-9; Ps. 80:8-16; Jud. 9:8-15.

Past historical events, instead of supposititious ones, are sometimes used for illustration. When thus used they serve as allegories, without affecting their original historical significance. Example.--Gal. 4: 22-31. See also Rom. 9:7, 8; 1 Cor. 9:9, 10, and 10:11.

33. A PARABLE is a similitude taken from natural things, to instruct us in the knowledge of spiritual. Examples.--Matt. 13th, and 21:28-41.

The Parable differs from the Allegory in that the acts ascribed are appropriate to the agents to which they are attributed. In the Allegory, acts may be ascribed to real objects which are not natural to those objects. Example.--See Judges 9:7-15.

The Parable is sometimes used to denote a prophecy, (Num. 23:7); sometimes a discourse, (Job 27:1); sometimes a lamentation, (Micah 2:4); sometimes a proverb, or wise saying, (Prov. 26:7); and sometimes to indicate that a thing is apocryphal. Ezek. 20:49. The terms parable and allegory, are often wrongfully applied.

34. A RIDDLE is an enigma--something to be guessed. Example.--See Judges 14:24-18. It is sometimes used to denote an allegory. Ezek. 17:1-10.

35. TYPES are emblems--greater events in the future being prefigured by typical observances, "which are a shadow of good things to come." Col. 2:17.

36. THE HYPOCATASTASIS, or substitution, is a figure introduced by Mr. LORD, in which the objects, or agents, of one class are, without any formal notice, employed in the place of the persons or things of which the passages in which they occur treat; and they are exhibited either as exerting, or as subjected to an agency proper to their nature, in order to represent by analogy, the agency which those persons are to exert, or of which those things are to be the subjects. Example.--"O, my people, they which lead thee cause thee to err, and destroy the way of thy paths."--Isa. 3:12,-- expressive of the manner in which they were misled by their rulers and kept from the truth.

37. A METONYMY is a reversion, or the use of a noun to express that with which it is intimately connected, instead of using the term which would literally express the idea. Thus the cause is used for the effect, the effect for the cause, the thing containing for that which is contained in it, &c. Example.--"Ye have eaten up the vineyard." Isa. 3:14--meaning the fruit of the vineyard.

38. A SYNECDOCHE is the use of a word expressive of a part, to signify the whole; or that expressive of the whole, to denote only a part--as the genus for the species, or the species for the genus, &c. Example.--"Man dieth and wasteth away; yea man giveth up the ghost, and where is he?" Job 14:10.

39. A HYPERBOLE is an exaggeration in which more is expressed than is intended to be understood. Example.--"I suppose that even the world itself could not contain the books that should be written." John 21:25--meaning that a great number might be written.

40. IRONY is the utterance of pointed remarks, contrary to the actual thoughts of the speaker or writer--not to deceive, but to add force to the remark. Examples.--"No doubt but ye are the people, and wisdom shall die with you." Job 12:2.

"And it came to pass at noon, that Elijah mocked them, and said, Cry aloud: for he is a god: either he is talking, or he is pursuing, or he is in a journey, or peradventure he sleepeth and must be awaked." 1 Kings 18:27.

41. THE INTERROGATION--while its legitimate use is to ask a question-- is also used to affirm or deny with great emphasis. Affirmative interrogations usually have no or not in connection with the verb. Example.--"Is not God in the height of the heavens?" Job 22:12. Examples of a negative.--"Shall the earth be made to bring forth in one day? or shall a nation be born at once?" Isa. 66:8. "Can the rush grow up without mire?" Job 8:11.

42. EXCLAMATIONS are digressions from the order of a discourse or

writing, to give expression to the emotions of the speaker, or writer. Example.--"O that I had wings like a dove! for then would I fly away and be at rest!" Psa. 55:6.

43. FABLES are fictions--additions to the word of GOD. All false theories and doctrines supposed to be based on the Bible, all interpretations of Scripture which do violence to the laws of language and falsify their meaning, and all opinions which are the result of mere traditions and doctrines of men, are to be classed as fables. Mark 7:8-13; 1 Pet. 1:18; 1 Tim. 1:4; 4:7; Tit. 1:14.

44. SYNCHRONOUS SCRIPTURES are the several passages which have reference to any one and the same event.

Each portion of Scripture respecting any subject, must be considered in connection with all the Scriptures that refer to the same subject.--Compare, for example, Dan. 2:34, 35, 44; 7:18, 27; Matt. 6:10; 13:37-43; 35:34; 1 Tim. 4:1; Rev. 11:15-18.

EXPOSITION OF THE APOCALYPSE.

The Title of the Book.

"The Revelation of Jesus Christ, which God gave to him, to show to his servants things which must shortly come to pass; and sending, he signified them through his angel to his servant John: who testified the word of God, and the testimony of Jesus Christ, and whatever he saw."--Rev. 1:1, 2.--Prof. Whiting's Translation.

"The very title of John's predictions, Apocalypse, implies the unveiling or 'revelation' of the mystic and hidden sense of the prophetic oracles, previously uttered by his inspired predecessors."--PROF. BUSH.

"The {~GREEK CAPITAL LETTER ALPHA~}{~GREEK SMALL LETTER PI~}{~GREEK SMALL LETTER OMICRON~}{~GREEK SMALL LETTER KAPPA~}{~GREEK SMALL LETTER ALPHA~}

{~GREEK SMALL LETTER LAMDA~}{~GREEK SMALL LETTER UPSILON~}{~GREEK SMALL LETTER PSI~}{~GREEK SMALL LETTER IOTA~}{~GREEK SMALL LETTER FINAL SIGMA~}, from which we have our word Apocalypse, signifies, literally, a revelation, or discovery, of what was concealed, or hidden."--DR. CLARKE.

The work of the apostles was "to make all men see what is the fellowship of the mystery, which, from the beginning of the world, hath been hid in God, who created all things by Jesus Christ," (Eph. 3:9); "even the mystery which hath been hid from ages and from generations, but now is made manifest to his saints," Col. 1:26. The entire record of the New Testament, is a revelation that God "hath in these last days spoken unto us by his Son;" in distinction from the records of the Old Testament, which He, "at sundry times and in divers manners, spake in time past unto the fathers by the prophets," Heb. 1:1. But the closing book of the new series is called, in distinction from the others, "THE REVELATION OF JESUS CHRIST."

It contains the "many things" he had to say to his disciples, in addition to those recorded by the evangelists; but which they could not then bear, John 16:12. It is the revelation "which God gave unto him;" for "there is a God in heaven that revealeth secrets, and maketh known ... what shall be in the latter days," Dan. 2:28. God communicated by his servants the prophets what should "come to pass hereafter," by visions which were "certain," and by "the interpretation thereof" which was "sure," Dan. 2:46. But Daniel was commanded to "shut up the words, and seal the book, even to the time of the end," when many should "run to and fro," and knowledge should "be increased." And it was added, "Go thy way, Daniel; for the words are closed up and sealed till the time of the end: Many shall be purified and made white, and tried; but the wicked shall do wickedly: and none of the wicked shall understand; but the wise shall understand." Dan. 12:4, 9, 10.

It will thus be seen, that provision had been made for the future unveiling of what was left obscure in the predictions of the Old Testament writers; and for the unsealing of what was then closed up and sealed. This revelation must come from God; for the Saviour has testified, that "of that day and hour knoweth no man, no, not the angels of heaven, but my Father only."

Matt. 24:36. "The secret things belong unto the Lord our God: but those things which are revealed belong unto us and to our children forever." Deut. 29:29.

As God had provided for a more full "revelation" respecting the events of the future, it was necessary that it should be communicated through "the appointed Heir of all things," by whom he was to speak in the last days, Heb. 1:2. The BAPTIST said of Christ, that "what he hath seen and heard, this he testifieth," John 3:22. And the Saviour said of him by whom he was sent, "I speak to the world those things which I have heard of him," Ib. 8:2, 6. And again, he saith, "I have not spoken of myself; but the Father which sent me, he gave me a commandment; what I should say, and what I should speak," Ib. 12:49. "The Lion of the tribe of Judah, the Root of David, hath prevailed to open the book, and to loose the seven seals thereof," Rev. 5:5.

The design of God in giving this additional revelation, was that he might "show unto his servants things which must shortly come to pass;" for "surely the Lord God doeth nothing, but he revealeth his secrets unto his servants the prophets," Amos 3:7. And he saith, "I have told you before it come to pass, that when it is come to pass ye might believe," John 14:29. When the old world was to be destroyed by water, "Noah, being warned of God of things not seen as yet, prepared an ark to the saving of his house," Heb. 11:7. And when the Lord had purposed the destruction of Sodom, he said, "Shall I hide from Abraham that thing which I do?" and angels were sent to Lot, that he might say to his children, "Up get ye out of this place; for the Lord will destroy this city," Gen. 18:17, and 19:14. So of the times and seasons of the second advent: while "the day of the Lord so cometh as a thief in the night," he has said to his chosen ones, "Ye brethren are not in darkness that that day should overtake you as a thief," 1 Thess. 5:1-4. He has condescended to give his people "a more sure word of prophecy: whereunto ye do well that ye take heed, as unto a light that shineth in a dark place, until the day dawn, and the day star arise in your hearts," 2 Pet. 1:19. Therefore it was said to John, "I will show thee things which must be hereafter," Rev. 4:1; which things were shortly to begin to come to pass,-- they being a series of successive events, commencing near the time in which John wrote, and extending to the end of the world and the establishment of the everlasting kingdom.

These were shown to John by symbolic representations, in a series of visions, the import of which was signified to him by an angelic interpreter. Said the Saviour, "I, Jesus, have sent my angel to testify unto you these things in the churches," 22:16. And these things were not to be sealed up, like the words of Daniel; for John was commanded to "seal not the sayings of the prophecy of this book: for the time is at hand," 22:10. He recorded the words which God thus gave him,--"the testimony of Jesus Christ, and of all things that he saw." He has given us, in graphic language, such descriptions of the visions shown, that we can easily imagine the symbols which he saw; and we have the inspired explanations of those which were "signified" to him. Therefore we may read, and receive the blessings promised to those who keep this testimony of Jesus.

The Benediction.

"Happy is he, who readeth, and those, who hear the words of this prophecy, and keep the things, written in it: for the season is near." Rev. 1:3.

Those who teach that the Apocalypse is a "sealed book," most clearly contradict the testimony of Christ respecting it. To discourage the study of it, is to treat with neglect, and to despise what God has spoken in these last days by his Son, Heb. 1:2; of whom it is said: "See that ye refuse not him that speaketh; for if they escaped not who refused him who spake on earth, much more shall not we escape, if we turn away from him that speaketh from heaven," Heb. 12:25. Those who thus neglect it, cannot regard the blessing promised to those who read, hear, and keep its sayings.

The Apocalypse is not to be undervalued as unprofitable; for "all scripture is given by inspiration of God, and is profitable for doctrine, for reproof, for correction, for instruction in righteousness: that the man of God may be perfect, thoroughly furnished unto all good works," 2 Tim. 3:16, 17. "For whatsoever things were written aforetime, were written for our learning, that we through patience and comfort of the scriptures might have hope," Rom. 15:4. "Search the scriptures; for in them ye think ye have eternal life:

and they are they which testify of me," John 5:39. "Thus saith the Lord, the Holy One of Israel, and his Maker, Ask me of things to come concerning my sons, and concerning the work of my hands command ye me," Isa. 45:11. "Behold, I come quickly: blessed is he that keepeth the sayings of the prophecy of this book," Rev. 22:7.

John's Salutation to the Churches.

"John to the seven congregations in Asia: grace be to you and peace, from Him who is, and who was, and who is to be; and from the seven Spirits, that are before his throne; and from Jesus Christ, the faithful Witness, and the First-born of the dead, and the Ruler of the kings of the earth. To him who loved us, and washed us from our sins in his own blood, and hath made us kings and priests to God even his father: to him be glory and dominion for ever and ever. Amen. Behold, he cometh with clouds; and every eye will see him, and those, who pierced him: and all the tribes of the earth will wail because of him. Yea, so be it! I am the Alpha and the Omega, saith the Lord God, who is, and who was, and who is to be, the Almighty."--Rev. 1:4-8.

The seven churches to which John sends salutation, were those of Ephesus, Smyrna, Pergamos, Thyatira, Sardis, Philadelphia, and Laodicea, 1:11. The Asia, in which they were situated, was a province in Asia Minor, distinct from Pontus, Gallatia, and Bithynia; which also were in Asia Minor, 1 Pet. 1:1, and Acts 2:9. Of the province of Asia, Ephesus was the capital, and was the principal place of John's residence. The seven cities which contained those churches, were situated in a kind of amphitheatre, surrounded by mountains. Smyrna was 46 miles north of Ephesus, and Pergamos 64 miles; Thyatira was 48 miles to the east, and Sardis 33 miles; Philadelphia 27 miles to the south, and Laodicea 42 miles. These churches had all been under the general supervision of John's ministry; and for this reason, doubtless, they are especially designated, instead of those with which he had not been so intimately connected.

John writes to the seven churches, in obedience to the command,--"What thou seest, write in a book, and send it unto the seven churches which are in Asia," 1:11. He seems to have written what he saw, at the time of its exhibition, and not at the close of the entire presentation; for when he was about to write the discordant utterances of "the seven thunders," he was told to "write them not," 10:4.

John observes the oriental custom of placing his name at the commencement, instead of the close of his communication. Few persons now deny that this was John the Evangelist. Irenæus, who was born only about 30 years after the death of John, speaks of the writer of the Apocalypse, as "the disciple of Christ,--that same John that leaned on his breast at the last supper."

Most beautiful reference is here made to the attributes of DEITY: "Him who is, and who was, and who is to be," can be no other than the great Preexistent, who said to Moses, "I AM THAT I AM," Ex. 13:14.

The seven Spirits, would seem to be irrelevantly placed between the Father and the Son,--the place always occupied by the Holy Spirit, when spoken of in connection with them,--if they were merely seven angels. Grace would also seem to be irreverently invoked from such,--its presence being implied where it is invoked,--unless they are expressive of the Holy Spirit, in which grace is inherent, and from whom it may be communicated; as it may not be from angels. Seven is a full and perfect number, and it may be here used because in another place "seven lamps of fire burning before the throne" are symbolic of "the seven Spirits of God," (4:5); which, if angels, would be expressly named, as in other inspired explanations,--as they are in that of the stars, 1:20. A burning flame is often used as a symbol of the Holy Spirit. Thus, when God would make a covenant with Abraham, and the victims between which the covenanting parties were to pass, were divided, the presence of God was symbolized by "a burning lamp that passed between those pieces," Gen. 15:17. And the descent of the Holy Spirit on the day of Pentecost, was manifested by "cloven tongues, like as of fire," which "sat upon each of them," Acts 2:3. In Zechariah 3:9, we read of the symbol of a stone laid before Joshua, that on it were engraved "seven eyes," which "are the eyes of the Lord which run to and fro, through the whole earth," (Zech. 4:10);--an expressive figure of God's Omniscience. The same is symbolized in Rev. 5:6, by the "seven eyes" of the LAMB.

Jesus Christ is the faithful Witness. He "was faithful to him that appointed him," (Heb. 3:2); and he was given as a Witness to the people, a Leader and Commander to the people, Isa. 55:4. He is the "first-begotten of the dead," having "risen from the dead, and become the first fruits of them that slept," 1 Cor. 15:20: he is "declared to be the Son of God, with power according to the spirit of holiness, by the resurrection from the dead," Rom. 1:4. He is "the Prince of the kings of the earth," the "King of kings and Lord of lords," 19:16; "all kings shall fall down before him: all nations shall serve him," Psa. 72:11. He hath shown how he "loved us," by giving himself for us, (Gal. 2:20); and hath cleansed his people from all sin, not "by the blood of goats and calves, but by his own blood, he entered in once into the holy place, having obtained eternal redemption for us," Heb. 9:12. He has redeemed us to God "out of every kindred, and tongue, and people, and nation," Rev. 5:9. He is the one who is to come in the clouds of heaven, in resplendent majesty, to reward his saints, and to destroy those who destroy the earth, 11:18. The announcement that he "cometh with clouds" is as if John had said that what he was commanded to write, was a revelation of the events which were to precede and usher in that coming.

Christ's Annunciation.

"I John, your brother, and partner in the affliction, and kingdom and patience of Jesus Christ, was in the island called Patmos, for the word of God, and for the testimony of Jesus Christ. I was in the Spirit on the Lord's day, and heard behind me a great voice, like that of a trumpet, saying, What thou seest, write in a book, and send it to the seven congregations, to Ephesus, and to Smyrna, and to Pergamos, and to Thyatira, and to Sardis, and to Philadelphia, and to Laodicea."--Rev. 1:9-11.

This gives a clue to the date of the Apocalypse. It was written when John was in the Isle of Patmos: "It is the general testimony of ancient authors, that St. John was banished into Patmos in the time of Domitian, in the latter part of his reign, and restored by his successor, Nerva. But the book could not be published till after John's release, and return to Ephesus, in Asia. Domitian died in 96, and his persecution did not commence till near the close of his reign."--DR. CLARKE.

"DOMITIAN, having exercised his cruelty against many, and unjustly slain no small number of noble and illustrious men at Rome, ... at length established himself as the successor of NERO, in his hatred and hostility to GOD. He was the second that raised a persecution against us. In this persecution, it is handed down by tradition, that the apostle and evangelist, JOHN, ... was condemned to dwell on the island of Patmos. IRENÆUS, indeed, in his fifth book against the heresies, where he speaks of the calculation formed on the epithet of Antichrist, in the above-mentioned Revelation of JOHN, speaks in the following manner respecting him: 'If, however, it were necessary to proclaim his name (i.e. Antichrist's), openly at the present time, it would have been declared by him who saw the Revelation, for it was not long since it was seen, but almost in our own times, at the close of DOMITIAN's reign.' "--EUSEBIUS.

Prof. Stuart, who dissents from the opinion, admits that "a majority of the older critics have been inclined to adopt the opinion of Irenes, viz.: that it was written during the reign of Domitian, i.e., during the last part of the first century, or in A. D. 95 or 96."--Com. Apoc., V. I., p. 263.

John's adherence to the word and testimony of Christ, had caused his banishment--as others "were slain--for the word of God, and for the testimony which they held," (6:9); and whose living again and reigning with Christ, was subsequently shown John in a vision, 20:4.

John was in the spirit; i.e., he was in a state of prophetic ecstasy, in which he was, as it were, caught away from a realization of the actual and the present, and shown "the things which must be hereafter." It was on the "Lord's day," the first day of the week, which was so called because on that day the Lord arose from the dead. It was a day which has been observed by all Christians in especial remembrance of that event. John does not appear to have anticipated any such announcement, until he was suddenly startled from his meditation by a voice in trumpet tones, announcing itself by the titles of Christ, and commanding him to write to the churches what he saw. Hearing the voice, he turned to see who had spoken to him, and beheld a

Vision of Christ.

"And I turned to see the voice, that spoke with me. And having turned, I saw seven golden lamp-stands; and in the midst of the seven lamp-stands one like a Son of man, clothed with a garment reaching the feet, and girded around the breasts with a golden girdle. His head, even his hair, was white like white wool, like snow; and his eyes were like a flame of fire; and his feet like fine brass, as if they burned in a furnace; and his voice like the sound of many waters. And he had in his right hand seven stars: and from his mouth went forth a sharp two-edged sword: and his countenance was like the sun shining in its strength. And when I saw him, I fell at his feet as if dead. And he laid his right hand on me, saying, Fear not; I am the first and the last, and am he, who liveth, and I became dead; and behold, I am alive for ever and ever, and have the keys of death and the pit. Therefore, write the things, which thou hast seen, and the things, which are, and the things, which will take place hereafter; the secret of the seven stars, which thou hast seen in my right hand, and the seven golden lamp-stands. The seven stars, are the messengers of the seven congregations: and the seven lamp-stands are the seven congregations."--Rev. 1:12-20.

The voice, by a metonymy, is used for the person speaking. He turned to see the glorious personage by whom the trumpet-tones were uttered. Being turned, he saw the commencement of those great panoramic presentations, by which the events of the future were revealed to him, and the significance of which were explained by an angelic interpreter.

The "seven golden candlesticks," symbolize "the seven churches" (1:20), to which John was commanded to write. By this, and other symbols which are divinely interpreted, are unfolded the principles on which symbols are used. A candle or lamp stand, supports the light placed on it, as churches are the recipients and dispensers of the light of the Holy Scriptures. They are therefore appropriate symbols of churches.

"In the midst of the candlesticks" is one in the form of humanity, surrounded by the insignia of Deity. It is the same appearance that Ezekiel saw, when he had a vision "of the likeness of the glory of the Lord," (Ezek. 1:26-28); and before which Daniel fell trembling, Dan. 10:5-9. The sublime spectacle was too overwhelming for John's endurance, and, like Isaiah,

Ezekiel, and Daniel, his strength turned to corruption. But the glorified Saviour was the same sympathetic being on whose breast John leaned, at the last supper, and he lays his endearing hand on John, and, by soothing words, restores his confidence. He explains the mystery contained in the symbols shown, and enjoins on him to write the things he had seen-- symbolic of the things which then were, and of those which were then in the future. As no created resemblance is a fit representative of Deity, Christ is shown to John by the symbol of his own likeness.

The "seven stars" in the right hand of the Saviour, are the angels,--the messengers, or pastors of the seven churches, 1:20. As the Saviour holds the stars in his hand, so does he sustain all his gospel ministers, enabling them to impart light to those who sit under their ministrations. And as he walked in the midst of the golden candlesticks, so the Lord is ever in the midst of those who fear him, and call upon his name.

Epistles to the Seven Churches.

Epistle to the Church in Ephesus.

"To the messenger of the congregation of Ephesus write: These things saith He who holdeth the seven stars in his right hand, who walketh in the midst of the seven golden lamp-stands: I know thy works, and thy toil, and thy patience, and that thou canst not endure the evil; and thou hast tried those, who say they are apostles, and are not; and hast found them liars; and hast patience, and hast endured on account of my name, and hast not fainted. Nevertheless, I have this against thee, that thou hast left thy first love. Remember therefore whence thou hast fallen, and repent and do the first works; or else I will come to thee quickly, and will remove thy lamp-stand out of its place, except thou repentest. But thou hast this, that thou hatest the deeds of the Nicolaitanes, which I also hate. He, who hath an ear, let him hear what the Spirit saith to the congregations: To him, who overcometh, I will grant to eat of the tree of life, which is in the paradise of God."--Rev. 2:1-7.

The seven churches are not, themselves, seen in vision; they were symbolized by seven golden candlesticks. Consequently, these are seven literal churches that are addressed, and not allegorical, as some teach. The symbolic portions of the Apocalypse, are the descriptions of what John saw, and the attendant utterances. What was addressed to the ear by way of explanation and instruction, does not come under the laws of symbolization.

As churches, in all ages, are often in the several conditions ascribed to the seven churches, the warnings, admonitions, and consolations addressed to them, may serve for instruction to all Christians, as implied in the declaration: "He that hath an ear, let him hear what the Spirit saith to the churches," 2:29.

"By {~GREEK SMALL LETTER ALPHA~}{~GREEK SMALL LETTER GAMMA~}{~GREEK SMALL LETTER GAMMA~}{~GREEK SMALL LETTER EPSILON~}{~GREEK SMALL LETTER LAMDA~}{~GREEK SMALL LETTER OMICRON~}{~GREEK SMALL LETTER FINAL SIGMA~}, angel [or messenger], we are to understand the messenger, or person sent by God to preside over the church; and to him the epistle is directed, not as pointing out his state, but the state of the church under his care. The Angel of the Church, here answers exactly to that officer of the synagogue among the Jews, called the messenger of the church, whose business it was to read, pray, and teach in the synagogue."--DR. CLARKE. Timothy is supposed to have had the care of the Ephesian church till A. D. 97, when he was martyred.

Ephesus was a large, idolatrous city, "a worshipper of the great goddess Diana, and of the image which," as they claimed, "fell down from Jupiter," Acts 19:35. The gospel was first preached there by Paul, and with such success, that "Many of them also which used curious arts, brought their books together, and burned them before all men; and they counted the price of them, and found it fifty thousand pieces of silver: So mightily grew the word of God, and prevailed," Ib. 19, 20. They continued a fine and prosperous church, but had fallen away from their first love. Therefore He who walketh in the midst of the seven golden candlesticks, and holdeth in his hand the messengers of the churches, admonished them that, unless they repented he would remove their candlestick, i.e., their church, of which the candlestick was a symbol, out of its place. They did not repent; and, says Gibbon, "In the year 1312, began the captivity, or ruin of the seven churches by the Ottoman power. In the loss of Ephesus, the Christians deplored the loss of the first Angel, the extinction of the first candlestick of the Revelations. The desolation is complete, and the temple of Diana, or the church of Mary, will equally elude the search of the curious traveller."

The Nicolaitanes, whose deeds God hated, were a sect of heretics, who assumed the name from Nicholas of Antioch, one of the first seven deacons of the church in Jerusalem. It is believed that he was rather the innocent occasion, than the author of the infamous practices of those who assumed his name,--who allowed a community of wives, and ate meats offered in sacrifice to idols. It was a short-lived sect.

For hating their deeds, the church of Ephesus was commended, and also for not giving countenance to false teachers, who claimed to be apostles, and were proved to be liars. Thus are Christians to "believe not every spirit, but try the spirits whether they are of God: because many false prophets are gone out into the world," 1 John 4:1. "Such are false apostles, deceitful workers, transforming themselves into the apostles of Christ," 2 Cor. 11:13. "There were false prophets also among the people, even as there shall be false teachers among you, who privily shall bring in damnable heresies," 2 Pet. 2:1.

The promise to him that overcometh, that he shall "eat of the tree of life," points to the resurrection and to the new creation. As in Eden was made to grow "the tree of life" (Gen. 2:9), so in Eden restored, "they that do his commandments ... may have right to the tree of life, and may enter in through the gates into the city," Rev. 22:2.

Epistle to the Church in Smyrna.

"And to the messenger of the congregation in Smyrna, write: These things saith the First and the Last, who became dead and is alive: I know thy works, and affliction, and poverty (but thou art rich); and I know the reviling of those, who say they are Jews, and are not, but are a synagogue of Satan. Fear none of the things, which thou wilt suffer. Behold, the devil will cast some of you into prison, that ye may be tried, and ye will have affliction ten days. Be thou faithful to death, and I will give thee the crown of life. He, who hath an ear, let him hear what the Spirit saith to the Congregations: he who overcometh, will not be hurt by the second death."-- Rev. 2:8-11.

The angel of the church in Smyrna is supposed to have been Polycarp, who, rather than to apostatize, was burnt alive in that city about A. D. 166. That church had passed through the trial of poverty, and was found "rich toward God," Luke 12:21. It had suffered from the blasphemy of unbelieving Jews, who had a synagogue there and were particularly active at the martyrdom of Polycarp. But "He is not a Jew, which is one outwardly; neither is that circumcision which is outward in the flesh: but he is a Jew which is one inwardly; and circumcision is that of the heart, in the spirit and not in the letter; whose praise is not of men, but of God," Rom. 2:28, 29. And the crucified and risen Saviour has said, that they are "of the synagogue of Satan which say they are Jews, and are not, but do lie," Rev. 3:9.

Not a word of reproof is addressed to this faithful flock; but they were to be still further tried, and a terrible persecution was foretold, which should continue ten prophetic days. Ten years was the duration of the last and bloodiest persecution under Diocletian, from A. D. 302 to 312, during which all the Asiatic churches were grievously afflicted.

This church passed triumphantly through all those trials; and Smyrna is now the most flourishing city of the Asiatic churches. It contains a population of 100,000, and is the seat of an archbishop. From 15,000 to 20,000 of its inhabitants are still professedly Christian.

The "crown of life," promised to those who are faithful unto death, is to be given at Christ's second coming, "who shall judge the quick and the dead at his appearing and kingdom," 2 Tim. 4:1: "Henceforth there is laid up for me a crown of righteousness, which the Lord, the righteous Judge, shall give me at that day; and not to me only, but unto all them also that love his appearing," Ib. 8. "Blessed is the man that endureth temptation: for when he is tried he shall receive the crown of life, which the Lord hath promised to them that love him," Jam. 1:12.

Those who shall not be hurt of the "second death," are those who shall attain unto the resurrection of the just, at the commencement of the millennium. "Blessed and holy is he that hath part in the first resurrection: on such the second death hath no power; but they shall be priests of God and of Christ, and shall reign with him a thousand years," Rev. 20:6. "But the fearful, and unbelieving, and the abominable, and murderers, and whoremongers, and sorcerers, and idolaters, and all liars, shall have their part in the lake which burneth with fire and brimstone: which is the second death," 21:8.

Epistle to the Church in Pergamos.

And to the messenger of the congregation in Pergamos write: These things saith He who hath the sharp two-edged sword: I know thy works, and where thou dwellest, even where Satan's throne is; and thou holdest fast my name, and hast not denied my faith, even in those days in which Antipas was my faithful witness: who was slain among you, where Satan dwelleth. But I have a few things against thee, because thou hast there those, who hold fast the doctrine of Balaam, who taught Balak to cast an enticement to sin before the children of Israel: to eat idol-sacrifices, and to commit fornication. So thou hast also those, who hold fast the doctrine of the Nicolaitanes, in like manner. Repent; or else I will come to thee quickly, and will fight against them with the sword of my mouth. He, who hath an ear, let him hear what the Spirit saith to the congregations: To him, who overcometh, I will grant to eat of the hidden manna, and will give him a white stone, and on the stone a new name written, which no one knoweth, but he, who receiveth it.--Rev. 2:12-17.

"He which hath the sharp sword with two edges," is the one who walked in the midst of the seven golden lamp-stands--out of whose "mouth went a sharp two-edged sword," 1:16. This identifies him as the one who was followed by the armies of heaven, when "the remnant were slain with the sword of him that sat upon the horse: which sword proceeded out of his mouth," 19:21. "The sword of the Spirit ... is the word of God," Eph. 6:17. "He shall smite the earth with the rod of his mouth, and with the breath of his lips shall he slay the wicked," Isa. 11:4. The One who indites this epistle is thus designated, probably, because, unless they repented of the things alleged against them, he would fight against them with the sword of his mouth.

The church of Pergamos had refrained from apostasy, although situated in a wicked and corrupt city,--even where Satan reigned almost supreme and received the obedience of its inhabitants. They had been faithful in those days when Antipas, a faithful Christian, and probably the former pastor of the church, was slain (Dr. Hales thinks) in Domitian's persecution, in A. D. 94. Yet, the Lord had some things against them.

The doctrine of Balaam is what that prophet counselled Balak to cast as a stumbling-block before Israel: For "the people began to commit whoredom with the daughters of Moab. And they called the people unto the sacrifices of their gods; and the people did eat and bowed down to their gods. And Israel joined himself unto Baal-peor," Num. 25:1-3. And Moses said of the women of Midian, "Behold, these caused the children of Israel, through the counsel of Balaam, to commit trespass against the Lord in the matter of Peor," Ib. 31:16. This was also, probably, the same as the doctrine of the Nicolaitanes, p. 34.

The "hidden manna" seems to be a reference to that hidden in the ark, where it was laid up before the Lord (Ex. 16:33), in memory of what was sent for the sustenance of Israel in the wilderness, where "man did eat angel's food," Ps. 78:25. The law having a shadow of good things to come (Heb. 10:1), the manna hidden in the ark may be typical of the angelic sustenance to be revealed in the future world. The Saviour said, "Verily, verily, I say unto you, He that believeth on me hath everlasting life. I am that bread of life. This is the bread which cometh down from heaven, that a man may eat thereof, and not die," John 6:47, 48, 50.

The "white stone" has received divers interpretations. In ancient trials, the votes of the judges were given by white and black pebbles. The former signified acquittal, and the latter condemnation. Conquerors in public games sometimes received a white stone with their name inscribed on it, which entitled them, during the remainder of their life, to be maintained at the public expense. Persons were sometimes invited to feasts or banquets, by the presentation of a white stone, with their name on it in connection with that of their hosts. The possession of the white stone evidently entitles the possessor to all the privileges of the heavenly inheritance.

The "new name" is unknown to all but its possessor; who, on its possession, becomes a child of God, and will receive, saith God, "in my house and within my walls, a place and a name better than of sons and of daughters: I will give them an everlasting name that shall not be cut off," Isa. 56:5. The Saviour has promised that "him that overcometh will I make a pillar in the temple of my God, and he shall go no more out: and I will write upon him the name of my God, and the name of the city of my God, which is new Jerusalem, which cometh down out of heaven from my God; and I will write upon him my new name," Rev. 3:12. And his new "name" "no man knew but he himself," Ib. 19:12.

Pergamos still contains a few thousand inhabitants.

Epistle to the Church in Thyatira.

"And to the messenger of the congregation in Thyatira write: These things saith the Son of God, who hath his eyes like a flame of fire, and his feet like fine brass: I know thy works, and love, and faith, and service, and thy patience, and thy works; and thy last works to be greater than the first. Notwithstanding, I have something against thee, because thou allowest thy woman Jezebel, who calleth herself a prophetess, to teach and seduce my servants to commit fornication, and to eat idol sacrifices. And I gave her time to repent, and she would not repent of her fornication. Behold, I will cast her into a bed, and those, who commit adultery with her, into great affliction, unless they repent of their deeds. And I will kill her children with pestilence; and all the congregations will know that I am he, who searcheth the reins and hearts: and I will give to each of you according to your works. But to you I say, and to the rest in Thyatira, As many as have not this doctrine, and who have not known the depths of Satan, as (they say;) I will not put on you another burden: but what ye have, hold fast till I come. And he, who overcometh, and keepeth my works to the end, to him, I will give power over the nations: (and he will rule them with a rod of iron; like the vessels of a potter they will be dashed in pieces:) even as I received of my Father. And I will give him the morning-star. He, who hath an ear, let him hear what the Spirit saith to the congregations"--Rev. 2:18-29.

In commending the general piety of this church, they are censured for permitting a woman to teach false doctrines among them. The church is not only made responsible for what it teaches, but also for what it suffers others to teach. In this particular the church in Thyatira appears in contrast with the church in Ephesus. The doctrines which this wicked woman taught appear to be similar to those of the Nicolaitanes, p. 34. She is probably called Jezebel, from her being a woman of power and influence, like the wife of Ahab, who "did sell himself to work wickedness in the sight of the Lord: whom Jezebel his wife stirred up," 1 Kings 21:25.

They who had not fallen into those depths of Satan, and should continue faithful to the end, were to have "power over the nations." "The saints of the Most High shall take the kingdom, and possess the kingdom for ever, even for ever and ever. And the kingdom and dominion, and the greatness of the kingdom under the whole heaven, shall be given to the people of the saints of the Most High, whose kingdom is an everlasting kingdom, and all dominions shall serve and obey him," Dan. 7:18, 27. "Ask of me, and I shall give thee the heathen for thine inheritance, and the uttermost parts of the earth for thy possession. Thou shalt break them with a rod of iron; thou shalt dash them in pieces like a potter's vessel," Ps. 2:8, 9. "To execute vengeance upon the heathen, and punishments upon the people; To execute upon them the judgment written: this honor have all the saints. Praise ye the Lord," Ib. 149:7, 9.

To receive the morning star, is to receive Christ, who testifieth of himself. "I am ... the bright and morning star," Rev. 22:16. We are commanded to take heed to the "sure word of prophecy ... as unto a light that shineth in a dark place, until the day dawn, and the day-star arise in your hearts," 2 Pet.

1:19. As "the testimony of Jesus is the spirit of prophecy" (19:10), those who refuse to consider the revelation he has given of things which shortly after began to come to pass, and which must now be verging towards their consummation, may fail of becoming illuminated by the day-star in their hearts.

Says Gibbon: "The God of Mahomet, without a rival or a Son, is invoked in the mosques of Thyatira and Pergamos."

Epistle to the Church in Sardis.

"And to the messenger of the congregation in Sardis write: These things saith He, who hath the seven Spirits of God, and the seven stars: I know thy works, that thou hast a name that thou livest, and art dead. Be watchful, and strengthen the things, which remain, which are about to die: for I have not found thy works complete before God. Remember therefore how thou hast received and heard, and hold fast and repent. If therefore thou shalt not watch, I will come on thee like a thief, and thou wilt not know what hour I will come on thee. But thou hast a few names in Sardis, that have not defiled their garments; and they will walk with me in white: for they are worthy. He, who overcometh, the same one will be clothed in white raiment; and I will not blot out his name from the book of life, but I will acknowledge his name before my Father, and before his angels. He, who hath an ear, let him hear what the Spirit saith unto the congregations."--Rev. 3:1-6.

The church in Sardis was Christian in name, but was destitute of spiritual life, with the exception of a few names who had not defiled their garments. Having become dead to the revivifying influences of the Holy Spirit, they are reminded that he who addresses them is the one who holds their messenger in his hand, and who hath the seven Spirits of God; i.e., that it was from the One who said of "the Comforter, which is the Holy Ghost" (John 14:26), "when the Comforter is come, whom I will send unto you from the Father, even the Spirit of truth which proceedeth from the Father, he shall testify of me," Ib. 15:26.

They had doubtless become greatly conformed to the corrupt worldly influences by which they were surrounded, without having actually denied the faith, or embraced the hated doctrines of the Nicolaitanes. Therefore they were exhorted to hold fast all that they still retained, and, by repentance, to recover what they had lost; and they were admonished that if they neglected those precautions, they would be suddenly visited; without its being designated what would be the precise nature, time, or manner, of their visitation: which made the threatening the more terrible.

The "few names" which had not defiled their garments, were used by a metonymy to signify persons. When an apostle was to be chosen in the place of Judas, "the number of the names together were about one hundred and twenty," Acts 1:15. Purity of raiment is significant of purity of character: "Blessed is he that watcheth and keepeth his garments," 16:15. White is an emblem of purity. To the "bride," it "was granted that she should be arrayed in fine linen clean and white: for the fine linen is the righteousness of the saints," 19:8. Those who came out of great tribulation, had "washed their robes and made them white in the blood of the Lamb," (7:13); and therefore they were symbolized as standing before the throne and before the Lamb, clothed with white robes, and palms of victory in their hands, 7:9. To be clothed in white raiment, is therefore to be accepted of the Saviour.

To blot one's name out of the book of life, is to erase his title to heaven. The figure seems to be an allusion to the ancient custom of enrolling in a book the names of all free citizens. If their names were confessedly written there, they were entitled to all the privileges and immunities of citizenship; but if blotted out, they had forfeited these. "They that dwell on the earth shall wonder, whose names were not written in the book of life from the foundation of the world, when they behold the beast that was, and is not, and yet is," 17:8. Moses said, if God would not forgive Israel, "blot me, I pray thee, out of thy book which thou hast written," Ex. 32:32. Of his enemies, David said, "Let them be blotted out of the book of the living, and not be written with the righteous," Ps. 67:28. Those only enter the New Jerusalem, "which are written in the Lamb's book of life," 21:27.

The church in Sardis, has long been utterly extinct; and what remains of the city is a miserable Turkish village.

Epistle to the Church in Philadelphia.

"And to the messenger of the congregation in Philadelphia write: These things saith the Holy, the True One, he who hath the key of David, he who openeth, and no one shutteth; and shutteth, and no one openeth: I know thy works: behold, I have set before thee an open door, and no one can shut it; for thou hast a little strength, and hast held fast my word, and hast not denied my name. Behold, I will make those of the synagogue of Satan, who say they are Jews, and are not, but who lie; behold, I will make them come and bow down before thy feet, and know that I have loved thee. Because thou hast kept the word of my patience, I also will keep thee from the hour of trial, which will come on all the world, to try those, who dwell on the earth. I come quickly: hold fast that which thou hast, that no one take thy crown. I will make him, who overcometh, a pillar in the temple of my God, and he will go out no more: and I will write on him the name of my God, and the name of the city of my God, the new Jerusalem, (which cometh down out of heaven from my God:) and my new name. He, who hath an ear, let him hear what the Spirit saith to the congregations."--Rev. 3:7-13.

The church of Philadelphia had maintained her integrity, and is therefore addressed in the language of commendation, without the rebukes which were directed to her sister churches. Having remained true to Him who "was called Faithful and True" (19:11), the epistle to this church makes mention of the Saviour by those titles, which are significant of his own faithfulness and inherent holiness.

"The key of David," brings to view the prediction of that which was to be laid "upon his shoulder;" so that "he shall open, and none shall shut; and he shall shut, and none shall open," Isa. 22:22. A key symbolizes that which will open or unlock, or will close fast: therefore said the Saviour, "I ... have the keys of hell and of death." By virtue of this power, an open door was set before the church of Philadelphia, which no man should be able to close.

The Jews in Philadelphia, who had claimed to be the only true church of God, but who were in reality of the synagogue of Satan, were to cease their opposition to the Christians, and to seek instruction and protection from them--recognizing the love of God to Gentiles as well as to Jews. History is silent respecting the fulfilment of this; but there is no reason to suppose that it was not literally fulfilled.

The "hour of temptation," which was to "come upon all the world, to try them that dwell on the earth," was to be one of peculiar trial. Some suppose it had reference to the persecution under Trajan, which was more severe and extensive than those under Nero, or Domitian: and others that it was the Mohammedan delusion. In such times there are peculiar temptations to apostatize, and the less faithful are in more danger of apostasy than others. But because the Philadelphian church had been faithful thus far, they were to be kept from that trying hour. When the scourge of Mohammedanism swept over all the other churches of Asia, this church maintained its integrity. Says Gibbon: "Among the Greek colonies and churches of Asia, Philadelphia is still erect, a column in a scene of ruins. At a distance from the sea, forgotten by the emperors, encompassed on all sides by the Turks, her valiant citizens defended their religion and their freedom above fourscore years, and at length capitulated with the proudest of the Ottomans." Philadelphia is still the seat of an archbishop, and contains from six hundred to seven hundred Greek houses, and several places of Christian worship. "The Lord knoweth how to deliver the godly out of temptations," 2 Pet. 2:9.

They are encouraged to constancy by the prospect of the coming coronation day, when "the Lord; the righteous Judge shall give" a "crown of righteousness," "unto all them that love his appearing," 2 Tim. 4:8. He has said "Be thou faithful unto death, and I will give thee a crown of life" (2:10); and therefore "when the chief Shepherd shall appear, ye shall receive a crown of glory that fadeth not away," 1 Pet. 5:4.

A pillar in the temple of God, is expressive of a position which shall give support to the church, which is erected "upon the foundation of the apostles and prophets, Jesus Christ himself being the chief corner-stone; In whom the building, fitly framed together, groweth unto a holy temple in the Lord: In whom ye also are builded together for a habitation of God through the Spirit," Eph. 2:20-22.

To receive the name of God, is to be recognized as belonging to God. As masters designated their servants by branding their name on them, or by some peculiar mark, so the children of God are referred to by the same figure. In a subsequent vision John saw with the Lamb on Mount Zion, "an hundred and forty and four thousand, having his Father's name written in their foreheads," 14:1. Their connection with new Jerusalem is similarly designated.

Epistle to the Church in Laodicea.

"And to the messenger of the congregation in Laodicea write: These things saith the Amen, the faithful and true Witness, the Ruler of the creation of God: I know thy works, that thou art neither cold nor hot: I would that thou wast cold or hot. So, because thou art lukewarm, and neither cold nor hot, I will cast thee out of my mouth: because thou sayest, I am rich, and have become wealthy, and have need of nothing; and knowest not that thou art wretched, and miserable, and poor, and blind, and naked: I counsel thee to buy of me gold tried by fire, that thou mayest be rich; and white raiment, that thou mayest be clothed, and that the shame of thy nakedness may not appear; and to anoint thine eyes with eye-salve, that thou mayest see. As many as I love, I rebuke and chastise: be fervent therefore, and repent. Behold, I stand at the door, and knock: if any one heareth my voice, and openeth the door, I will come in to him, and will sup with him, and he shall sup with me. To him, who overcometh I will grant to sit with me in my throne, even as I also overcame, and have sat down with my Father in his throne. He, who hath an ear, let him hear what the Spirit saith to the congregations."--Rev. 3:14-22.

By his titles of truth and verity, the Saviour prepares the Laodiceans for the humiliating threatenings, which are uttered against them. By that of "the beginning of the creation of God," is indicated Christ's kingship as head and governor of all; and hence the authority on which his declarations are founded.

The Laodiceans seemed to have been very well satisfied with their own condition, without possessing any very marked characteristics. They were neither good, nor very wicked; but supposed that they abounded in all spiritual wealth, when they were destitute of all the Christian graces. They could not appreciate their own condition; and not realizing their need, were unlikely to heed the counsel given them, and therefore they have long since ceased to have a name and a place on the earth. Says Gibbon: "The circus and three stately temples of Laodicea, are now peopled with wolves and foxes."

The great majority of them seemed to have become unworthy even of the chastisement which God bestows on those he loves. "Behold, happy is the man whom God correcteth; therefore despise not the chastening of the Almighty," Job 5:17. "My son, despise not the chastening of the Lord: neither be weary of his correction: For whom the Lord loveth he correcteth, even as a father the son in whom he delighteth," Prov. 3:11, 12. "Blessed is the man that endureth temptation: for when he is tried, he shall receive the crown of life, which the Lord hath promised to them that love him," Jas. 1:12.

The Saviour shows his readiness to receive those who will open unto him. He is saying, "Open to me ... for my head is filled with dew, and my locks with the drops of the night," Cant. 5:2. "Blessed are those servants, whom the Lord, when he cometh, shall find watching: verily I say unto you, That he shall gird himself, and make them to sit down to meat, and will come forth and serve them," Luke 12:37. Said Jesus, "If any man love me, he will keep my words: and my Father will love him, and we will come unto him, and make our abode with him," John 14:23.

To him that overcometh, as in another place he is promised a crown, so now there is the promise of a seat with the Saviour in his throne. Said the Saviour, "Ye which have followed me, in the regeneration when the Son of man shall sit in the throne of his glory, ye also shall sit upon twelve thrones, judging the twelve tribes of Israel," Matt. 19:28. "And I appoint unto you a kingdom, as my Father hath appointed unto me," Luke 22:29. "If we suffer" i.e. with Christ, "we shall also reign with him," 2 Tim. 2:12.

Vision of the Deity.

"After this, I looked, and behold, a door opened in heaven: and the first voice, which I heard, was like a trumpet talking with me; saying, Ascend here, and I will show thee things, which must take place hereafter. And immediately I was in the Spirit: and behold, a throne was set in heaven, and One sat on the throne. And, He, who sat, was in appearance like a jasper and a cornelian stone: and there was a rainbow around the throne, in appearance, like an emerald. And around the throne were twenty-four thrones; and on the thrones I saw twenty-four elders sitting, clothed in white raiment; and crowns of gold on their heads. And from the throne came forth lightnings, and voices and thunders. And seven lamps of fire were burning before the throne, which are the seven Spirits of God. And before the throne there was a transparent sea like crystal: and in the midst of the throne, and around the throne, were four living beings, full of eyes before and behind. And the first living being was like a lion, and the second living being like a calf, and the third living being had a face like a man, and the fourth living being was like a flying eagle. And each of the four living beings had six wings around him; and within they were full of eyes: and they rest not day or night, saying, Holy, holy, holy, Lord God Almighty, who was, and is, and is to be! And when the living beings give glory, and honor, and thanks to Him seated on the throne, who liveth for ever and ever, the four and twenty elders fall down before Him seated on the throne, and worship Him, who liveth for ever and ever, and cast their crowns before the throne, saying, Worthy art thou, O Lord, our God, to receive glory, and honor, and power: for thou hast created all things, and for thy pleasure they existed and were created."--Rev. 4:1-11.

This vision is preparatory to the revelations of "things which must be hereafter," which were given John in the series of visions following. Their divine origin, and, consequently, the deference with which they are to be received as a revelation from God, are demonstrated by this symbolization of the presence chamber of the Almighty.

The revelator had before heard a voice speaking to him, (1:10); and turning to look, he beheld the risen Saviour. He then writes the epistles which the Saviour dictated to the churches; and again he turns his eyes to the place where the voice spake to him.

The opening of a door in heaven, appears to be no part of the "things which must be hereafter;" and is, therefore, no symbol. It was doubtless an appearance of an aperture in the sky above, through which the revelator saw the vision. It indicates that he looked through and beyond the limits prescribed to human vision; and the summons to "come up hither," indicates that he was to have free access to the secrets there to be unfolded.

A "throne set in heaven," is a symbol of sovereignty there. Consequently the one who sits thereon is the Almighty--his greatness, glory and majesty, being indicated by the "lightnings, thunderings and voices," the "rainbow round about the throne," and the resemblance to brilliant gems. It is the same Being, seen in vision by Ezekiel (1:28), round about whom was "as the appearance of the bow in the day of rain;" and who was explained to be "the appearance of the likeness of the glory of the Lord."

The "elders" seated about the throne, and the "four living creatures," improperly rendered beasts, are representatives of the redeemed of our race; for they subsequently unite in the new song, saying to Christ, "Thou wast slain, and hast redeemed us to God by thy blood, out of every kindred and tongue, and people and nation; and hast made us unto our God kings and priests, and we shall reign on the earth," 5:8-10. The difference between the two orders, is not fully apparent. They have "vials full of odors, which are the prayers of saints." The four beasts are evidently of the same order as the "living creatures" in Ezek. 1:5; the cherubim of Ezek. 10:20, and the seraphim of Isa. 6:1. The entire hosts of the redeemed are thus represented as interested spectators in the visions which are to be unfolded.

The "seven lamps of fire," are explained to be "the seven Spirits of God," which, as before shown, is expressive of the Holy Spirit.

The "sea of glass," corresponds to the brazen sea, or laver, under the law, which stood at the door of the tabernacle, Ex. 38:8. It was an emblem of purity. Before entering the tabernacle the priest must there wash. Those admitted on the sea of glass, are those who are purified and made white in the blood of the Lamb, 15:2.

With this preliminary representation, the first series of events extending to the final consummation, is shown under the symbol of:

The Sealed Book.

"And I saw in the right hand of Him seated on the throne, a book written within and without, sealed with seven seals. And I saw a mighty angel proclaiming with a loud voice, Who is worthy to open the book, and to loose its seals? and no one in heaven, or on the earth, or under the earth, was able to open the book nor to look in it. And I was weeping much, because no one was found worthy to open, and to read the book, nor to look in it. And one of the elders saith to me, Weep not: behold, the Lion of the tribe of Judah, the Root of David, hath prevailed to open the book, and to loose its seven seals. And I saw in the midst of the throne, and of the four living beings, and in the midst of the elders, the Lamb standing, as having been slain, having seven horns, and seven eyes, which are the seven Spirits of God sent forth into all the earth. And he came and took the book out of the right hand of Him seated on the throne. And when he took the book, the living beings, and twenty-four elders fell down before the Lamb, all of them having harps, and golden bowls full of incense, which are the prayers of saints. And they sung a new song, saying, Worthy art thou to take the book and to open its seals: for thou wast slain, and hast redeemed us to God by thy blood out of every tribe, and tongue, and people, and nation; and hast made us kings and priests to our God, and we shall reign on the earth! And I beheld, and I heard the voice of many angels around the throne, and the living beings, and the elders: and the number of them was ten thousand times ten thousand, and thousands of thousands; saying with a loud voice, Worthy is the Lamb, that was slain, to receive power, and riches, and wisdom, and strength, and honor, and glory, and blessing. And every creature which is in heaven, and on the earth, and under the earth, and those on the sea, even all that are in them, I heard saying, Blessing, and honor, and glory, and power, be to Him sitting on the throne, and to the Lamb, for ever and ever! And the four living beings said, Amen. And the elders fell down and worshipped."--Rev. 5:1-14.

The written book, must symbolize God's purposes, which were about to be unfolded on the loosening of the seals. Its being written within and without, indicates the fulness of its contents, the completeness of the record:--God's purposes being fully and unalterably formed. In like manner Ezekiel was shown "a roll of a book ... written within and without," symbolizing the "lamentations, mourning and woe" (Ezek. 2:9), which were soon to overtake Israel.

A sealed book is one whose contents are hidden: "The vision of all is become unto you as the words of a book that is sealed, which men deliver to one that is learned, saying, Read this I pray thee: and he saith, I cannot; for it is sealed," Isa. 29:11. God said to Daniel, "Shut up the words, and seal the book, till the time of the end," Dan. 12:4.

To open the seals, no one was found worthy. There was no being in heaven among the angels, no human being on the earth, and no disembodied spirit, or demon, under the earth, who was able to unfold the future. The tears of the revelator are, however, dried, and his drooping spirits cheered, by the announcement of one of the elders, that "the LION of the tribe of JUDAH, the ROOT of DAVID, hath prevailed to open the book," and to unfold its mysteries. He stood in the midst of the assembled intelligences,--his human nature and sacrificial office, being designated by his metaphorical title of the "Lamb:"--John seeing Jesus coming to him said, "Behold the Lamb of God, which taketh away the sin of the world," John 1:29. His sovereignty is shown by the "seven horns," the symbols of power; and his relation to the Godhead, by the seven eyes, the seven Spirits of God;--expressive of the Holy Spirit. See p. 25.

The rejoicings on the announcement of Christ's ability to take the book, and to open the seals, indicate the greatness of the blessing which God gives the church, when he thus reveals a knowledge of the future. All creatures should join in these hosannas, and praise the Lord for his great condescension, in showing his servants the things which must shortly come to pass. To neglect this revelation, is not joining in the ascription of praise.

The golden vials, full of odors, symbolize the prayers of saints. Under the Mosaic dispensation, the frankincense and odors offered at the tabernacle were emblematic of prayer and praise to God. "Let my prayer be set forth before thee as incense; and the lifting up of my hands as the evening sacrifice," Psa. 141:2.

Christ takes the book from the hand of him who sits on the throne, and opens the seals. Thus he makes known unto his servants the revelation which God had given him, 1:1. As each successive seal is opened, successive portions of the writing in the book become accessible,--an epoch is marked, following which, and previous to that symbolized by the opening of the next seal, are to be fulfilled, the events symbolized under it.

The First Seal.

"And I saw when the Lamb opened one of the seven seals, and I heard one of the four living beings, saying, with a voice like thunder, Come! And I saw, and behold, a white horse: and he, who sat on him, had a bow; and a crown was given him: and he went forth conquering and to conquer."--Rev. 6:1, 2.

The voice is evidently addressed to the personage on the white horse, or to the agencies thus symbolized. It is the signal for their appearance on the stage of action.

The symbol is that of a victorious warrior, armed with weapons of conquest,--success being indicated by the crown given him. As there is no analogous order, except in the religious world, Mr. Lord very properly regards it as a symbol of the body of religious teachers, those faithful soldiers of the cross, who, from the middle of the first to the middle of the third century, as "soldiers of Jesus Christ" (2 Tim. 2:3), went forth to war "against principalities and powers, against the rulers of the darkness of this world, against spiritual wickedness in high places," Eph. 6:12. The apostle, when they received their commission, said to them, "Take unto you the whole armor of God, that ye may be able to withstand in the evil day, and having done all, to stand. Stand, therefore, having your loins girt about with truth, and having on the breast-plate of righteousness; and your feet shod with the preparation of the gospel of peace; above all, taking the shield of faith, wherewith ye shall be able to quench all the fiery darts of the wicked. And take the helmet of salvation, and the sword of the Spirit, which is the word of God," Ib. 13-17.

Thus equipped, they went forth, conquering and to conquer. They assailed the strong-holds of sin and Satan, and planted the standard of the cross in all portions of the then civilized world. And at the end of their warfare thousands of them could say with the apostle: "I have fought a good fight, I have finished my course, I have kept the faith: henceforth there is laid up for me a crown of righteousness, which the Lord, the righteous Judge, shall give me at that day: and not to me only, but unto all them also that love his appearing," 2 Tim. 4:7, 8.

The period symbolized under this seal, was distinguished for purity of faith in the church, and devotion to the cause of Christ,--indicated by the whiteness of the horse that the warrior rides.

The Second Seal.

"And when he opened the second seal, I heard the second living being say, Come! And there went out another horse that was red: and power was given to him, who sat on him, to take peace from the earth, and that they should kill each other: and a great sword was given to him."--Rev. 6:3, 4.

This symbol, like the former, is that of a mounted warrior, and must also symbolize a body of religious teachers. The color of the horse, indicates that the doctrine and character of the body symbolized will have lost the original purity of the church, and become more sanguinary; which is also indicated by the great sword given him.

The warfare under this seal is not against outside enemies; for they kill each other. This, then, indicates an era when the church shall be disquieted, and her peace interrupted by internal dissensions. Such was its history during the third, fourth, and fifth centuries. This period was distinguished for the contentions of the clergy; their usurpation of power not conferred by the apostles; their divisions and sub-divisions into parties; their opposing councils; their collisions and distractions; their love of power; their pride, discord, strife, and tyranny; their mutual anathemas and excommunications; the envy, jealousy, and detraction they indulged in, and the other hateful passions which they exercised. Thus they marred the peace of the church; and by causing many to apostatize, killed each other with spiritual death.

The Third Seal.

"And when he opened the third seal I heard the third living being say, Come! And I beheld, and lo, a black horse; and he, who sat on him, had a balance in his hand. And I heard a voice in the midst of the four living beings say, A measure of wheat for a penny, and three measures of barley for a penny; and injure thou not the oil and the wine."--Rev. 6:5, 6.

This foreshadows a period of great scarcity and cruel exactions. Applying it to the only department of society which is analogous to civil life, and the famine symbolized, is like that predicted by Amos: "Behold, the days come, saith the Lord God, that I will send a famine into the land, not a famine of bread, nor a thirst for water, but of hearing the words of the Lord: and they shall wander from sea to sea, and from the north even to the east; they shall run to and fro to seek the word of the Lord, and shall not find it," Amos 8:11, 12.

This, then, marks a period when the traditions and opinions of men are substituted for the word of God. With Origen was introduced a new mode of interpreting scripture, which afterwards became prevalent. The scriptures, instead of being received in their natural and obvious sense, were regarded as mystical and allegorical. Milner, in his Church History, says: "From the fanciful mode of allegory, introduced by him, and uncontrolled by scriptural rule and order, there arose a vitiated method of commenting on the sacred pages." And Mosheim says: "The few who explained the sacred writings with judgment and a true spirit of criticism, could not oppose, with any success, the torrent of allegory that was overflowing the church." Following this example, Luther says, "men make just what they please of the Scriptures, until some accommodate the word of God to the most extravagant absurdities."

Substituting the conceptions of their own fancy for the word of God, they withheld from the people the bread of life, and produced a famine for the word of the Lord. Crude notions took the place of Bible doctrines; and pernicious speculations were substituted for the teachings of Christ and his apostles. Baptism and the Lord's supper, lost their emblematic significance, and were regarded as saving ordinances. Heaven was sought to be merited by works, and sanctification was supposed to be gained by penance and mortification of the flesh. In short, all the corruptions of the apostasy were substituted for the primitive faith, and the Bible became a sealed book to the great mass of the people.

The Fourth Seal.

"And when he opened the fourth seal, I heard the voice of the fourth living being saying, Come! And I looked, and behold, a pale horse: and his name, who sat on him, was Death, and the pit followed with him. And power was given to them over the fourth part of the earth, to kill with sword, and with famine, and with pestilence, and with the wild beasts of the earth."--Rev. 6:7, 8.

The Christian church alone being analogous to the civil power, it is within its pale that the fulfilment of this symbol is to be looked for. During this period, violence is substituted for famine; and men are compelled to apostatize, which results in spiritual death. The Papacy having the power to enforce her decrees, Christians had to embrace her faith, or be handed over to the secular power for punishment. They produced death by compelling men to apostatize, by withholding from them the word of life, by infusing into their minds pestiferous doctrines, and by the fear of the civil power,-- symbolized by the sword, famine, pestilence, and beasts of the earth.

The Fifth Seal.

"And when he opened the fifth seal, I saw under the altar the souls of those slain on account of the word of God, and on account of the testimony, which they held: and they cried with a loud voice, saying, How long, O Lord, holy and true, dost thou not judge and avenge our blood on those, who dwell on the earth? And a white robe was given to each of them; and it was said to them, that they should rest yet for a short time, until their fellow-servants also and their brethren, that were to be slain as they were, should be filled up."--Rev. 6:9-11.

This symbolized a period intervening between the time of the martyrdom, of those whose souls are seen in vision, and another time of persecution to follow. Consequently, the symbol represents the disembodied spirits of those who had already been slain. They symbolize the souls of martyrs who counted not their lives dear unto themselves for the sake of Christ; and being faithful unto death, were in expectation of a crown of life. Says Mr. Lord: "The term {~GREEK SMALL LETTER TAU~}{~GREEK SMALL LETTER ALPHA~} {~GREEK SMALL LETTER PI~}{~GREEK SMALL LETTER TAU~}{~GREEK SMALL LETTER OMEGA~}{~GREEK SMALL LETTER MU~}{~GREEK SMALL LETTER ALPHA~} {~GREEK SMALL LETTER TAU~}{~GREEK SMALL LETTER ALPHA~} is used in the prophecy to denote the dead bodies of the martyrs (chap. 11:9), and {~GREEK SMALL LETTER ALPHA~}{~GREEK SMALL LETTER IOTA~} {~GREEK SMALL LETTER PSI~}{~GREEK SMALL LETTER UPSILON~}{~GREEK SMALL LETTER PSI~} {~GREEK SMALL LETTER ALPHA~}{~GREEK SMALL LETTER IOTA~} (20:4) to denote their disembodied spirits. They are represented as having been slain, and as uttering their appeal to God because of their blood having been shed." Also: "The martyr souls are exhibited in their own persons; and obviously because no others could serve as their symbol,--there being no others that have undergone a change from a bodied to a disembodied life, nor that sustain such relations to God, of forgiveness, acceptance, and assurance of a resurrection from death, and a priesthood with Christ during his victorious reign on the earth," Ex. Apoc. p. 155.

The altar, symbolizes the atonement made by Christ for sin; and, consequently, the position of the souls of the martyrs under it, indicates their reliance on him for an inheritance in his everlasting kingdom,--when "he shall come to be glorified in his saints," and to "take vengeance on them that know not God, and obey not the gospel," 2 Thess. 1:8, 10.

The presentation of white robes to them, symbolizes their acceptance and justification.

The declaration that they must rest till their fellow-servants are killed, as they have been, implies another persecution, to be subsequent to the period symbolized by the opening of this seal. The persecutions which followed the Reformation, in which the fires of Smithfield were lighted in England, the Huguenots were driven from France, and thousands suffered martyrdom, probably fulfilled this.

The interest taken by the souls of the martyrs in the avenging of their blood on the earth, shows that the spirits of departed saints look forward with intense interest to the time of their glorification. And although the dead who die in the Lord are blessed, the glories of the resurrection morn are not less desired by those who are absent from the body and present with the Lord, than by humble, devoted, waiting Christians here.

The opening of this seal evidently synchronizes with the commencement of the reformation, when they might have supposed the kingdom of God would immediately appear.

The Sixth Seal.

"And I beheld when he opened the sixth seal, and there was a great earthquake; and the sun became black like sackcloth of hair, and the moon became like blood: and the stars of heaven fell to the earth, as a fig-tree casteth its unripe figs, when shaken by a mighty wind. And the heaven departed like a scroll rolled together; and every mountain and island were removed from their places. And the kings of the earth, and the nobles, and the rich, and the commanders, and the strong men, and every bond-man, and every freeman, hid themselves in the dens and in the rocks of the mountains; and said to the mountains and rocks, Fall on us, and hide us from the face of Him seated on the throne, and from the wrath of the Lamb: for the great day of his wrath is come; and who can stand?"--Rev. 6:12-17.

The laws of symbolization require that symbols should not be representatives of their own order when there is any analogous order to be representatives of. In other places in the Apocalypse, these symbols are used, under circumstances where it is impossible to regard them as symbols of their own order. And here, as the kings of the earth call on the rocks and mountains to fall on them after the heaven has departed as a scroll and every mountain and island is moved out of its place, it is necessary to regard them as symbols of objects of analogous orders.

The earthquake, then, as in corresponding Scriptures, symbolizes a political revolution. The darkening of the sun and moon, would represent a change in the character of the rulers and legislators of the world, so that instead of extending a genial influence over their subjects, they should exert a deleterious one; and the fall of the stars, their ejection from their stations-- synchronizing with the first five vials (16:1-11), and fulfilled in the political revolutions of Europe during the past century.

By the passing away of the heavens and the removal of mountains and islands from their places, is symbolized the total dissolution of all human governments--corresponding to the seventh vial (16:20).

On the occurrence of this unprecedented state of anarchy, the inhabitants of earth will be aware of the proximity of the Advent. They flee from the face of the Lamb, which indicates his appearance in the clouds of heaven at his personal advent. The great day of wrath will have come; but before the infliction of merited punishment on his enemies, the servants of God are to be designated, the righteous dead are to be raised, and they with the righteous living are to be caught up to meet the Lord in the air, 1 Thess. 4:17. The living righteous are designated by:

The Sealing of the Servants of God.

"And after these things I saw four angels standing on the four corners of the earth, holding fast the four winds of the earth, that a wind might not blow on the earth, nor on the sea, nor on any tree. And I saw another angel ascending from the rising of the sun, having a seal of the living God: and he cried with a loud voice to the four angels, to whom it was given to injure the earth and the sea, saying, Injure not the earth, nor the sea, nor the trees, till we have sealed the servants of our God on their foreheads! And I heard the number of those sealed: a hundred and forty-four thousand were sealed out of all the tribes of the children of Israel. Of the tribe of Judah, twelve thousand were sealed. Of the tribe of Reuben twelve thousand were sealed. Of the tribe of Gad twelve thousand were sealed. Of the tribe of Asher twelve thousand were sealed. Of the tribe of Naphtali, twelve thousand were sealed. Of the tribe of Manasseh twelve thousand were sealed. Of the tribe of Simeon twelve thousand were sealed. Of the tribe of Levi twelve thousand were sealed. Of the tribe of Issachar twelve thousand were sealed. Of the tribe of Zebulon twelve thousand were sealed. Of the tribe of Joseph twelve thousand were sealed. Of the tribe of Benjamin twelve thousand were sealed."--Rev. 7:1-8.

The symbols here presented, were seen immediately subsequent to the exhibition of the preceding ones. This alone would not prove that the events symbolized follow in order, but it is indicated by their being a continuation of the symbolization under the sixth seal, and before the opening of the seventh.

In the sixth chapter, the great men and rich men, as well as bond-men, are aware of the proximity of the day of the Lord, and seek for a refuge from the face of the Lamb. The next events in consecutive order, would be the resurrection of the righteous dead, the change of the living, their ascension to meet the Lord in the air, and the infliction of the wrath of God on the wicked.

After the wicked seek to escape from God's presence, the righteous are still unchanged upon the earth. But before the wrath of God is poured upon his enemies, the winds of heaven are to be holden while the angel of the living God seals his servants in their foreheads. The holding of the winds and the sealing are, consequently, subsequent to the terror of the wicked, at the appearance of the Saviour.

The four winds are the winds coming from all directions; and symbolize strife, war, and commotion among men, analogous to the violent action of the winds of heaven.

In Dan. 7:2, the striving of the four winds upon the great sea preceded the rising of the four beasts: in other words, the various contests and strifes among the different people and tongues of earth resulted in the establishment of the successive empires which have arisen to universal dominion. The blowing of the wind seems to be any influence exerted upon men. In Ezek. 37:9 the breathing of the wind revives the dead; and in Zech. 5:9 it symbolizes the removal of the wickedness of the Jews.

The angels holding the winds, consequently, must symbolize the agencies which have the power to excite or quell these disturbing influences. They do the bidding of the Lord in restraining or exerting the influences which should produce the effect symbolized. The holding of them indicates the proximity and certainty of their blowing unless they are restrained. The earth, sea, and trees, which would be hurt by the blowing of the wind, evidently symbolize the different classes of inhabitants of the earth, on whom an effect would be produced by the blowing of the winds, analogous to the effect produced on those elements by a violent tempest, or hurricane. The storm here symbolized is evidently that of which the Scriptures speak. "On the wicked he shall rain snares, fire and brimstone, and an horrible tempest," Psa. 11:6. "Thou shalt be visited of the Lord of hosts with thunder, and with earthquake, and great noise, with storm and tempest, and the flame of devouring fire," Isa. 29:6. "The Lord hath a mighty and strong one, which as a tempest of hail, and a destroying storm, as flood of waters overflowing, shall cast down to the earth with the hand," Ib. 28:2.

The sealing of the servants of God in their foreheads, designates them, but does not constitute them such; for none are sealed, only those who are previously his. This is in allusion to the ancient custom of stamping with a hot iron the name of the owner on the forehead or shoulder of his slave.

Before the final destruction of Jerusalem by the Babylonians, Ezekiel saw in vision a man clothed in linen, with a writer's ink-horn by his side, who was commissioned to go through the midst of Jerusalem and set a mark on the foreheads of the men that sigh and that cry for all the abominations that be done in the midst thereof. And the destroying angels who were commanded to slay all, both old and young, to spare not, nor to have pity, were expressly told to "come not near any man upon whom is the mark," Ezek. 9:2-6. When the destroying angel passed through Egypt, on the night of the Passover, "to slay all the first-born of that nation, the houses of the Israelites were indicated by the blood of the Paschal Lamb sprinkled on their lintels and door-posts; and by these the angels passed," Ex. 12:23. Thus in the present instance, before the descent of the impending storm, the servants of the Lord are to be indicated by the seal of the living God in their foreheads, and will be spared the horrible tempest which will "hurt" all those on whom it shall fall.

The 144,000,--the whole number sealed, is a perfect number,--an appropriate symbol of all the living righteous on the earth. The twelve tribes, then, would symbolize all the branches of Christ's mystical body in which the servants of God are found. The pious dead would need no mark indicative of their acceptance, having previously, in the white robes given them, received the symbols of their justification, 6:11. That their resurrection and the changing of the living, immediately succeeded, is evident from:

The Palm-bearing Multitude.

"After these things I looked, and lo, a great crowd, which no one could number, out of all nations, and tribes, and people, and tongues, stood before the throne, and before the Lamb, clothed with white robes, and palm-branches in their hands; and they cried with a loud voice, saying, Salvation to our God seated on the throne, and to the Lamb! And all the angels stood around the throne, and the elders and the four living beings, and fell before the throne on their faces, and worshipped God, saying, Amen: blessing and glory, and wisdom, and thanksgiving, and honor, and power, and might, be to our God for ever and ever. Amen! And one of the elders answered, saying to me, Who are these arrayed in white robes? and whence came they? And I said to him, My Lord, thou knowest. And he said to me, These are they who came out of great affliction, and have washed their robes, and made them white in the blood of the Lamb. For this, they are before the throne of God, and serve him day and night in his temple: and He, who sitteth on the throne, will dwell among them. They will hunger no more, and will thirst no more; nor will the sun light on them, nor any heat. For the Lamb, who is in the midst of the throne, will tend them, and lead them to fountains of living waters: and God will wipe away every tear from their eyes."--Rev. 7:9-17.

This great multitude of white-robed palm-bearers, must include those who, under the preceding seal, anxiously inquired how long was to be deferred the avenging of their blood on those who dwell on the earth. That epoch had now arrived; and they come forth arrayed in the white robes then given them. The palm-branches in their hands, are emblems of victory. They symbolize the subjects of the first resurrection, caught up to meet the Lord in the air. That they are gathered from every land and every age, is asserted when it is said they are from every kindred, tongue, and people; and that they triumph over death and the grave, is evident from the answer of one of the elders to the questions: "What are these?" and "Whence came they?"

The epoch, is a point of time intervening between the first resurrection, and the descent of the new Jerusalem, 21:2. The loud and united voice, with which the redeemed multitude cry "Salvation to our God which sitteth upon the throne, and unto the Lamb,"--synchronizes with that of the "great multitude," which, like the voice of many waters, and of "mighty thunderings," shouted "Alleluia: for the Lord God omnipotent reigneth" (19:6), immediately preceding the marriage-supper of the Lamb (19:6-9). They are removed above the troubles of earth, which are impending upon the wicked, under:

The Seventh Seal.

"And when he opened the seventh seal, silence took place in heaven for about half an hour. And I saw the seven angels, who stood before God; and seven trumpets were given to them. And another angel came and stood by the altar, having a golden censer; and much incense was given to him, that he should offer it with the prayers of all the saints on the golden altar before the throne. And the smoke of the incense, with the prayers of the saints, ascended before God from the angel's hand. And the angel took the censer, and filled it with the fire of the altar, and out it into the earth: and there were voices, and thunders, and lightnings, and an earthquake."--Rev. 8:1-5.

The epoch of this seal, is sometimes regarded as anterior to that of the trumpets; and those are often supposed to be included in the events of this seal; but no conclusive reason has ever been given for removing it from its obvious position as the closing one, of a series of successive periods, commencing with the gospel, and extending to the end of the world. If the first six are successive in their respective order, analogy would require that the seventh be thus considered.

Under the sixth seal, the great men and rich, are seen fleeing to the rocks for refuge from the wrath of the Lamb; and the risen saints symbolized, are in the Saviour's presence; but the infliction of the wrath of God on the wicked is not there symbolized. The events of that seal come down as far as those in the 19th chapter, which precede the marriage of the Lamb, 19:7.

The half-hour's silence, is the first thing indicated under the seventh seal. Being so expressly noticed, it would seem to be of some significance. As a period of symbolic time, on the scale of a day for a year, "about half an hour," would equal a week's duration--corresponding to the time which intervened between the entrance of Noah into the ark, and the commencement of the deluge, Gen. 7:1-4. As the period evidently synchronizes with the parable of the Saviour, when "the Bridegroom came; and they that were ready went in with him to the marriage, and the door was shut" (Matt. 25:10),--the others being still without,--it would seem to symbolize the time, between the entrance to the marriage of the Lamb (19:7), and the going forth of the Word of God with his armies, to judge, make war, and to slay the remnant with the sword, 19:11-21. It would be a period of holy joy to the righteous in the Saviour's presence, and of awful suspense to the wicked.

The seven angels, to whom were given seven trumpets, being introduced here, have doubtless caused the events of this seal to be regarded as anterior to the first trumpet. As those immediately following, evidently synchronize with occurrences of the closing epoch, the angels can only be introduced here in anticipation of the symbolization which they are to unfold under the sounding of the successive trumpets--the same as the seven angels with the last plagues are introduced, before the epoch of the commencement of their allotted work, 15:1.

The golden censer was the instrument in which incense was burned in the Jewish worship. Incense symbolizes prayers (5:8). The offering of much incense with the prayers of all saints and the smoke of the incense ascending up before God, indicates the acceptance of their offerings in heaven--the act being before the throne, and not on the earth. The acceptance of their prayers, also implies their own acceptance, when presented "faultless before the presence of his glory with exceeding joy," Jude 24.

The fire from the altar, symbolizes the instruments of divine justice; and the filling the censer with coals after the acceptance of the saints, and the casting of both the censer and fire to the earth, indicate that thenceforth there would be no more acceptance of prayer from those left on the earth, but the speedy infliction of impending judgments.

The "voices, and thunderings, and lightnings, and an earthquake," which followed, evidently synchronize with the same events which follow the seventh trumpet: when the "wrath of God" has come, with "the time of the dead that they should be judged;" and when those are to be destroyed who have destroyed the earth, 11:19. They are the same, also, as those under the seventh vial, (16:18); and symbolize the final overturn and commotion, previous to the cleansing of the earth and the ushering in of a better day: Then will the

"fire purge all things new, Both Heaven and Earth, wherein the just shall dwell."--MILTON, BOOK XI.

The Seven Trumpets.

"And the seven angels having seven trumpets prepared themselves to sound."--Rev. 8:6.

The sounding of each successive trumpet marks the commencement of an era, of a longer or shorter duration, as the striking of a clock does the succession of hours. During each era, were to be fulfilled the events symbolized in connection with its respective trumpet. Those under the trumpets are more of a political character than those presented in connection with the seals.

The First Trumpet.

"And the first angel sounded, and there was hail and fire mingled with blood, and they were cast into the earth; and the third part of the earth was burnt up, and the third part of the trees was burnt up, and every green herb was burnt up."--Rev. 8:7.

The earth of the Apocalypse is regarded by most expositors as the Roman empire, in a state of comparative quiet. As no tornado like this described has ever happened, its correspondence must be sought for in the political relations of the empire. There is great unanimity among commentators respecting the period and the agents here symbolized,--that it refers to the invasions of the Goths and other barbarians, from A. D. 363 to 410. After 395, their incursions were more severe than during the earlier portion of that period. The third part of the earth, would be the third part of the Roman empire, in distinction from the other two-thirds.

The green grass of the earth, the trees, &c., are distinguished from "those men which have not the seal of God in their foreheads" (9:4), and must therefore symbolize the people of God in the third part of the empire. As all the green grass is burnt up, while only one-third of the trees suffer, the latter cannot include one-third of all the trees in the empire, but only one-third in the parts affected,--the grass indicating the more weakly, and the trees the more hardy classes of Christians.

The infidel historian, Gibbon, has given the events which fitly correspond with the symbolization of these trumpets. After the death of Theodosius, in January, A. D. 395, Alaric, the bold leader of the Gothic nation, took arms against the empire. The terrible effects of this invasion, are thus described:--

"The barbarian auxiliaries erected their independent standard; and boldly avowed hostile designs, which they had long cherished in their ferocious minds. Their countrymen, who had been condemned, by the conditions of the last treaty, to a life of tranquillity and labor, deserted their farms at the first sound of the trumpet, and eagerly assumed the weapons which they had reluctantly laid down. The barriers of the Danube were thrown open; the savage warriors of Scythia issued from their forest; and the uncommon severity of the winter, allowed the poet to remark, that 'they rolled their ponderous wagons over the broad and icy back of the indignant river.' The unhappy nations of the provinces to the south of the Danube, submitted to the calamities, which, in the course of twenty years, were almost grown familiar to their imagination; and the various troops of barbarians, who gloried in the Gothic name, were irregularly spread from the woody shores of Dalmatia, to the walls of Constantinople. The Goths were directed by the bold and artful genius of Alaric. In the midst of a divided court, and a discontented people, the emperor, Arcadius, was terrified by the aspect of the Gothic arms. Alaric disdained to trample any longer on the prostrate and ruined countries of Thrace and Dacia, and he resolved to seek a plentiful harvest of fame and riches in a province which had hitherto escaped the ravages of war.

"Alaric traversed, without resistance, the plains of Macedonia and Thessaly. The troops which had been posted to defend the Straits of Thermopyl? retired, as they were directed, without attempting to disturb the secure and rapid passage of Alaric; and the fertile fields of Phocis and Boeotia were instantly covered with a deluge of barbarians, who massacred the males of an age to bear arms, and drove away the beautiful females, with the spoil and cattle of the flaming villages. The travellers who visited Greece several years afterwards, could easily discover the deep and bloody traces of the march of the Goths. The whole territory of Attica was blasted by his baneful presence; and if we may use the comparison of a cotemporary philosopher, Athens itself resembled the bleeding and empty skin of a slaughtered victim. Corinth, Argos, Sparta, yielded without resistance to the arms of the Goths; and the most fortunate of the inhabitants were saved, by death, from beholding the slavery of their families, and the conflagration of their cities."--Gibbon's Rome, vol. v., p. 177.

Being tempted by the fame of Rome, Alaric hastened to subjugate it. He put to flight the Emperor of the West; but deliverance soon came, and Rome was saved from his hands. Alaric was first conquered in 403. But another cloud was gathering, and is thus described by Gibbon:--

"About four years after the victorious Toulan had assumed the title of Khan of the Geougen, another barbarian, the haughty Rhodogast, or Radagaisus, marched from the northern extremities of Germany almost to the gates of Rome, and left the remains of his army to achieve the destruction of the West. The Vandals, the Suevi, and the Burgundians, formed the strength of this mighty host; but the Alani, who had found a hospitable reception in their new seats, added their active cavalry to the heavy infantry of the Germans; and the Gothic adventurers crowded so eagerly to the standard of Radagaisus, that, by some historians, he has been styled the King of the Goths. Twelve thousand warriors, distinguished above the vulgar by their noble birth, or their valiant deeds, glittered in the van; and the whole multitude, which was not less than two hundred thousand fighting men, might be increased by the accession of women, of children, and of slaves, to the amount of four hundred thousand persons.

"The correspondence of nations was, in that age, so imperfect and precarious, that the revolutions of the North might escape the knowledge of the court of Ravenna, till the dark cloud, which was collected along the coast of the Baltic, burst in thunder upon the banks of the Upper Danube, &c. Many cities of Italy were pillaged or destroyed; and the siege of Florence by Radagaisus, is one of the earliest events in the history of that celebrated republic, whose firmness checked or delayed the unskilful fury of the barbarians.

"While the peace of Germany was secured by the attachment of the Franks, and the neutrality of the Alemanni, the subjects of Rome, unconscious of the approaching calamities, enjoyed a state of quiet and prosperity, which had seldom blessed the frontiers of Gaul. Their flocks and herds were permitted to graze in the pastures of the barbarians: their huntsmen penetrated, without fear or danger, into the darkest recesses of the Hercynian wood. The banks of the Rhine were crowded, like those of the Tiber, with elegant houses and well-cultivated farms; and if the poet descended the river, he might express his doubt on which side was situated the territory of the Romans. This scene of peace and plenty was suddenly changed into a desert; and the prospect of the smoking ruins, could alone distinguish the solitude of nature, from the desolation of man. The flourishing city of Mentz was surprised and destroyed; and many thousand Christians were inhumanly massacred in the church. Worms perished, after a long and obstinate siege; Strasburg, Spires, Rheims, Tournay, Arras, Amiens, experienced the cruel oppression of the German yoke; and the consuming flames of war spread from the banks of the Rhine over the greatest part of the seventeen provinces of Gaul. That rich and extensive country, as far as the ocean, the Alps, and the Pyrenees, was delivered to the barbarians, who drove before them, in a promiscuous crowd, the bishop, the senator, and the virgin, laden with the spoils of their houses and altars."-- Ibid., vol. v., p. 224.

After this invasion of the empire by Radagaisus, Alaric again returned, invaded Italy in 408, and in 410 he besieged, took, and sacked Rome, and died the same year. In 412 the Goths voluntarily retired from Italy.

In this last year, "a public conference was held in Carthage, by order of the magistrate;" and it was there agreed to inflict the most severe penalties on those who dissented from the Catholic doctrines, in the African part of the Roman empire. Says Gibbon:--"Three hundred bishops, with many thousands of the inferior clergy, were torn from their churches, stripped of their ecclesiastical possessions, banished to the islands, and proscribed by the laws, if they presumed to conceal themselves in the provinces of Africa. Their numerous congregations, both in the cities and country, were deprived of the rights of citizens, and of the exercise of religious worship."

The Second Trumpet.

"And the second angel sounded, and it was as if a great mountain burning with fire were cast into the sea: and the third part of the sea became blood; and the third part of the creatures in the sea, and having life, died; and the third part of the ships was destroyed."--Rev. 8:8, 9.

A mountain differs from a tornado, and must symbolize a compact, organized body of invaders. Its being of a volcanic nature, renders it so much the more terrible and destructive.

As waters symbolize "peoples, multitudes, nations, and tongues," the sea into which the mountain is cast, is a people already agitated by previous commotions.

The ships and fish in the sea, must necessarily symbolize agents sustaining a relation to the Roman Sea, analogous to the relation of such to the literal sea. They are those who live upon, and are supported by, the people:--the rulers and the officers of state.

The symbol of a burning mountain fitly represents the armed invaders under Genseric. In the year 429, with fifty thousand effective men he landed on the shores of Africa, established an independent government in that part of the Roman empire, and from thence, harassed the southern shores of Europe and the intermediate islands, by perpetual incursions. Says Gibbon:--"The Vandals, who, in twenty years, had penetrated from the Elbe to Mount Atlas, were united under the command of their warlike king; and he reigned with equal authority over the Alarici, who had passed within the term of human life, from the cold of Scythia, to the excessive heat of an African climate.

"The Vandals and Alarici, who followed the successful standard of Genseric, had acquired a rich and fertile territory, which stretched along the coast from Tangiers to Tripoli; but their narrow limits were pressed and confined on either side by the sandy desert and the Mediterranean. The discovery and conquest of the black nations that might dwell beneath the torrid zone, could not tempt the rational ambition of Genseric; but he cast his eyes towards the sea; he resolved to create a new naval power, and his bold enterprise was executed with steady and active perseverance. The woods of Mount Atlas afforded an inexhaustible nursery of timber; his new subjects were skilled in the art of navigation and ship-building; he animated his daring Vandals to embrace a mode of warfare which would render every maritime country accessible to their arms; the Moors and Africans were allured by the hope of plunder; and, after an interval of six centuries, the fleet that issued from the port of Carthage again claimed the empire of the Mediterranean. The success of the Vandals, the conquest of Sicily, the sack of Palermo, and the frequent descents on the coast of Lucania, awakened and alarmed the mother of Valentinian, and the sister of Theodosius."

"The naval power of Rome was unequal to the task of saving even the imperial city from the ravages of the Vandals. Sailing from Africa, they disembarked at the port of Ostia, and Rome and its inhabitants were delivered to the licentiousness of Vandals and Moors, whose blind passions revenged the injuries of Carthage. The pillage lasted fourteen days and nights; and all that yet remained of public and private wealth, of sacred or profane treasure, was diligently transported to the vessels of Genseric. In the forty-five years that had elapsed since the Gothic invasion, the pomp and luxury of Rome were in some measure restored; and it was difficult either to escape, or to satisfy the avarice of a conqueror, who possessed leisure to collect, and ships to transport, the wealth of the capital."--Gibbon.

The Third Trumpet.

"And the third angel sounded, and a great star fell from heaven, burning like a torch, and it fell on the third part of the rivers, and on the fountains of waters; and the name of the star is called Wormwood: and the third part of the waters became wormwood; and many men died by the waters, because they were made bitter."--Rev. 8:10, 11.

The sounding of the third trumpet marks the advent of a third invader of the Roman empire. And such was Attila, the king of the Huns, who invaded Gaul A. D. 451. Gibbon says:--

"The kings and nations of Germany and Scythia, from the Volga perhaps to the Danube, obeyed the warlike summons of Attila. From the royal village in the plains of Hungary, his standard moved towards the west; and, after a march of seven or eight hundred miles, he reached the conflux of the Rhine and the Necker." "The hostile myriads were poured with resistless violence into the Belgic provinces." "The consternation of Gaul was universal." "From the Rhine and the Moselle, Attila advanced into the heart of Gaul, crossed the Seine at Auxerre, and, after a long and laborious march, fixed his camp under the walls of Orleans." "An alliance was formed between the Romans and Visigoths." The hostile armies approached. " 'I myself,' said Attila, 'will throw the first javelin, and the wretch who refuses to imitate the example of his sovereign, is devoted to inevitable death.' The spirit of the barbarians was rekindled by the presence, the voice, and the example, of their intrepid leader; and Attila, yielding to their impatience, immediately formed his order of battle. At the head of his brave and faithful Huns, Attila occupied, in person, the centre of the line." The nations from the Volga to the Atlantic were assembled on the plains of Chalons; and there fought a battle, "fierce, various, obstinate, and bloody, such as could not be paralleled, either in the present, or in past ages! The number of the slain amounted to one hundred and sixty-two thousand, or according to another account, three hundred thousand persons; and these incredible exaggerations suppose a real or effective loss, sufficient to justify the historian's remark, that whole generations may be swept away, by the madness of kings, in the space of a single hour."

Attila was compelled to retreat; but neither his forces nor reputation suffered. He "passed the Alps, invaded Italy, and besieged Aquileia with an innumerable host of barbarians." "The succeeding generation could scarcely discover the ruins of Aquileia. After this dreadful chastisement, Attila pursued his march; and, as he passed, the cities of Altinum, Concordia, and Padua were reduced into heaps of stones and ashes. The inland towns, Vicenza, Verona, and Bergamo, were exposed to the rapacious cruelty of the Huns. Milan and Pavia submitted, without resistance, to the loss of their wealth;" and "applauded the unusual clemency which preserved from the flames the public as well as private buildings, and spared the lives of the captive multitude." "Attila spread his ravages over the rich plains of modern Lombardy; which are divided by the Po, and bounded by the Alps and

Apennines." He took possession of the royal palace of Milan. "It is a saying worthy of the ferocious pride of Attila, that the grass never grew on the spot where his horse had trod."

He advanced into Italy, only as far as the plains of Lombardy and the banks of the Po, reducing the cities he passed to stones and ashes; but there his ravages ceased. He concluded a peace with the Romans in the year of his invasion of Italy (451), and the next year he died. Thus he appeared like a fiery meteor, exerted his appointed influence upon the tongues and people, who were tributary to the Romans,--as rivers and fountains of waters are to the sea; and like a burning star, he as suddenly expired. As a specimen of the bitterness which followed his course, it is recorded of the Thuringians who served in his army, and who traversed, both in their march and in their return, the territories of the Franks, "that they massacred their hostages as well as their captives. Two hundred young maidens were tortured with exquisite and unrelenting rage; their bodies were torn asunder by wild horses, or were crushed under the weight of rolling wagons; and their unburied limbs were abandoned on public roads, as a prey to dogs and vultures."

The Fourth Trumpet.

"And the fourth angel sounded, and the third part of the sun was smitten, and the third part of the moon, and the third part of the stars; so that the third part of them was darkened, and the day shone not for a third part of it, and the night in like manner."--Rev. 8:12.

The sun, moon, and stars cannot here, any more than under the sixth seal (6:12,13), symbolize agents of their own order, but must represent the rulers of the Roman empire. Says Dr. Keith:--

"At the voice of the first angel, and the blast of his trumpet, the whole Roman world was in agitation, and 'the storms of war' passed over it all. 'The union of the empire was dissolved;' a third part of it fell; and the 'transalpine provinces were separated from the empire.' Under the second trumpet, the provinces of Africa, another, or the maritime, part, was in like manner reft from Rome, and the Roman ships were destroyed in the sea, and even in their harbors. The empire of Rome, hemmed in on every side, was then limited to the kingdom of Italy. Within its bounds, and along the fountains and rivers of waters, the third trumpet reechoed from the Alps to the Apennines. The last barrier of the empire of Rome was broken. The plains of Lombardy were ravaged by a foreign foe: and from thence new enemies arose to bring to an end the strife of the world with the imperial city.

" 'In the space of twenty years since the death of Valentinian' (two years subsequent to the death of Attila), 'nine emperors had successively disappeared; and the son of Orestes, a youth recommended only by his beauty, would be the least entitled to the notice of posterity, if his reign, which was marked by the extinction of the Roman empire in the west, did not leave a memorable era in the history of mankind.' "

The throne of the Caesars had been for ages the sun of the world; while other kings were designated as stars. The imperial power had first been transferred to Constantinople by Constantine; and it was afterwards divided between the east and the west; but the eastern empire was not yet doomed to destruction. The precise year in which the western empire was extinguished, is not positively ascertained, but it is usually assigned to A. D. 476. Some place it in 479. The imperial Roman power, of which either Rome or Constantinople had been jointly or singly the seat, whether in the West or the East, ceased to be recognized in Italy; and the third part of the sun was smitten, till it emitted no longer the faintest rays. The power of the Cæsars became unknown in Italy; and a Gothic king reigned over Rome.

Dr. Keith considers that "the concluding words of the fourth trumpet imply the future restoration of the Western empire: 'The day shone not for a third part of it, and the night likewise.' In respect to civil authority, Rome became subject to Ravenna; and Italy was a conquered province of the Eastern empire. But, as more appropriately pertaining to other prophecies, the defence of the worship of images first brought the spiritual and temporal powers of the Pope and of the emperor into violent collision; and, by conferring on the Pope all authority over the churches, Justinian laid his helping hand to the promotion of the papal supremacy, which afterwards assumed the power of creating monarchs. In the year of our Lord 800, the Pope conferred on Charlemagne the title of Emperor of the Romans. The title was again transferred from the King of France to the Emperor of Germany. By the latter it was formally renounced, within the memory of the existing generation. In our own days the iron crown of Italy was on the head of another 'emperor.' " Then the sun was suddenly darkened, as symbolized under the sixth seal, 6:12. p. 66.

The Woe-denouncing Angel.

"And I beheld, and heard an eagle flying in the midst of heaven, saying with a loud voice, Woe, woe, woe, to the inhabitants of the earth, from the remaining voices of the trumpet of the three angels, who are to sound."-- Rev. 8:13.

The word eagle, instead of angel, is in accordance with the more recent revised editions of the Greek. It must symbolize persons peculiarly apprehensive at this crisis, of disasters to follow the extinction of the Roman empire in the west. During the first half of the sixth century, the Sclavonians invaded the east, "spread from the suburbs of Constantinople to the Ionian Gulf, destroyed thirty-two cities or castles which Athens had built, and Philip had besieged, and repassed the Danube, dragging at their horses' heels one hundred and twenty thousand of the subjects of Justinian."--Gibbon. And they continued their inroads, until the citizens became apprehensive that the Empire of the East would be extinguished like that of the West.

This symbol also indicates that the events under the trumpets which were to follow, would be far more dreadful and terrible than those of the preceding ones. For this reason, the last three are sometimes denominated THE WOE TRUMPETS.

The Fifth Trumpet.

"And the fifth angel sounded, and I saw a star, which had fallen from heaven to the earth: and to him was given the key of the pit of the abyss. And he opened the pit of the abyss: and a smoke arose out of the pit, like the smoke of a great furnace; and the sun and the air were darkened by the smoke of the pit. And locusts came out of the smoke into the earth: and power was given to them, as the scorpions of the earth have power. And it was said to them that they should not injure the herbage of the earth, nor any green thing, nor any tree; but only those men who have not the seal of God on their foreheads. And they were not allowed to kill them, but to torment them five months: and their torment was like the torment of a scorpion, when he striketh a man. And in those days men will seek death, and will not find it; and will desire to die, and death will flee from them. And the shapes of the locusts were like horses prepared for battle; and on their heads were as it were crowns like gold, and their faces were like the faces of men. And they had hair like the hair of women, and their teeth were like those of lions. And they had breast-plates, like breast-plates of iron; and the sound of their wings was like the sound of chariots with many horses rushing into battle. And they had tails like scorpions, and there were stings in their tails: and their power was to injure men five months. They had a king over them, the messenger of the abyss, whose name in Hebrew is Abaddon, but in the Greek tongue he hath the name Apollyon. One woe is past away; and behold, there come yet two woes hereafter."--Rev. 9:1-12.

The previous trumpets reveal the agencies which effected the dismemberment and overthrow of Western Rome. The fifth and sixth unfold those which terminated that empire in the east, embracing the territory between the Adriatic and Euphrates, the Lybian desert and the Danube.

A star (1:20) symbolizes a messenger, or head of a religious body, p. 31. Mohammed is generally regarded as represented by this symbol. He was, by birth, of the princely house of the Koreish, Governors of Mecca, a family of eminence.

The star had fallen to the earth before opening the pit of the abyss, which illustrates the flight of Mohammed from Mecca, and the seeming termination of all his hopes. To save his life, he took refuge, with one companion, in a cave near Medina, in A. D. 622, which forms the epoch of the Hegira, i.e., of his flight.

The bottomless pit, is where Satan is subsequently cast (20:3); and the key of it being given to this agent, symbolizes his power to open and to cause the smoke to issue from it; the Satanic origin of which is thus indicated:

Smoke is an appropriate representative of error, and symbolizes the Mohammedan doctrines; which, like the smoke of a great furnace, were disseminated far and wide, subverting the religion, and, in time, effecting the overthrow of the remaining portion of the Roman empire--the sun, one-third of which was smitten under the fourth trumpet.

The locusts were generated in the smoke from whence they issued. In a corresponding manner, the spread of Mohammedanism resulted in the organization of hordes of Saracens, who propagated the religion of the false prophet by the sword, and founded the famous Arabian empire, which extended from the Atlantic ocean to the river Euphrates.

The shapes of the locusts were like horses prepared for battle; and the Saracenic hordes, thus symbolized, were mounted horsemen, famous for the swiftness of their flight or pursuit, and ever ready for the contest.

Their crowns, faces, hair, teeth, breast-plates, &c., seem to be indicative of their personal appearance: on their heads they wore yellow turbans, like coronets; their demeanor was grave and firm; their hair, like that of women, was suffered to grow uncut; they were defended by the cuirass or breast-plate; and in rushing to battle, their onset was like that of chariots and many horses.

They had a king over them, named Abaddon in the Hebrew, and Apollyon in the Greek, both of which signified the Destroyer. The Saracens acknowledged the authority of Mohammed during the whole period of their conquests; not only recognizing him as their prophet and king during his lifetime, but his successors, after his death, considered and called themselves Mohammed's Caliphs, or Vicars.

Their mission was not against the grass, green things, and trees, but had express reference to the men who had not the seal of God in their foreheads. The antithesis here expressed, shows that by the former were symbolized the servants of God, and that these locust-warriors were particularly commissioned against infidels and apostates. Christians were not to be molested; and provision was made for their protection, in the circular letter which Abubekir sent to the Arabian tribes, A. D. 633. He said:

" 'Remember, that you are always in the presence of God, on the verge of death, in the assurance of judgment, and the hope of paradise: avoid injustice and oppression; consult with your brethren, and study to preserve the love and confidence of your troops. When you fight the battles of the Lord, acquit yourselves like men, without turning your backs; but let not your victory be stained with the blood of women and children. Destroy no palm-trees, nor burn any fields of corn. Cut down no fruit-trees, nor do any mischief to cattle, only such as you kill to eat. When you make any covenant, or article, stand to it, and be as good as your word. As you go on, you will find some religious persons who live in retired monasteries, and propose to themselves to serve God that way; let them alone, and neither kill them nor destroy their monasteries; and you will find another sort of people that belong to the synagogue of Satan, who have shaven crowns; be sure you cleave their skulls, and give them no quarter till they either turn Mohammedans or pay tribute.' "

At this epoch, the Greek church at Constantinople had been preserved from the reproach of image worship, and still later it made strenuous efforts against it; but the churches of the north of Africa, and the Asiatic portion of the Eastern empire, had become greatly debased, and worshipped saints and images. And while the territories of these were speedily subverted to Mohammedanism, and became a part of the Arabian empire, the east of Europe was wonderfully preserved from their inroads.

Their power was not to kill, but to torment men five months. To kill, symbolically, according to the significance of the second seal, p. 60, is to compel men to apostasize; and they could not be in a condition to force their religion on the men of the eastern empire, without first subjecting it by force of arms.

The time of this torment was limited to five prophetic months. In one hundred and fifty years from the Hegira the Saracen empire had ceased to be aggressive. In 762 Bagdad, the city of peace, was founded on the Tigris, by Al-Mansur, who died in 774. "From this time," says ROTTICK, "the Arabian history assumes an entirely different character." It was no longer progressive; the proud Saracen empire became dismembered, and three independent and hostile Caliphates, and several fragments of kingdoms, were formed from its ruins. In 841, the reigning Caliph at Bagdad, distrusting the spirit of his own troops, hired a body of fifty thousand Turkish soldiers, which he distributed in his dominions. These accelerated the ruin of the Caliphate, and, in time, the whole of the Saracen territory became subject to the Tartar rule, which had become Mohammedan, and also aimed to subject the eastern empire.

The declaration that "one woe is past," v. 12, implies an interval between that and the woe following. In a corresponding manner, the crusaders from Europe, like the successive overflowing of a mighty river, restrained the Tartars from the conquest of Constantinople, which had now consented to image worship, till the sounding of:

The Sixth Trumpet.

"And the sixth angel sounded, and I heard a voice out of the four horns of the golden altar before God, saying to the sixth angel having the trumpet, Loose the four messengers bound near the great river Euphrates. And the four messengers were loosed, prepared for an hour, and day, and month, and year, to slay the third part of men. And the number of the army of the horsemen were two hundred thousand thousand: I heard the number of them. And thus I saw on the horses in the vision, and those, who sat on them, having red, blue and yellow breast-plates: and the heads of the horses were like the heads of lions; and fire, and smoke, and brimstone issued from their mouths. By these three plagues the third part of men was killed; by the fire, and by the smoke, and by the brimstone, which issued from their mouths. For the power of the horses is in their mouth, and in their tails: for their tails having heads were like serpents, and they injure with them. And the rest of the men, who were not killed by these plagues, yet repented not of the works of their hands, that they should not worship demons, and idols of gold, and silver, and brass, and stone, and of wood: which can neither see, nor hear, nor walk; nor did they repent of their murders, nor of their sorceries, nor of their fornication, nor of their thefts."--Rev. 9:13-21.

The great river, the Euphrates,--waters being a symbol of people, (17:15)--must symbolize those who sustain a relation to the Roman hierarchy, as its defenders and supporters; analogous to that sustained by the river Euphrates to the city of Babylon; which was situated on, and drew its wealth and support from it.

The angels bound near the Euphrates, must then be those powers, which, approaching and attacking the Roman Empire, were restrained from effecting its conquest and enforcing the profession of Mohammedanism. Their being loosed, signifies the removal of those restraints. Mr. Lord suggests that they symbolize leaders of the four armies of the Tartars, which successively overran the surrounding provinces. He says:

"The first horde were the Seljukians, who invaded the Eastern empire about the middle of the eleventh century, under Togrul Beg. He suddenly overran, with myriads of cavalry, the frontier, from Taurus to Arzeroum, and spread it with blood and devastation. Alp Arslan, his successor, soon renewed the invasion, conquered Armenia and Georgia, penetrated into Cappadocia and Phrygia, and scattered detachments over the whole of lesser Asia. His troops being subsequently driven back, he renewed the war, and recovered those provinces. His descendants, and others of the race, soon after extended their conquests, and established the kingdoms in the east of Persia and Syria, and Roum, in lesser Asia, which they maintained through many generations, and made their sway a scorpion scourge to the idolatrous inhabitants. The Christians were allowed the exercise of their religion on the conditions of tribute and servitude, but were compelled to endure the scorn of the victors, to submit to the abuse of their priests and bishops, and to witness the apostasy of their brethren, the compulsory circumcision of many thousands of their children, and the subjection of many thousands to a debasing and hopeless slavery.

"The second army was that of the Moguls, who, in the thirteenth century, after the conquest of Persia, passed the Euphrates, plundered and devastated Syria, subdued Armenia, Iconium, and Anatolia, and extinguished the Seljukian dynasty. Another army advancing to the west, devastated the country on both sides of the Danube, Thrace, Bulgaria, Servia, Bosnia, Hungary, Austria, and spread them with the ruins of their cities and churches, and the bones of their inhabitants. This horde had been prepared for this invasion by vast conquests in the East.

"The third were the Ottomans, who in the beginning of the fourteenth century conquered Bithynia, Lydia, Ionia, Thrace, Bulgaria, Servia, and in the following century Constantinople itself, and have maintained their empire to the present time. They were released from restraint on the one hand by the decay of the Mogul Khans, to whom they had been subject, and on the other by the dissensions and weakness of the Greeks.

"The last was that of the Moguls under Tamerlane, who in the beginning of the fifteenth century overran Georgia, Syria, and Anatolia, and spread them with slaughter and desolation. He also had been prepared for this incursion by his previous victories and conquests."--Ex. Apoc., pp. 225, 226.

These armies, the number of which is literally "myriads of myriads," were not all subsequent to the time when they had power to subject the Eastern Roman empire; but may be the four, from the fact that the Mohammedan power was extended by these armies, which till this time had been restrained from accomplishing the subjugation of Constantinople.

The restraints being removed, they were now to have power to kill, by compelling the third part of men to embrace the doctrines of Mohammed,-- evident reference being had to the men of the eastern empire; the conquest of which was now to be effected, the dial of heaven having indicated the arrival of the predicted epoch.

In 1449 Constantine Deacoses, being entitled to the throne of

Constantinople by the death of John Paleologus, did not venture to take possession till he had sent ambassadors and gained the consent of Amurath, the Turkish Sultan. From this fact, Ducas, the historian, counts Paleologus as the last Greek emperor--for he did not consider as such, a prince who did not dare to reign without permission of his enemy. Amurath died and was succeeded in the empire, in 1451, by MAHOMET II., who set his heart on Constantinople, and made preparations for besieging the city. The siege commenced on the 6th of April, 1453, and ended in the taking of the city, and death of the last of the Constantines, on the 16th of May following, when the eastern city of the Caesars became the seat of the Ottoman empire; and its "religion was trampled in the dust by the Moslem conquerors." Thus the two-horned beast (13:11), became merged in, and identified with the false prophet, 16:13, and 19:20.

The description of the horses, and those who sat on them (v. 17), is strikingly emblematic of the Turkish warriors who subjugated Constantinople. Says Dr. Keith: "The breast-plates of the horsemen, in reference to the more destructive implements of war, might then, for the first time, be said to be fire, and jacinth, and brimstone. The musket had recently supplied the place of the bow. Fire emanated from their breasts. Brimstone, the flame of which is jacinth, was an ingredient both of the liquid fire and of gunpowder.... A new mode of warfare was at that time introduced, which has changed the nature of war itself, in regard to the form of its instrument of destruction; and sounds and sights unheard of and unknown before, were the death-knell and doom of the Roman empire. Invention outrivalled force, and a new power was introduced, that of musketry as well as of artillery, in the art of war, before which the old Macedonian phalanx would not have remained unbroken, nor the Roman legions stood. That which JOHN saw 'in the vision,' is read in the history of the times."

By these three, the fire, smoke, and brimstone, were the third part of men killed (v. 18), and by these was the conquest of Constantinople effected. Says Gibbon: "At the request of Mahomet II., Urban produced a piece of brass ordnance of stupendous and almost incredible magnitude. A measure of twelve palms was assigned to the bore, and the stone bullet weighed about six hundred pounds. A vacant place before the new palace was chosen for the first experiment; but to prevent the sudden and mischievous effects of astonishment and fear, a proclamation was issued that the cannon would be discharged the ensuing day. The explosion was felt or heard in a circuit of a hundred furlongs; the ball, by the force of the gunpowder, was driven about a mile, and on the spot where it fell, it buried itself a fathom deep in the ground. For the conveyance of this destructive engine, a frame or carriage of thirty wagons was linked together, and drawn along by a train of sixty oxen; two hundred men, on both sides, were stationed to poise or support the rolling weight; two hundred and fifty workmen marched before to smooth the way and repair the bridges, and near two months were employed in a laborious journey of a hundred and fifty miles.

"In the siege, the incessant volleys of lances and arrows were accompanied with the smoke, the sound, and the fire of their musketry and cannon. Their small arms discharged at the same time five or even ten balls of lead of the size of a walnut, and according to the closeness of the ranks, and the force of the powder, several breast-plates and bodies were transpierced by the same shot. But the Turkish approaches were soon sunk into trenches, or covered with ruins. Each day added to the science of the Christians, but their inadequate stock of gunpowder was wasted in the operation of each day. Their ordnance was not powerful either in size or number, and if they possessed some heavy cannon, they feared to plant them on the walls, lest the aged structure should be shaken and overthrown by the explosion. The same destructive secret had been revealed to the Moslems, by whom it was employed with the superior energy of zeal, riches, and despotism. The great cannon of MAHOMET was flanked by two fellows almost of equal magnitude: the long order of the Turkish artillery was pointed against the walls: fourteen batteries thundered at once on the most accessible places, and of one of these it is ambiguously expressed that it was mounted with one hundred and thirty guns, or that it discharged one hundred and thirty bullets."

The conquest of Constantinople being accomplished, they were to have power to kill men during an hour, day, month, and year of prophetic time-- i.e. three hundred and ninety-one years, fifteen days. If reckoned from the conquest of the city, this would extend to June 1844. Whether any particular act has transpired to mark the precise point of its termination, may not be important; but it is interesting to consider that within a few years the Mohammedan government has formally granted permission for the full enjoyment of the Protestant religion; and has renounced the right of punishing by death, apostates from Islamism.

In August 1843, an Armenian, who had become a Mussulman and subsequently returned to the religion of his fathers, was beheaded at Constantinople. The Christian powers of Europe immediately remonstrated, and it was hoped that the law against apostates from Mohammedanism would be permitted to become a dead letter. In a few months, however, a firman issued from the government ordering the decapitation of a young man near Brooza, who was put to death for having promised in a passion, but had afterwards refused, to become a Mohammedan. Lord Aberdeen, the British Secretary of Foreign Affairs, then demanded of the Turkish Sultan that the Porte should not insult and trample on Christianity, "by treating as a criminal any person who embraces it;" but should "renounce, absolutely and without equivocation, the barbarous practice which has called forth the remonstrance now addressed to it." To this communication the following answer was made early in 1844: "The Sublime Porte engages to take effectual measures to prevent, henceforward, the execution and putting to death of the Christian who is an apostate." On the 15th of November, 1847, for the first time, a firman was issued recognizing Protestant Christians as a distinct community, forbidding any molestation or interference "in their temporal or spiritual concerns," and permitting them "to exercise the profession of their creed in security." This coming from the Vizier, did not necessarily survive a change of ministry; but in November, 1850, a firman was issued from the Sultan himself, establishing the policy of the empire in respect to Protestants, and confirming them in all needed civil and religious privileges. Thus has the Mohammedan government formally and forever renounced the power it had so long wielded, of causing spiritual death by compelling men to apostatize from Christianity.

The rest of the men not killed, must be those in portions of the Roman territory not included in the eastern third. The Roman Catholics in the western parts, were not reformed by the judgments inflicted on the east. They continued to worship the canonized dead, and to bow down to images of the saints. Under this trumpet, a mighty movement was to be there effected, which was symbolized by the descent of:

The Rainbow Angel.

"And I saw another mighty angel descending from heaven, clothed with a cloud: and the rainbow was over his head, and his face was like the sun, and his feet like pillars of fire; and he had in his hand a little book opened: and he set his right foot on the sea, and his left foot on the land. And shouted with a loud voice, as a lion roareth: and when he shouted, seven thunders uttered their voices. And when the seven thunders had uttered their voices, I was about to write: and I heard a voice from heaven saying, Seal up those things, which the seven thunders uttered, and write them not. And the angel, whom I saw standing on the sea and on the land, raised his hand to heaven, and swore by him who liveth for ever and ever, who created heaven, and the things in it, and the earth, and the things in it, and the sea, and the things in it, that the time should not yet be; but in the days of the voice of the seventh angel, when he will sound, the secret of God will be finished, as he hath announced to his servants the prophets. And the voice, which I heard from heaven, spoke with me again, and said, Go, take the little book, which is opened in the hand of the angel, who standeth on the sea and on the land. And I went away to the angel, and said to him, Give me the little book. And he said to me, Take, and eat it up; and it will make thy stomach bitter, but in thy mouth, it will be sweet as honey. And I took the little book from the angel's hand, and ate it up; and it was in my mouth sweet as honey: and when I had eaten it my stomach was bitter. And he said to me, Thou must prophesy again concerning many people, and nations, and tongues, and kings."--Rev. 10:1-11.

This angel, like those in corresponding passages, must symbolize a body of men, whose importance is indicated by the might and splendor of the symbol.

His descent from heaven, the cloud, the rainbow, the sun-like face, and the fire-like feet of the Mighty Messenger, attest the heaven-inspired origin of his utterances. His "eyes as a flame of fire, and his feet like unto fine brass, as if they burned in a furnace," would not be given to one who came to announce other than heaven-inspired truths.

The open book in the hand of the angel, fixes the chronology of the fulfilment of this vision at an epoch when the Scriptures cease to be a closed and sealed book, and the people are permitted to have free access to them.

His position--one foot resting on the sea, and one on the land--attests the universality of the movement which is to date from that epoch.

His lion voice, must symbolize the manner in which would be announced the great truths, at which the whole world would be startled.

The singleness of his cry, is also symbolic of the simplicity of the truth, which is never symbolized by discordant multitudinous sounds.

The responsive thunders, unlike the single voice of the angel, are multitudinous and discordant; and consequently symbolize errors. Their following so immediately on the shout of the angel, shows the proximity of their promulgation to the utterance of the truths to which they are responsive.

JOHN'S readiness to write what the seven thunders uttered, shows that what they uttered was professedly in harmony with the truths previously announced, and that men would be liable to be deceived, by their promulgation.

His being forbidden by the cloud-robed angel, to write what they uttered--while he was commanded to "seal not the sayings of the prophecy of this book" (22:10),--shows that their utterances were not heaven-inspired, and constituted no part of "the word of GOD, and of the testimony of JESUS CHRIST," which JOHN bare record of.

The subsequent oath of the angel, by Him who liveth forever, that "the time is not yet," shows that those thunders, however erroneous in their form manner and connection with other errors, had respect to some great event foretold in Scripture; but which the thunders had antedated and presented in an unscriptural form.

His further announcement that it would be fulfilled under the sounding of the "seventh trumpet," and that then the mystery of GOD should be finished in the manner foretold to his servants the prophets, shows that the great event, the time of which was "not yet,"--i.e., under the sixth trumpet, was the coming of the kingdom of GOD--the fifth universal empire; that at a period anterior to the time when it might rationally be expected, it would be proclaimed in a form repugnant to the teachings of the prophets; and that when thus heralded, it would be met by the party uttering the heaven-inspired truths, with the denial that the time had arrived, and by arguments to show its true nature and epoch, under the seventh trumpet.

The command to take and eat the little book, shows that its contents were such as the soul might feed on; which should be sweet to the believer's taste, but would subject him to bitter persecution. And the announcement that they were to prophesy again before many nations and peoples and tongues and kings, marks this as the commencement of an era when the Gospel should again begin to go forth into distant lands.

All of the above particulars harmonize in the time of the reformation of LUTHER in the sixteenth century, and with no other epoch. The great truths then promulgated, of which "justification by faith" was the cardinal one, electrified the whole world, as the loud roaring of a lion would startle the passer-by. These were immediately responded to by the multitudinous errors of the Anabaptists and others, who thought to set up the kingdom of GOD in this world, and before the resurrection, by putting to death the ungodly and sparing only the saints.

As in all efforts for good Satan is careful to attempt a counterfeit, or to mingle impure elements to the injury of the truth, so in the Reformation there were false reformers. THOMAS MUNZER, and others, in 1525, incited vast numbers on the borders of the Danube to make physical war on the Papal ecclesiastics. He denounced LUTHER, also, with the same violence that he did the Pope. In his mad attempt to slay the ungodly, he took possession of Muhlhausen, appointed a new city council, pillaged the houses of the rich, proclaimed a community of goods, and committed various excesses; but they were finally defeated in a pitched battle, with a loss of from five thousand to seven thousand killed. Others succeeded him, teaching that GOD spake to them in person, instructing them how to act. They professed the most extravagant doctrines, setting aside both LUTHER and the Bible. The former did not go near far enough for them; and the latter was in their view insufficient for man's instruction, who could only be taught of God. They taught that the world was to be immediately devastated; and no priest or ungodly person be left alive; and that then the kingdom of GOD would commence, and the saints possess the earth. Those who adhered to LUTHER, united with him in bearing a faithful testimony against such extravagances, adhered to the written word, denounced new revelations, and showed from the Bible that Antichrist was to be overthrown by the personal advent of CHRIST, and not by the sword of man. The following extracts are from MR. LORD:

"The pretences of the Anabaptists to inspiration were in like manner denounced by Melancthon. 'The Anabaptists, infatuated by the devil, have boasted a new species of sanctity, as though they had left the earth, and ascended to the skies; and given out, moreover, that they enjoy extraordinary inspiration. But as the pretence was hypocritical, and designed merely to subserve appetite and ambition, they soon plunged into debauchery, and then excited seditions, and undertook to establish a New Jerusalem, as other enthusiasts have often attempted. A like tragedy was formerly acted at Pepuza in Phrygia, which fanatical prophets denominated the new Jerusalem.'

"He also refuted by the Scriptures, the expectation of the Anabaptists of the immediate establishment of Christ's millennial kingdom. He regarded the term Antichrist as denoting both the Mohammedan empire and the Papacy, and held that they were not to be overthrown till the time of the resurrection of the dead, and that a considerable period was to pass before that event.

'God showed to Daniel a series of monarchies and kingdoms, which it is certain has already run to the end. Four monarchies have passed away. The cruel kingdom of the Turks, which arose out of the fourth, still remains, and as it is not to equal the Roman in power, and has certainly, therefore, already nearly reached its height, must soon decline, and then will dawn the day in which the dead shall be recalled to life.' He then repeats the saying ascribed to Elias, that six thousand years were to pass before the advent of Christ; two thousand before the law, two under the law, and two under the gospel; and proceeds to show that four hundred and fifty-eight years were, therefore, to intervene before the advent of the Redeemer, the destruction of Antichrist, and the establishment of the kingdom of the saints. 'It is known that Christ was born about the end of the fourth millenary,(1) and one thousand five hundred and forty-two years have since revolved. We are not, therefore [in 1542], far from the end.'

"These views corresponding so conspicuously with the symbol, continued to be repeated by a crowd of writers, till at the distance of sixty-seven years from the death of Melancthon, the celebrated Joseph Mede published his 'Clavis Apocalyptica,' in which he showed from the coincidence of the periods of the wild beast and the witnesses, that the advent of the Redeemer, and the destruction of the anti-Christian powers were not to be expected until twelve hundred and sixty years had passed from the rise of the ten kingdoms, and that near one hundred of them, therefore, were still to revolve. As that period expired and the knowledge of the prophecy advanced, the catastrophe of the wild beast was referred to a later time. Many recent expositors regard the twelve hundred and sixty years as having reached their end in 1792; and most refer the fall of the anti-Christian powers to the last half of the present, or the beginning of the next century."--Ex. of Apoc., pp. 238-240.

All the vagaries of the various sects of heretics were connected with an expectation of the immediate establishment of CHRIST'S kingdom. That the seven thunders gave utterance to such an expectation, is evident from the response of the angel, when he lifted up his hand to heaven and with the solemnity of an oath, by Him who liveth forever, affirmed that "the time should not yet be;" but that "in the days of the voice of the seventh angel, when he delays to sound,(2) the secret of GOD will be finished, as he hath announced to his servants the prophets." Why such an annunciation at this stage of the vision? It must be to correct a misapprehension which would exist at a corresponding time in its fulfilment, respecting the immediate appearance of the kingdom. Thus did PAUL correct the Thessalonian brethren, when he wrote to them in his second epistle not to be shaken in mind, as that the day of the LORD was then impending, 2 Th. 2:2.

The Bible, was, at this epoch, first opened to the common people. Before, it was only found in languages which they were entirely ignorant of. It was translated by LUTHER into their own language, and thus made accessible. The art of printing, discovered at about that time, enabled all who wished, to avail themselves of its unsealed contents. They feasted on the words of inspiration, which were sweeter to them than honey, or the honey-comb. But afterwards, they had to endure bitterness for the sake of the Gospel. Divisions and subdivisions followed, parties multiplied, and heresies abounded, accompanied with bitter and mischievous discussions, and fierce and rancorous contentions. These being based on the understanding which the several parties attached to portions of scripture, were fitly symbolized by the bitterness that followed the eating of the book. At this time, also, was revived a system of religious teachings which has gone forth into many lands.

The reorganization of the church at this epoch, is next symbolized.

The Measuring Reed, Temple, &c.

"And there was given me a measuring reed like a rod, and it was said, Arise, and measure the temple of God, (and the altar,) and those who worship in it. But the court which is without the temple, leave out, and measure it not; for it is given to the Gentiles: and they will tread the holy city under foot forty-two months."--Rev. 11:1, 2.

These symbols are evidently taken from the temple and altar of Jewish worship, and represent corresponding analogies under the Christian dispensation.

To measure anything, is to examine and take notice of its parts and proportions; and that by which it is measured, is the standard or rule to which it should conform.

The temple, is a proper symbol of the church of God; which is "built upon the foundation of the apostles and prophets, Jesus Christ himself being the Chief Corner Stone, in whom all the building, fitly framed together, groweth unto a holy temple in the Lord," Eph. 2:20, 21.

At the epoch of the Reformation, the nominal church was subjected to the scrutiny of the word of God; and its pretensions were measured by the scriptural rule. The reformers found the Man of Sin, "as God sitting in the temple of God," (2 Thess. 2:4); and they had to re-model their church relationship, in accordance with the pattern presented in the New Testament. This involved the consideration of what constituted the church,--its organization, its ministry, its sacraments, and its membership,--their mutual relation to God, and to each other.

The altar, must symbolize the sacrifice and atonement of Christ,--the "altar whereof they have no right to eat which serve the tabernacle," Heb. 13:10. The great question, of justification by faith in the death of Christ, was the rallying cry of the Reformation. The fundamental principles of Christian truth were then unfolded anew, and the doctrines of the Papacy, including the sacrifice of the mass, were rejected as contrary to Bible teachings.

The worshippers in the temple, who were to be measured by the same rule, are Christians. All who were to be recognized as such, were to give evidence of conformity to the Bible standard. Regeneration by the Holy Ghost, was held by the reformers to be necessary to church membership. The Papists required only baptism and confirmation.

The court without the temple, was that to which the Gentiles had access, and beyond which their entrance was prohibited. Devout foreigners were there permitted to pay their devotions to the God of heaven. As the Gentiles must symbolize those who are not Christians, the occupants of the outer court, must be the congregation--the nominal worshippers who throng the outer courts of the Lord, in distinction from the true worshippers. Such were to have free and unrestricted access to the places of Christian worship.

The holy city is that in which the temple is situated, and must embrace the church as a whole, subjected to Gentile rule. Its being trodden under foot, indicates that the civil polity under which the church would subsist, should, during the period specified, be under the control of those who worship only in the outer court.

The forty and two months, is a period of time, corresponding with the thousand two hundred and three score days of the verse following, the time and times and half a time of Rev. 12:14, and the corresponding periods of Rev. 12:6; 13:5; Dan. 7:25; and 12:7; symbolizing a period of twelve hundred and sixty years, according to the almost unanimous opinion of Protestant writers.

This period does not commence with this epoch, but began with the subjection of Christianity to the power of the civil arm, which was to continue during the time predicted,--notwithstanding the readjustment of the temple-worship,--when Christians should cease to be responsible to any human tribunal for the orthodoxy of their faith.

During the same period, also, power to prophesy, though shrouded in sackcloth, was to be given to:

Christ's Two Witnesses.

"And I will give charge to my two witnesses, and they will prophesy one thousand two hundred sixty days, clothed in sackcloth. These are the two olive-trees, and the two lamp-stands, standing before the Lord of the earth. And if any one wisheth to injure them, fire proceedeth from their mouth, and devoureth their enemies: and if anyone wisheth to injure them, he must thus be killed. These have power to shut heaven, that it may not rain in the days of their prophecy: and they have power over the waters to turn them to blood, and to smite the earth with every plague, as often as they wish. And when they shall have finished their testimony, the wild beast that ascendeth out of the abyss will make war with them, and will overcome them, and kill them. And their dead body will lie on the wide street of the great city, which is spiritually called Sodom and Egypt, where also their Lord was crucified. And those of the people, and tribes, and tongues, and nations, will see their dead body three days and a half, and will not allow their dead body to be put into a tomb. And those, who dwell on the earth, will rejoice over them, and exult, and send gifts to each other; because these two prophets tormented those, who dwell on the earth. And after the three days and a half the Spirit of life from God entered them, and they stood on their feet; and great fear fell on those, who saw them. And they heard a great voice from heaven, saying to them, Ascend here! And they ascended into heaven in a cloud; and their enemies saw them. And in that hour there was a great earthquake, and the tenth part of the city fell, and in the earthquake seven thousand names of men were slain: and the remnant became terrified, and gave glory to the God of heaven. The second woe is past away; behold, the third woe cometh quickly."--Rev. 11:3-14.

The two witnesses are not symbolically exhibited, but are referred to by an elliptical metaphor, and are explained to be the "two olive-trees, and the two candlesticks." Therefore, they are not two living men, as some suppose, shown to John in vision, symbolizing analogous agents; but their nature is to be determined by a consideration of the olive-trees and candlesticks which symbolize them.

Candlesticks symbolize churches. Thus the Saviour said to John: "The seven candlesticks which thou sawest are the seven churches," 1:20. When "men light a candle," they put "it on a candlestick, and it giveth light unto all that are in the house," Matt. 5:15. The candlestick does not originate, but sustains the light in a position to be seen and exert a beneficial influence. It is thus that the church is said to be "the light of the world," and is required to let her light "shine before men," Ib. vs. 14-16,--i.e. She is to disseminate the light committed to her; and in so doing, she becomes a witness for Jesus.

The church comprises all the holy persons who have lived on earth, and is symbolized by two candlesticks, corresponding to the two dispensations of its existence. Those who lived under the former dispensation, are called "a great cloud of witnesses," Heb. 12:1. Of Christ, "give all the prophets witness," Acts 10:43. They constitute the voice of the church in that age. Under the gospel dispensation, also, Christ had chosen witnesses of himself. He said to his disciples, "Ye shall be witnesses unto me, both in Jerusalem and in all Judea, and in Samaria, and unto the uttermost parts of the earth," (Ib. 1:8); and they said, "We are his witnesses," Ib. 5:32. "We are witnesses of all things which he did, ... witnesses chosen before of God," (Ib. 10:39-41);--"his witnesses unto the people," Ib. 13:31. They and their successors have "testified and preached the word of the Lord," (Ib. 8:25), overcoming "by the word of their testimony," (Rev. 12:11),--many of them being "slain for the word of God, and for the testimony which they held," 6:9. The church, one in all ages, symbolized by the two candlesticks, is thus a witness of Jesus.

The two olive-trees, symbolize the other witness, which must sustain a relation to the church, analogous to that sustained by the olive-trees to the candlesticks. The declaration, that the witnesses are the two olive-trees and candlesticks, implies the existence of some previous symbolization, where those objects and their relation to each other are presented. And the connection shows clearly that reference is made to the vision, wherein Zechariah beheld "a candlestick all of gold, with a bowl upon the top of it, and his seven lamps thereon, and seven pipes to the seven lamps, which are upon the top thereof; and two olive-trees by it, one upon the right side of the bowl, and the other upon the left side thereof," Zech. 4:2, 3. The relation which the olive-trees sustain to the candlestick, is shown by the questions of the prophet: "What are these, my Lord?" (Ib. v. 4); "What are these two olive-trees upon the right side of the candlestick and upon the left side thereof? What be these two olive-branches which through the two golden pipes empty the golden oil out of themselves?" Ib. vs. 11, 12. The office of the olive-trees, was to supply the candlestick with oil which alone enabled them to give light. The oil of the olive-tree, was burned before the Lord continually. The light committed to the church, is the truth of God's word. And thus the angel explains the meaning of the olive-trees: "This is the word of the Lord unto Zerubbabel," (Ib. v. 6); "These are the two anointed ones [mar, sons of oil], that stand by the Lord of the whole earth," Ib. v. 14. And this expression, corresponding with that in Rev. 11:4, shows that this vision of Zechariah is the one referred to, and that it is explanatory of the witnesses.

The Scriptures, as well as the church, testify of Christ: "Search the Scriptures," said the Saviour, speaking of those then written; "they are they which testify [or bear witness] of me," (John 5:39); and of the New Testament, he said: "This gospel of the kingdom shall be preached in all the world for a witness unto all nations," Matt. 24:4. Like two olive-trees supplying the candlesticks with oil, the Scriptures of the Old, and of the New Testament give light to the church, and testify of Christ. They stand on either side of him,--the one beginning with the creation and pointing to a Messiah to come, testifying of him by types and shadows; and the other looking back to the death and resurrection of Christ, and cheering the heart of the believer by the evidence of his second coming at the end of the world. Thus stood within the oracle of the temple the two cherubim, which Solomon made "of olive-tree," and whose wings met over the ark of the covenant: "He set the cherubim within the inner house, and they stretched forth the wings of the cherubim, so that the wing of the one touched the one wall, and the wing of the other cherub touched the other wall; and their wings touched one another in the midst of the house," 1 Kings 6, 27. Thus symbolized, the Scriptures and the church are Christ's two witnesses.

To prophesy, is to make known the truths of God. Thus, at the epoch of the Reformation, they were to prophesy again before many peoples, and nations, and tongues and kings, 10:11. It was to enable the witnesses to do this, that the necessary power was to be given them.

Sackcloth, is a symbol of humiliation and sorrow; and the witnesses being thus clothed, indicates that during the time specified, they should be in a despised and oppressed condition.

The one thousand two hundred and sixty days, symbolize years. God said to Israel, after the evil report of the twelve spies: "Your children shall wander in the wilderness forty years ... after the number of the days which ye searched the land," Num. 14:33, 34. And to Ezekiel, "This shall be a sign to the house of Israel: Lie thou upon thy left side, and lay the iniquity of the house of Israel upon it, ... for I have laid upon thee the years of their iniquity, according to the number of the days, three hundred and ninety days.... And when thou hast accomplished them, lie again on thy right side, and thou shalt bear the iniquity of the house of Judah forty days: I have appointed thee each day for a year," Ezek. 4:3-6.

This period of one thousand two hundred and sixty years, is not the whole time in which the witnesses prophesy, but marks the duration of their prophesying in sackcloth. It commenced when the light of the Bible began to be obscured by the secondary place which was accorded to it in the estimation of the Papal church, and the living witnesses were no longer permitted to preach the gospel in its purity.

In A. D. 533, the Emperor Justinian, wrote a letter to the Pope declaring him to be "the head of all the holy churches," and subjecting to his control "all the priests of the whole East." By the edicts and mandates of Justinian, who was master of the Roman world, the supremacy of the Pope received the fullest sanction; and the highest authorities among the civilians and annalists of Rome, refer to these as evidence of the right of the Pope to the title of "Universal Bishop," and date it from A. D. 533. p. 200.

With this supremacy, the power of the Papacy commenced. The Bible was permitted only in a dead language, and the faithful Christian was obliged to seek refuge in the wilderness. False doctrines obscuring the Bible, and persecuting enactments oppressing the church, clothed the witnesses in sackcloth; and thus only did they testify, till the power of the papacy was broken.

Fire proceeded out of their mouth, when they made known the fiery judgments predicted in the Scriptures against all their enemies. And they shut heaven, smite with plagues, turn water to blood, &c., when, in accordance with the inspired record, are fulfilled the predictions which, in various places, are thus symbolized.--See Rev. 15:6; 16:4, &c.

The finishing of their testimony, refers to the termination of the sackcloth period,--twelve hundred and sixty years from A. D. 533; i.e. in 1793,--if the former date is correct.

The beast that ascendeth out of the bottomless pit, is that on which, in a subsequent vision, the woman is seated, 17:7, 8. John saw this beast arise out of the sea, (13:1); and the subsequent exposition given of it, will show that it symbolized the civil power of the Roman empire in its divided form.--See p. 169. As the ten kingdoms constitute the beast, what is done by any of these kingdoms, is done by the beast. France was one of the more prominent of these kingdoms, and at one period, under Napoleon, controlled the greater portion of the whole.

To war against the witnesses, is to oppose, resist, and endeavor to crush them; and to overcome them, is to be successful in such efforts.

To kill, when used symbolically and applied to Christians, is to cause them to apostatize--producing spiritual death, 9:5. When applied to the Scriptures, it can only denote their prohibition.

The great city, as shown in connection with Rev. 16:19, p. 290, is the Roman hierarchy:--symbolized by Babylon, and "spiritually called Sodom and Egypt." By being thus "spiritually called Sodom," some understand that it is a "spiritual Sodom," &c., which would be a contradiction of terms; others understand that it is called figuratively by those names, and deduce from it an argument for spiritualizing the Scriptures; but the use of the word "spiritually," it is believed, will not sanction any such meaning. It occurs only in two other passages:--in Rom. 8:7, to be "spiritually minded," is to have a mind in accordance with the will of the Spirit; and in 1 Cor. 2:14, things "spiritually discerned," signifies that they are discerned by the aid of the Spirit. The great city, then, is called by the Spirit, "Sodom and Egypt;" and is so called because of her licentiousness and idolatries, and her subjecting the saints to bondage. To crucify the Lord afresh, is to apostatize from his teachings, Heb. 6:6.

In 1793, twelve hundred and sixty years from the date of the Papal supremacy, the Bible was abolished in France, by the solemn decree of the government, which declared that the nation acknowledged no God. A copy of the Bible could not be found in a single bookstore in Paris. Inquiry also was made for it in Rome, in all the book establishments of that city, and the invariable reply was, that it was prohibited. All the churches of Paris were shut, and the church plate was declared the property of the nation. Professors of religion, at the same time, in large numbers openly apostatized and embraced infidelity. Says Dr. Croley:--

"On the 1st of November, 1793, Gobet, with the republican priests of Paris, had thrown off the gown and abjured religion. On the 11th, a 'grand festival,' dedicated to 'Reason and Truth,' was celebrated instead of divine service in the ancient cathedral of Notre Dame, which had been desecrated, and been named, 'the Temple of Reason;' a pyramid was erected in the centre of the church, surmounted by a temple, inscribed, 'To Philosophy.' The torch of 'Truth' was on the altar of 'Reason,' spreading light, &c. The National Convention, and all the authorities, attended at this burlesque and insulting ceremony. In February, 1794, a grand fête was ordered by the convention, in which hymns to Liberty were chanted, and a pageant in honor of the abolition of slavery in the colonies, was displayed in the 'Temple of Reason.' In June another festival was ordered--to the Supreme Being: the God of Philosophy. But the most superb exhibition was the 'general festival,' in honor of the republic. It was distinguished by a more audacious spirit of scoffing and profanation than the former. Robespierre acted the 'high-priest of Reason' on the day, and made himself conspicuous in blasphemy. He was then at the summit of power,--actual sovereign of France."

The dead bodies of the witnesses, would be their existence in that prohibited condition, when, in France, neither the Scriptures, nor the church showed any symptoms of life. In the street, would be the conspicuous and public manner in which indignities should be heaped on them. France had been one of the principal states yielding homage to the Roman church. Surrounding nations beheld, but would not permit the extermination of the Bible and Christianity.

The French made merry over their blasphemous work. Says Dr. Croley:--

"A very remarkable and prophetic distinction of this period, was the spirit of frenzied festivity which seized upon France. The capital, and all the republican towns, were the scene of civic feasts, processions, and shows of the most extravagant kind. The most festive times of peace under the most expensive kings were thrown into the shade by the frequency, variety, and extent of the republican exhibitions. Yet this was a time of perpetual miseries throughout France. The guillotine was bloody from morn till night. In the single month of July, 1794, nearly eight hundred persons, the majority, principal individuals of the state, and all possessing some respectability of situation, were guillotined in Paris alone. In the midst of this horror, there were twenty-six theatres open, filled with the most profane and profligate displays in honor of the 'triumph of reason.' "

In Lyons a Bible was tied to the tail of an ass and dragged in a procession through the streets of that city. Thus they rejoiced over the supposed end of religion in France; and congratulated themselves that the terrors of God's word, and the church would no more torment them.

"After three days and a half," would be that number of years from the suppression of Christianity in November, 1793. On the 17th day of June, 1797, three and a half years from the abolition of the Bible and religious worship, CAMILLE JOURDAN, in the Council of Five Hundred, brought up the memorable report on the Revision of the Laws Relative to Religious Worship, by which France gave permission to all citizens to buy or hire edifices for the free exercise of it; repealing all opposing laws, and subjecting those to a heavy fine who should in any way impede or interrupt any religious service. The Bible and the church again stood erect, to the dismay of all who had rejoiced over their overthrow. Those two witnesses were again in a position to resume their testimony.

They were not only to be thus restored, but were to be elevated far above their former position. Since that epoch, have been made all those great efforts to evangelize the world, by means of missionary, tract, Bible, and other benevolent societies, which have caused the Scriptures to be translated into nearly all known languages, and carried by the living preacher to the ends of the earth. The very room in which Voltaire uttered his famous prediction--that "the time would arrive when the Bible would be regarded only in the light of an old curiosity,"--is now used for a Bible depository, and is "piled to the ceiling with that rare old book." Copies of the Bible have been multiplied a million fold, and scattered broadcast over the earth. The other witness,--the church, has since then, also, been greatly magnified. In this age of missions and Bibles, the number of believers has been greatly multiplied; and missionaries have penetrated all lands. The last half-century has been distinguished for its wonderful revivals; and the servants of the cross have "prophesied [or testified] again before many peoples, and nations, and tongues, and kings," 10:11.

The same hour, is the time of the slaughter of the witnesses. Its epoch was to be marked by a great political revolution, which, in the Apocalypse, is symbolized by an earthquake. In the year in which Christianity was suppressed by France, they beheaded their king, abolished the monarchy, and entirely revolutionized the government. In the reign of terror following, the best blood of the nation was shed like water, and no man of influence could consider his life secure. Men, women and children were dragged before the revolutionary tribunals, had their accusations read to them, and were immediately condemned, and hurried off in crowds without a trial, to be shot, drowned or beheaded. At Lyons thirty-one thousand persons were thus slain; at Nantes thirty-two thousand,--and throughout France in proportion. The number thus slain, has been estimated at over one million,-- a number hardly credible, and which might well be symbolized by seven thousand--a perfect number. Well might the remnant be affrighted, and hasten to give glory to the GOD of heaven, by the restoration of that book, the setting aside of which had involved them in such dire calamities.

The tenth of the city which fell, must be the tenth of the Roman hierarchy, which is symbolized by the city. With the suppression of religion, the Catholic church was prohibited, with all others. France was one of the ten kingdoms, and the overthrow of the church in France, would be the fall of one-tenth of that city.

Thus passed the second woe--the prelude to the third woe, which cometh quickly.

The Seventh Trumpet.

"And the seventh angel sounded; and there were loud voices in heaven, saying, The kingdom of the world hath become the kingdom of our Lord, and of his Anointed; and he will reign for ever and ever. And the twenty-four elders, who sat before God on their thrones, fell on their faces, and worshipped God, saying, We thank thee, O Lord God Almighty, who art, and who wast, because thou hast taken to thyself thy great power, and reigned. And the nations were enraged, and thy wrath is come, and the season of the dead, when they should be judged, and a reward should be given to thy servants the prophets, and to the saints, and to those who fear thy name, small and great; and when thou shouldest destroy those, who destroy the earth. And the temple of God was opened in heaven, and the ark of his covenant in his temple appeared, and there were lightnings, and voices, and thunders, and an earthquake, and great hail."--Rev. 11:15-19.

The seventh, like the preceding trumpets, marks an epoch from which an era dates. "The days of the voice of the seventh angel" (10:7), are indicative of a period of time to follow its sounding, in which will be fulfilled the events predicted of that era.

The voices in heaven, which immediately follow its sounding, are prophetic utterances of events then to transpire; and are distinct from the response of the elders. When Christ "shall be revealed from heaven," he will be accompanied "with his mighty angels," 2 Thess. 1:7. He will descend "with a shout, with the voice of the archangel, and with the trump of God," (1 Thess. 4:16); and the shout is evidently that of the attending angels, symbolized by those voices, which will announce the revolution which is to be made in the empire of the earth, and of the substitution of the kingdom of God in the place of human governments.

The kingdom here established, is the long promised consummation, foretold by prophets, and anticipated by saints of every age. It is that predicted by Daniel, when he says: "In the days of these kings shall the GOD of heaven set up a kingdom, which shall never be destroyed: and the kingdom shall not be left to other people, but it shall break in pieces and consume all these kingdoms, and it shall stand forever." Dan. 2:44. He also "saw in the night visions, and behold, one like the Son of Man came with the clouds of heaven, and came to the Ancient of Days, and they brought him near before him. And there was given him dominion, and glory, and a kingdom, that all people, nations, and languages, should serve him: his dominion is an everlasting dominion, which shall not pass away, and his kingdom that which shall not be destroyed.... And the kingdom and dominion, and the greatness of the kingdom under the whole heaven, shall be given to the people of the saints of the Most High, whose kingdom is an everlasting kingdom, and all dominions shall serve and obey him." Ib. 7:13, 14, 27. It is that referred to in the simple petition, "Thy kingdom come" (Matt. 6:10), which was to be the great object of our prayer till the final consummation; which the disciples thought was to appear immediately, when they journeyed towards, and were nigh to, Jerusalem, and which misapprehension the Saviour corrected by the parable of a nobleman going into a far country to receive for himself kingly authority, and to return, Luke 20:12. It is that respecting which they inquired, as the SAVIOUR was about to be taken from them, if he would at that time restore it to Israel, (Acts 1:6); and to which the apostle refers, when he declares to TIMOTHY that the Lord JESUS CHRIST will judge the living and the dead at his appearing and kingdom, 2 Tim. 4:1.

"Thy kingdom come! Thus, day by day We lift our hands to God and pray; But who has ever duly weighed The meaning of the words he said?"

This kingdom is to be an eternal kingdom: "He will reign for ever and ever." This is in accordance with the declaration in Daniel, that "the saints of the Most High shall take the kingdom, and possess the kingdom forever, even for ever and ever," Dan. 7:18. To its eternity Nathan testifies when he says to David, "Thy house and thy kingdom shall be established forever before thee: thy throne shall be established forever," 2 Sam. 7:16. Though this was spoken to David, it was to be fulfilled in Christ; for we read in Luke (1:32, 33), "He shall be great, and shall be called the Son of the Highest: and the Lord God shall give unto him the throne of his father David: and he shall reign over the house of Jacob forever; and of his kingdom there shall be no end." It is predicted in Isaiah, that "Unto us a child is born, unto us a son is given, and the government shall be upon his shoulder; and his name shall be called Wonderful, Counsellor, the Mighty God, the Everlasting Father, the Prince of Peace. Of the increase of his government and peace there shall be no end; upon the throne of David, and upon his kingdom, to order it and to establish it with judgment and with justice, from henceforth, even forever," Isa. 9:6, 7. To the Son the Father saith, "Thy throne, O God, is for ever and ever," (Heb. 1:8); and the blood-washed throng ascribe to him "glory and dominion for ever and ever," 1:5, 6.

"Thy kingdom come! O day of joy, When praise shall every tongue employ; When hate and strife and war shall cease, And man with man shall be at peace. Jesus shall reign on Zion's hill, And all the earth with glory fill; His word shall Paradise restore, And sin and death afflict no more. God's holy will shall then be done By all who live beneath the sun; For saints shall then as angels be, All changed to immortality."

The four-and-twenty elders,--symbolizing those who are redeemed "out of every kindred and tongue and people and nation," 5:8, 9,--at the establishment of the kingdom, are to be made "kings and priests," and are to "reign on the earth," 5:10. They are "saints of the Most High," who are to "take the kingdom," and possess it "forever." With the announcement of its establishment, they immediately respond with glad hosannas, which spontaneously and unitedly burst forth from the enraptured hosts of the ransomed ones, as they find themselves clothed upon with immortality, and in the joyful presence of their Lord. They are raised from the dead at this epoch; or are among the living who will then be translated, as says the apostle:

"Behold I show you a mystery; we shall not all sleep, but we shall all be changed, in a moment, in the twinkling of an eye, at the last trump,"--the last of the seven;--"for the trumpet shall sound, and the dead shall be raised incorruptible, and we shall be changed."

The nations who are angry, will be the nations out from whom the righteous are taken, and who are left to the recompense of their reward;--"when the Lord Jesus shall be revealed from heaven with his mighty angels, in flaming fire taking vengeance on them that know not God and obey not the gospel of our Lord Jesus Christ: who shall be punished with everlasting destruction from the presence of the Lord, and from the glory of his power; when he shall come to be glorified in his saints, and to be admired in all them that believe," 2 Thess. 1:7-10.

The heathen had raged, and the people imagined a vain thing. The kings of the earth had set themselves, and the rulers taken counsel against the Lord, and against his anointed. Now the time of their anger is to end: the time for the exercise of the wrath of Jehovah upon them, has arrived, and they are filled with fear, consternation, and shame. The time has come when the dead are to be avenged,--when those who had been slain for the word of God, and for the testimony which they held, whose souls under the altar during the fifth seal, cried with a loud voice, saying,

"How long, O Lord, holy and true, dost thou not judge and avenge our blood on them that dwell on the earth?" (6:10) find their expectations answered, and the destroyers, or perverters of the earth, in like manner perverted and destroyed. This winds up the kingdom of Satan on earth; his reign terminates, and his subjects are banished. The absence of all the wicked, with the transfiguration of all the righteous living and resurrection of the just, leave for subjects only those who have passed the period of their probation, and are introduced into the everlasting kingdom of God.

The opening of the temple in heaven, and the presentation of the Ark of the Covenant, symbolize the unfolding of the mystery, in which the administration of God may have been shrouded, making apparent all which may have been inexplicable in his dealings with men; and rendering evident the verity of his promises to his chosen ones.

The voices, lightnings, thunders, earthquake, and hail, are appropriate symbols of the plagues which will fall upon the wicked. These are fearfully depicted in the Scriptures. God says to Job, "Hast thou seen the treasures of hail which I have reserved against the time of trouble, against the day of battle and war," 38:22, 23. Judgment then will be laid "to the line, and righteousness to the plummet, and the hail shall sweep away the refuge of lies. The Lord shall cause his glorious voice to be heard, and shall show the lighting down of his arm with the indignation of his anger, and with the flame of devouring fire, with scattering, and tempest, and hailstones," Isa. 28:17.

This prepares the way for the purification of the earth as foretold by Peter (2 Pet. 3:12, 13), the restitution of all things (3:21), the new heavens and new earth (21:1), the descent of the saints (21:2), and the kingdom of God on the earth, 21:3. Assuming the correctness of the view here given, how near to the time now present does it seem to fix the consummation!

"So shall the world go on, To good malignant, to bad men benign, Under her own weight groaning: till the day Appear, of respiration to the just, And vengeance to the wicked; at return Of him--thy Saviour and thy Lord: Last in the clouds from heaven, to be revealed In glory of the Father, to dissolve Satan, with his perverted world; then raise From the conflagrant mass, purged and refined, New heavens, new earth, ages of endless date, Founded in righteousness, and peace, and love, To bring forth fruits, joy, and eternal bliss."--Milton.

"The world shall burn, and from her ashes spring New heavens and earth, wherein the just shall dwell, And after all their tribulations long, See golden days, fruitful of golden deeds, With joy and love triumphing, and fair truth."--Ib.

The Woman and Dragon.

"And a great sign appeared in heaven: a woman clothed with the sun, and the moon was under her feet, and on her head a crown of twelve stars; and she, being with child, cried, travailing in birth, and pained to be delivered. And another sign appeared in heaven: and behold, a great red dragon, having seven heads and ten horns, and seven diadems on his heads. And his tail dragged the third part of the stars of heaven, and cast them to the earth: and the dragon stood before the woman, who was about to be delivered, to devour her child as soon as it was born. And she brought forth a male child, who was to rule all nations with a rod of iron; and her child was snatched up to God, and to his throne. And the woman fled into the desert, where she hath a place there prepared of God, that they should feed her there one thousand two hundred and sixty days."--Rev. 12:1-6.

With this chapter commences a new series of events, extending through the entire gospel dispensation; the former series being terminated by the events of the last trumpet.

The heaven, where these great "wonders" are exhibited, must symbolize the theatre of their fulfilment--the station to be occupied by the agents symbolized, which must be as conspicuous as heaven is relatively high above the earth.

The woman, according to the use of the symbol in other places, must be a representative of the church. As the harlot on a scarlet-colored beast (17:3), is a symbol of a corrupt and apostate church, so a virtuous woman is a chosen symbol of the true church.

The "Jerusalem which is above is the mother" of all true Christians (Gal. 4:26); she is also "the bride, the Lamb's wife" (21:9); and "the remnant of her seed," are those "which keep the commandments of God, and have the testimony of Jesus Christ," v. 17. Her robe of light, her position above the moon, and her crown of stars, indicate her greatness and glory.

The epoch symbolized, as appears from the relative position of the woman and dragon, is evidently just prior to the first advent of the Messiah, when his coming was eagerly anticipated and ardently desired by the church, and the Roman power had thereby been excited to jealousy.

The church is the same in all ages, comprising only the true people of God; all of whom will have part in the first resurrection, 20:6. The Jewish church was continued by the breaking off of unbelieving branches, and the grafting in of believing Gentiles with believing Jews, who alike partake of the root and fatness of the same olive-tree, Rom. 11:17.

Previous to the first advent, the Jewish church occupied a high political position, above that of the inferior officers of state, and was in the enjoyment of imperial favor. Patriarchs and prophets--the messengers of the church--were stars in her crown of rejoicing, 1:20. From the utterance of the prediction that the woman's seed should bruise the serpent's head (Gen. 3:15), the coming of the promised deliverer was the great desire of the church. Even Eve exclaimed, at the birth of her first-born (literally), "I have gotten the man from the Lord," Gen. 4:1. For his coming,

"Kings and prophets waited long But died without the sight."

They "inquired and searched diligently, who prophesied of the grace that should come unto you: searching what, or what manner of time the spirit of Christ which was in them did signify, when it testified beforehand the sufferings of Christ, and the glory that should follow," 1 Pet. 1:10, 11. "Many righteous men desired" to see his day (Matt. 13:17); Abraham rejoiced and was made glad at its prospect, when in the distant future (John, 8:56); and Hezekiah lamented that because of death he should not see "the Lord in the land of the living," Isa. 38:11.

The seventy weeks indicated to the Jews the time of "the Messiah, the Prince," Dan. 9:26-27. When these were near their termination, to the pious and devout Simeon who was "waiting for the consolation of Israel," it "was revealed by the Holy Ghost, that he should not see death before he had seen the Lord's Christ," Luke 2:25, 26. And the opinion was so general, that when the Baptist preceded him, "the people were in expectation, and all men mused in their hearts of John, whether he were the Christ or no," Luke 3:15. This expectation is testified to by the Jewish historians Philo and Josephus; and it was that which so troubled Herod, when wise men came, saying, "Where is he that is born King of the Jews?" Matt. 2:1-3.

The belief that some remarkable personage was about to appear in Judea, was not confined to Palestine, but extended to Egypt, Rome, Greece, and wherever the Jews were scattered abroad. Says Suetonius, a Roman historian: "An ancient and settled persuasion prevailed throughout the East, that the Fates had decreed some one to proceed from Judea, who should attain universal empire." And Tacitus, another Roman historian, says: "Many were persuaded that it was contained in the ancient books of their priests, that at that very time the East should prevail, and that some one should proceed from Judea, and possess the dominion."

The great red dragon sustains a relation to the woman, analogous to that sustained by the nondescript beast (of Dan. 7:7), to the saints of the Most High; and his position respecting the man-child is like that of the exceeding great horn (Dan. 8:9), to the Prince of princes, Dan. 8:25. Like the beast referred to, the dragon has ten horns; and its characteristics indicate that it also symbolizes the Roman empire,--"the fourth kingdom upon earth," Dan. 7:23. The dragon is a monster serpent. "That old serpent" who seduced Eve (Gen. 3:5), "called the devil" (Matt. 4:1-12), and "Satan" (2 Cor. 2:11), "who deceiveth the whole world," is an appropriate representative of Rome.

The "head" of a beast, sustains a relation to the beast analogous to that of the government to the people of an empire. It is that by which the beast is directed and governed. When distinguished from the body of the beast (Dan. 7:11), according to the analogy, it must be understood as a symbol of the directing and controlling power, in the kingdom indicated by the beast. Several heads on the same beast, on this principle, must indicate the several forms of government to which the nation is subject. As these cannot be contemporary, like the divisions of a kingdom represented by the horns, they must be successive. To suppose they represent different governments, destroys the analogy, and makes them separate beasts, instead of heads of the same beast; and no government can be subject to more than one head at the same time.

The "seven heads" of the dragon, then, symbolize the directing and controlling powers which ruled the Roman empire,--the seven successive forms of government under which it existed. Rome was founded about B. C. 753, from small beginnings, on the summit of Mount Palatine, and gradually increased in extent, till it spread over seven hills: the Palatine, Capitoline, Aventine, Esquiline, Coelius, and Quirinalia; and its population of about three thousand in the time of Romulus, increased to about two millions in the time of Augustus Caesar.

Previous to the subversion of the empire, Rome existed under different forms of government, as follows:--

1. Kingly.--The first government established was a monarchy, and lasted two hundred and forty-four years, under seven kings, viz., Romulus, Numa, Tullus Hostilius, Ancus Martius, Tarquin Priscus, Servius Tullius, and Tarquin the Proud, who was afterwards expelled from the throne. This was denominated the infancy of the Roman empire.

2. Consular.--In B. C. 509, the constitution of Rome was remodelled, and the executive power committed to two consuls, to be elected annually. This commenced the "Commonwealth of Rome."

3. Dictatorial.--The office of dictator was the highest known in Rome, and was only resorted to in cases of emergency. He was elected for six months only, and usually resigned his authority, which, for the time, was nearly absolute, as soon as he had effected the object for which he was chosen.

4. Decemviral.--In B. C. 451, the government was so changed, that, instead of the two consuls, the government was committed to ten men, to be chosen annually, and jointly exercise the sovereign power. After two years the decemvirs were banished, and the consular government was restored.

5. Tribunitial.--In B. C. 426, Rome having become a military state, military tribunes were substituted for the consular power, till B. C. 366, when the latter was again restored.

6. Pagan Imperial.--With the battle of Actium, B. C. 31, the Roman Commonwealth terminated; and Augustus Caesar united in his own person not only the offices of Consul, Tribune, &c., but also that of Supreme Pontiff,--the head of the pagan hierarchy. This last office, says Gibbon, "was constantly exercised by the emperors." Thus were united the highest civil and ecclesiastical powers of the state.

7. Christian Imperial.--In A. D. 312, the government was revolutionized, by the accession of Constantine to the throne. He effected important changes in

the relations of the people to the monarch, opposed idolatry, and by the introduction of Christianity, effected a political change in the laws and administration of the empire. This continued, with a slight interruption under Julian the Apostate, till the subversion of the Western empire, A. D. 476.

Mr. Elliott, in explanation of the first five heads, says: "I adopt, with the most entire satisfaction, that generally-received Protestant interpretation, which, following the authoritative statement of Livy and Tacitus (the latter great historian, St. John's own contemporary), enumerates kings, consuls, dictators, decemvirs, and military tribunes, as the first five constitutional heads of the Roman city and commonwealth; then as the sixth, the Imperial head, commencing with Octavian."--Hor?Apoca., vol. III., p. 106, 4th ed.

Those heads are shown to symbolize seven forms of government, by the explanation that "they are seven mountains where the woman sits on them [mountains also symbolizing governments], and are seven kings," 17:9, 10. And they are shown to be successive, by the fact that, when John wrote, the first five had passed away, one only then existed,--the Pagan Imperial,--and the other head was then in the future, 17:10.

The "ten horns" also symbolize kings, or dynasties; but, unlike the heads, instead of being successive, they are contemporaneous. According to the explanation, they had received no kingdom when John wrote, and were all to exercise power at the same time: "The ten horns which thou didst see, are ten kings who have not yet received a kingdom; but they receive power as kings, one hour with the wild beast," 17:12. These will be more particularly noticed in connection with the thirteenth chapter, and there shown to be the ten contemporaneous governments which succeeded to the dominion, on the subversion of the Western Empire. See p. 169.

The "seven crowns" on the heads of the dragon, indicate that the acts here symbolized, would be fulfilled during the period when the sovereignty of Rome should be vested in the forms of government symbolized by the heads, and not during that symbolized by the horns.

The woman appeared in the symbolic heavens anterior to the dragon. Prior to the birth of Christ, the church was conspicuous and honored. The sacrifices which smoked on Jewish altars, were offered to Jehovah. The subjects of the divine government conducted their service with all the splendor imparted by the Jewish ritual. Royalty was an appendage of the nation: the sceptre did not depart from Judah, nor a law-giver from between his feet, till Shiloh came, Gen. 49:10. By an alliance with the Romans, B. C. 135, Rome took its position in the presence of the woman.

The first act of the dragon was by a sweep of its tail to draw down one-third of the stars, and to cast them to the earth. This was before the birth of the man-child. After Rome attained the supremacy, Judea proportionably suffered. Her glory was measurably dimmed by many indignities before her subjugation to Rome was consummated. Jerusalem was repeatedly besieged. At one time (B. C. 94) Alexander Jannæus slew six thousand persons on account of their meeting in the temple at the feast of tabernacles. In B. C. 63, Judea was conquered by Pompey, the Roman general. In B. C. 54, Crassus plundered the temple of Jerusalem. In B. C. 37, Jerusalem was taken, after a siege of six months. Various other difficulties occurred between Judea and Rome, previous to the Saviour's advent, on account of which she was greatly depressed and humbled, so that it might with propriety be said that one-third of her stars were cast to the ground. This depression was one great reason why the church within her borders looked so earnestly for a Deliverer.

The Man-child is the one "who was to rule all nations with a rod of iron," according to the prediction of Christ in the second Psalm; which proves its reference to the Saviour.

The purpose of the dragon to destroy the child of the woman as soon as it should be born, in accordance with the view here taken, would symbolize the purpose of the Roman power, by the agency of Herod the Roman governor in Judea, to destroy the infant Saviour. "When he had gathered all the chief priests and scribes of the people together, he demanded of them where Christ should be born. And they said unto him, In Bethlehem, in Judea: for thus it is written by the prophet." And Herod "sent forth and slew all the children that were in Bethlehem, and in all the coasts thereof, from two years old and under, according to the time which he had diligently inquired of the wise men," Matt. 2:1-16. Thus Rome sought to slay the Saviour as soon as he was born; but Joseph took the child and fled into Egypt. Afterwards Christ was crucified by Roman soldiers, and deposited in the tomb, arising again the third day.

His being caught up to God and to his throne, symbolizes his resurrection from the dead, and ascension from the Mount of Olives (Acts 1:9), to the right hand of the Majesty on high; "whom the heaven must receive until the times of restitution of all things," Ib. 3:21.

The flight of the woman into the wilderness, denotes her descent from the conspicuous position she had occupied, and the dispersion of the church. With the crucifixion of Christ, Judaism was no longer the casket in which the church was enshrined. It left its place in the moral heavens, and the followers of Christ were scattered abroad, Acts 8:1-4. Thus she virtually fled into the wilderness--into the condition, where, subsequently, she was to be nourished for 1260 prophetic days.

It is objected to the application of the man-child to the Saviour, that it should be prophetic, and not retrospective. This objection would be equally valid to the application of the symbolic heads, against which it is never urged. That which is retrospective, to be appropriately symbolized, must be in harmony with, and explanatory of other parts. Thus, by the man-child and previous travail of the woman, she is identified, and her relation to the dragon established. No other subject could fulfil the conditions of the symbol, for of no other was it predicted: "Thou art my Son; this day have I begotten thee.--Ask of me, and I shall give thee the heathen for thine inheritance, and the uttermost parts of the earth for thy possession.--Thou shalt break them with a rod of iron; thou shalt dash them in pieces like a potter's vessel," Psa. 2:8-10.

The War in Heaven.

"And a war took place in heaven: Michael and his angels fought with the dragon;, and the dragon fought and his angels, and he prevailed not; nor was their place found any more in heaven. And the great dragon was cast out, the old serpent, called the Devil, and Satan, who deceiveth the whole world: he was cast out into the earth, and his angels were cast out with him."--Rev. 12:7-9.

The churches,--which on the persecution subsequent to the Pentecostal season were scattered abroad, and went everywhere preaching the word (Acts 8:4),--afterwards had rest, and were multiplied, Ib. 9:31. They were thus enabled again to act a conspicuous part, as symbolized by the contest between Michael and the dragon.

The contest symbolized, is a religious one; for the dragon is overcome "by the word of their testimony," v. 11.

Michael and his angels, then, must symbolize the body of Christ,--the apostles, and their successor, under the guidance of the Lord,--who constituted an army of religious teachers. With the arrows of truth they assailed the idolatrous combinations of their opponents. Under the first seal, they are represented by a mounted warrior, with bow and crown, going forth conquering and to conquer, 6:2. See p. 58.

The dragon, with the appendages of heads, horns, and diadems, was seen to be a symbol of the Roman government. Divested of those, it would simply represent the Pagan hierarchy with which the contest was waged. The heathen priests and their adherents, thus warred with the preachers of Christianity.

Its prevailing not, shows the relative success of the two parties. The struggle continued from the day of Pentecost till the accession of Constantine. The church waded through bloody scenes of bitter persecution, which, instead of diminishing, greatly added to her numbers--"the blood of the martyrs" proving "the seed of the church."

The heathen priests were not deficient in logic, philosophy, and artful sophistry, by which to defend their mythology. They exhausted these, and then resorted to persecution, torture, and death; yet they prevailed not. With the weapons of truth, the teachers of Christianity successfully assailed those antiquated forms of error,--overcoming "by the blood of the Lamb, and by the word of their testimony." "They loved not their lives unto the death," but freely gave themselves for Christ, till, in time, the current of popular favor ceased to flow in the direction of paganism. The accession of Constantine to the throne, put an end to the dragonic period of Rome; the Pagan service gave place to the worship of Jehovah. The rites of heathenism were no longer the religion of the state, and its ministers were displaced from the exalted position they had so long occupied. Their place was no longer in the symbolic heavens, but in a less conspicuous station.

The casting out of the dragon, would then be this expulsion of the pagan hierarchy from its national importance, and the dejection of the priesthood and their adherents to the earth,--below their former high station,--and to the sea, among the unsettled tribes and nations outside of Rome. This being a religious and not a political event, it does not immediately affect Rome's nationality. That it is not the overthrow of a kingdom, but of religious rites, is shown by the rejoicings which followed.

Rejoicings of the Victors.

"And I heard a loud voice in heaven, saying, Now is come the salvation and the strength, and the Kingdom of or God, and the power of his Anointed: for the accuser of our brethren it cast out, who accused them before our God day and night. And they overcame him by the blood of the Lamb, and by the word of their testimony; and they loved not their lives to death. On this account, rejoice, ye heavens, and ye who dwell in them."-- Rev. 12:10-12.

The loud voice is heard in the symbolic heaven from which the Dragon had been cast. By the displacement of the Pagan hierarchy, and the substitution of Christianity under Constantine, the adherents of the latter succeeded to the place of the former, and rejoiced over them.

A loud voice symbolizes the utterance of the thoughts and feelings of an interested multitude. The nature of the voice indicates the nature of the utterance--whether it be one of expectation, fear, warning, or instruction. This voice is expressive of the then prevalent expectation, that, with the displacement of Paganism commenced the establishment of the Kingdom of God on earth. This belief was not necessarily well founded;--its existence only being symbolized.

On the triumph of Constantine over Licinius, Eusebius says:--"There were illuminations everywhere. They who were before dejected looked on one another with joyful aspects and smiles, and with choirs and hymns through the cities and country, gave honor first to God, the Supreme Ruler of all, as they were taught, and then to the pious emperor and his children." Says Mr Lord:

"Eusebius represents the victors at the precipitation of Maxentius and his attendants into the Tiber, as saying, like Moses at the overthrow of the Egyptians in the Red Sea: 'Let us sing to the Lord, for he is signally glorified. Horse and rider he has thrown into the sea. The Lord my helper and defender was with me unto salvation. Who, O Lord, is like to thee among gods? Who is like to thee, glorified by the holy, admirable in praise, doing wonders? Constantine entered Rome in triumph, hymning these and similar passages to God, the author of the victory.' And on the fall of Licinius he represents the church as uniting in thanksgiving for the deliverance, and congratulations at the overthrow of idolatry, and establishment of Christ's kingdom; and devotes the tenth book of his history to the edicts of the emperor by which the church was nationalized and endowed, and to the restoration of the temples, and the public rejoicings at their dedication. 'Let thanks be given by all to the Almighty Ruler of the universe, and to Jesus Christ, our Saviour and Redeemer, through whom we pray that peace from external foes may be uninterruptedly preserved to us, and tranquillity of mind.'

" 'Let us sing to the Lord a new song, for he has done wonderful things. His right hand has saved him and his holy arm. The Lord has made known his salvation; he has revealed his righteousness in the presence of the nations. We may now appropriately respond to the inspired command to sing a new song, inasmuch as after such direful spectacles and narrations we now have the happiness to see and celebrate what many holy men before us and the martyrs for God desired to see on earth, and did not see, and to hear, and have not heard. But advancing more rapidly they attained far superior gifts in heaven, being caught up to the paradise of celestial joy; while we acknowledge the gifts we enjoy are greater than we deserve, and contemplate with wonder the largeness of the divine bounty. Admiring and adoring with all our souls, we testify to the truth of the prophet's words, "Come and see the works of the Lord, what wonders he has wrought in the earth, abolishing wars to the ends of the world. The bow he has broken, he has dashed the arms, the shield he has burned in the fire." Rejoicing at the manifest fulfilment of these predictions to us, we go on with our history.' He goes on accordingly to represent the whole population, freed from the domination of the tyrants, and relieved from oppression, as acknowledging the only true God and protector of the pious, and these especially who had placed their hope in Christ, as filled with inexpressible joy; the ministers everywhere delivering commemorative addresses, and the whole multitude offering praises and thanksgiving to God.

"Lactantius also: 'Let us celebrate the triumph of God with gladness; let us commemorate his victory with praise; let us make mention in our prayers day and night of the peace which, after ten years of persecution, he has conferred on his people.' "--Ex. of Apoc., pp. 343-4.

Multitudes actually supposed the long-predicted kingdom of God was now being established. Says Mr. Elliott:

"Can we wonder, then, at the exultation that was felt at this time by many, perhaps by most, that bore the Christian name: or at their high-raised expectations as to the future happy destiny of the Roman, now that it had been changed into the Christian, nation? It seemed to them as if it had become God's covenanted people, like Israel of old: and the expectation was not unnatural,--an expectation strengthened by the remarkable tranquillity which, throughout the extent of the now reunited empire, followed almost immediately on Constantine's establishment of Christianity,--that not only the temporal blessings of the ancient Jewish covenant would thenceforth in no small measure attach to them, but even those prophesied of as appertaining to the latter day. Hence on the medals of that era the emblem of the phoenix, all radiant with the rising sunbeams, to represent the empire as now risen into new life and hope, and its legend which spoke of the happy restoration of the times. Hence, in forgetfulness of all former prognostications of Antichrist and fearful coming evils, the reference by some of the most eminent of their bishops to the latter-day blessedness, as even then about fulfilling. The state of things was such, Eusebius tells us, that it looked like 'the very image of the kingdom of Christ.' The city built by the emperor at Jerusalem, beside the new and magnificent Church of the Holy Sepulchre,--the sacred capital, as it were, to the new empire,--might be, perhaps, he suggested, the New Jerusalem, the theme of so many prophecies. Yet again, on occasion of the opening of the new church at Tyre, he expressed in the following glowing language, not his own feelings only, but those, we may be sure, of not a few of the congregated Christian ministers and people that heard him: 'What so many of the Lord's saints and confessors before our time desired to see, and saw not, and to hear, and heard not, that behold now before our eyes! It was of us the prophet spake when he told how the wildernesses and solitary places should be glad, and the desert rejoice and blossom as the lily. Whereas the church was widowed and desolate, her children have now to exclaim to her, Make room, enlarge thy borders! the place is too strait for us. The promise is fulfilling to her, In righteousness shalt thou be established: all thy children shall be taught of God: and great shall be the peace of thy children.' "--Hor?Apoc., v. i., pp. 230-1.

They rejoiced over the downfall of the dragon as over "the Accuser of our brethren, who accused them before our God day and night." The phrase "our brethren," proves that those who unite in this song are the living saints on the earth. The reference to Satan as an Accuser bears a close resemblance to Zech. 3:1, where Joshua, as a symbol of the people of Israel, is represented as standing before the angel of the LORD, and Satan standing at his right hand to resist him.--"{~HEBREW LETTER SHIN~}{~HEBREW LETTER TET~}{~HEBREW LETTER FINAL NUN~} Satan signifies an adversary. {~HEBREW LETTER RESH~}{~HEBREW LETTER SHIN~}{~HEBREW LETTER TET~}{~HEBREW LETTER NUN~}{~HEBREW LETTER VAV~} lesiteno, to be his adversary or accuser."--Dr. Clark.

Satan's most common work is to invent false accusations against those whose efforts tend to frustrate his designs. The Christians had endured false accusations and bitter persecutions, and therefore rejoiced the more over the defeat of the Pagans.

The Flight of the Woman.

"Woe to the inhabitants of the earth, and of the sea! for the devil is come to you, having great wrath, because he knoweth that he hath but a short season."

"And when the dragon saw that he was cast out into the earth, he persecuted the woman, who brought forth the male child. And two wings of a great eagle were given to the woman, that she might fly into the desert, into her place, where she is nourished for a time, and times, and half a time, from the presence of the serpent. And the serpent cast out of his mouth water like a river, after the woman, that he might cause her to be carried away by the river. And the earth helped the woman; and the earth opened its mouth and swallowed up the river, which the dragon cast out of his mouth. And the dragon was enraged against the woman, and went away to make war with the remnant of her seed, that keep the commandments of God, and have the testimony of Jesus."--Rev. 12:12-17.

The rejoicing of Christians, according to this symbolization, is afterwards followed by renewed triumphs of the Pagans over them. The hatred of the Pagan worshippers to Christianity, is strikingly evinced; but it is manifested in a manner different from the former contest.

When the church sought only to overcome by "the blood of the Lamb, and by the word of their testimony," it was owned of Christ; but as it became proud and worldly, and cared more for popular favor than for purity of faith and practice, the true church which the woman symbolized, was represented only by those who continued faithful to their profession. Historians inform us that with the success of Constantine, the visible church became speedily corrupt. As it became popular, unconverted men sought to be enrolled as members. The Pagans, instead of approaching as enemies, came as professed friends. As a profession of Christianity was alone necessary for admission to the church, multitudes sought connection with it. This caused a condition of things, of which Dr. Milner thus speaks:--"In the general appearance of the church, we cannot see much of the spirit of godliness. External piety flourished. But faith, love, heavenly-mindedness appear very rare. The doctrine of real conversion was very much lost, and external baptism placed in its stead: and the true doctrine of justification by faith, and true practical use of a crucified Saviour for troubled consciences were scarcely to be seen at this time. Superstition and self-righteousness were making vigorous shoots; and the real gospel of Christ was hidden from the men that professed it."

To the same effect is the report of Mosheim:--Of the life and morals of the professing Christians of the fourth century, he says: "Good men were, as before, mixed with bad; but the bad were by degrees so multiplied, that men truly holy and devoted to God appeared more rarely; and the pious few were almost oppressed by the vicious multitude." Of their doctrines he says: "Fictions, of early origin" (about saint veneration and relics, a purifying fire, celibacy, &c., &c.), "now so prevailed as in course of time almost to thrust true religion aside, or at least to exceedingly obscure and tarnish it."

Says Mr Lord:--"Constantine and his successors introduced a flood of false doctrines, superstitions and idolatries, into the church, which were incompatible with a pure worship, and swept all who yielded to their impulse to the gulf of apostasy. Such were the veneration of the cross, and ascription to it of miraculous powers, the homage of relics, the invocation of saints, the conversion of religion into gorgeous ceremonies, the encouragement of celibacy, and the arrogation of the throne and prerogatives of God by civil and ecclesiastical rulers. These falsehoods, follies, and impieties, introduced or adopted by the emperors, encouraged by their example, sanctioned by their laws, and enforced by the penalties of excommunication, imprisonment, the forfeiture of civil rights, banishment, and death, came armed with an overpowering force to all who were not fortified against them by the special aids of the divine spirit, and like a resistless torrent bore away the great mass of the church."--Exp. of Apoc., p. 350.

With the accession of multitudes of unworthy members, and the prevalence of false doctrines, the true church would have been speedily overwhelmed had not the people of God been sustained from such deleterious influences. To the woman, therefore, were given two wings of a great eagle that she might escape. Wings are symbolic of power of flight--for succor, or escape. The four-winged leopard of Daniel used his speed to approach and demolish the enemy; the woman, to escape hers. The church of old was sustained in like manner. Thus God said to Israel, "Ye have seen what I did unto the Egyptians, and how I bare you on eagles' wings, and brought you to myself."--Ex. 19:4.

On the introduction of new rites and doctrines into the church, multitudes withdrew from the public assemblies, and worshipped apart. They retired from the observation of their rulers and lived secluded for a long period.

Some may inquire for the historical evidence of the time when such a body withdrew. This, from the nature of the case, it may be difficult to give. If the withdrawal of the true worshippers had been an occurrence of so much notoriety as to be prominently historically noticed, it might have defeated their withdrawal. It is sufficient that the prophecy makes such a withdrawal necessary; and that at a later period such a body was found existing as predicted. See p. 198. Says Mr. Lord:

"Her retreat into her place from the face of the serpent, denotes that the scene of her residence was unknown to the rulers. The anger of the serpent indicates their continued disposition to destroy her, if in their power; while its going on to make war with such of her seed as had not retreated to the desert, denotes that they continued, after her disappearance, to persecute the isolated individuals that from time to time dissented from the corrupt church, and professed the pure faith.

"As it was by spiritual aids that the true worshippers were enabled to resist the temptations and force by which the rulers endeavored to constrain them to apostasy, and to fly to the desert, no specific record of those aids is to be sought on the page of history. The only evidence that we can ask or possess, that they were conferred, is presented in the fact that a body of dissentients from the corrupt church were in a latter age found in a secluded scene, who had survived the endeavors of the rulers of the fourth, fifth, sixth, and following centuries, to compel all their subjects to conformity, and who have continued to maintain a separate existence, and offer an unidolatrous worship to the present time.

"And such a body were the Waldenses, inhabiting the eastern valleys of the Cottian Alps. They are known, from the testimony of cotemporary Catholics and their own authors, to have existed there as early as the eleventh century. It was then, and is now, claimed by themselves, and admitted by their enemies, that they had subsisted there from a much earlier age. These were a Christian church, having the Scriptures of the Old and New Testaments, regarding them as a revelation from God, and making them the rule of their faith; having a ministry of their own, holding religious assemblies, professing and teaching the doctrines of the gospel, and celebrating the sacraments.

"They were distinguished for the simplicity and purity of their lives. It was asserted by them, and repeated by the Catholics, that they were induced to retreat to the secluded valleys which they inhabit, to escape the despotism of the rulers and the corruptions and tyranny of the church, soon after its nationalization by Constantine. They have continued to subsist there to the present time, as a separate and evangelical church."--Exp. Apoc., pp. 348, 349, 359.

Says Mr. Elliott:--"I must not pass on without pressing on the reader's notice this notable pre-figuration of the seclusion of Christ's church in the wilderness, as the true and fittest answer to the Romish anti-Protestant taunt, 'Where was your religion before Luther?' Protestants have not duly, as it seems to me, applied the answer here given. For the wilderness-life necessarily, as I must repeat,--and that on Bossuet's own showing,--implies the invisibility of her who lives in it. And consequently, instead of the long previous invisibility of a church like the Lutheran, or Anglican Reformed, of the sixteenth century, in respect of doctrine and worship, being an argument against it, it is an argument for it. The Romish church, which never knew the predicted wilderness-life, could not, for this very reason, be the woman of the 12th Apocalyptic chapter; that is, could not be the true church of Christ.

"For 1260 prophetic days, then, or years, she was to disappear from men's view in the Roman world. Is it asked how her vitality was preserved? Doubtless in her children, known to God, though for the most part unknown to men; just like the 7000 that Elijah knew not of, who had not bowed the knee to Baal; some, it might be, in monasteries, some in the secular walks of life; but all alike insulated in spirit from those around them, and as regards the usual means of grace, spiritually destitute and desolate; even as in a barren and dry land, where no water is.--Besides whom, some few there were of her children,--some very few,--prepared, like Elijah of old, to act a bolder part, and stand forth, under special commission from God, as Christ's witnesses before Christendom."--Hor?Apoc., pp. 55-57.

The flood of water cast out after the woman, is an appropriate symbol of the various tribes which subsequently overran the Western empire. Waters symbolize peoples, 17:15; and by hordes of barbarian Huns, Goths, and Vandals, Rome was inundated as by a flood, in the 5th century; and in A. D. 476 its government was entirely subverted.

Such an irruption of barbarians might be expected to extirpate Christianity from the earth; but help came from an unexpected quarter. The woman had retired to her secure retreat, and the earth swallowed up the flood. Those barbarous tribes were absorbed by, and mixed with, the previous population of the empire, and constituted the clay ingredient with the iron, in the feet of the metallic image.--Dan. 2:41. They rapidly assimilated to the character and habits of the previous inhabitants; and ultimately adopted the forms of government and religion which for a time they subverted; and within the limits of the Western empire, in the place of the Imperial head, constituted ten contemporary kingdoms. These were a continuation of the former government, and were symbolized by:

The Ten-Horned Beast.

"And I was standing on the sand of the sea, and saw a wild beast ascending out of the sea, having ten horns and seven heads, and on his horns ten diadems, and on his heads names of reviling. And the wild beast, which I saw was like a leopard, and his feet were like those of a bear, and his mouth like the mouth of a lion: and the dragon gave him his power, and his throne, and great authority. And I saw one of his heads as it were wounded to death; and his deadly wound was healed: and all the world admired and followed the beast. And they worshipped the dragon, for he gave power to the wild beast: and they worshipped the wild beast, saying, Who is like the wild beast, and who is able to make war with him?"--Rev. 18:1-4.

The sea, from which this beast emerged, is evidently the turbulent state of anarchy, to which the people of the fourth kingdom had been reduced, on its subversion. And the beast which came up out of the sea, represents the forms of government which then arose.

Its heads and horns synchronize with those of the dragonic monster, which had preceded it, and disappeared from the view of the revelator. And they doubtless symbolize the same forms of government. See pp. 145-148.

The ten crowns encircling its horns, indicate that an era is foreshadowed, when the sovereignty of the kingdom shall have been transferred from the forms of government symbolized by the heads,--which had before been encircled by the crowns,--to that represented by the horns. There is great unanimity among Protestant writers, in regarding these as the first ten kingdoms which existed in the western empire arising during the period of its decline, viz:

1. The Huns in Hungary, from A. D. 356.

2. The Ostrogoths in Mysia, from A. D. 377. They invaded Italy, and conquered the Heruli in 493; and were defeated in 538 by Justinian, when the Pope was placed in quiet possession of the capital of Rome.

3. The Visigoths in Pannonia, from A. D. 378 to 408, when they removed to the south of France till 585. They then removed to, and subjugated Spain.

4. The Franks in France, from A. D. 407.

5. The Vandals in Spain, from A. D. 407 till 427, when they removed to Africa, and continued an independent kingdom till subjugated by Justinian in 533.

6. The Suevi and Alans in Gascoigne and Spain, from 407 till 585.

7. The Burgundians in Burgundy, from A. D. 407 till 524, when they became subject for a time to the Franks; but afterwards they arose again to an independent kingdom.

8. The Heruli, who advanced into Italy under Attila, and in 476 terminated the imperial rule by the dethronement of Agustulus. They were in turn conquered by the Ostrogoths in A. D. 493.

9. The Saxons and Angles in Britain from about A. D. 450. And,

10. The Lombards in Germany, from A. D. 483.

The name of blasphemy, on the heads of this beast, identifies it as the successor and representative of the persecuting power which sought the life of the Man-child, (12:4), and caused the woman to flee to the wilderness, 12:14.

Its characteristics resemble those of the lion, bear, and leopard, of Daniel's vision (Dan. 7:4-6), which respectively symbolized the Babylonian, Medo-Persian, and Grecian kingdoms. These mark it as their successor--synchronizing with Daniel's ten-horned nondescript beast, (Dan. 7:7); which was the fourth kingdom that should exist on the earth, and the ten horns of which, symbolized the same ten-fold partition of the Roman empire.

His power, seat, and great authority being given by the dragon, is another evidence that it is a continuation of that fourth kingdom succeeding to its sovereignty. The laws of the ancient empire were generally adopted by the ten kingdoms, which assumed and exercised the prerogatives of ancient

Rome. Says Bossuet: "Whoever carefully examines the laws of the Theodosian and Justinian codes against heretics, will see that they are the source of the decrees against them, that the church, aided by the edicts of princes, enacted in the third and fourth Lateran councils."

The head, which was as it were wounded to death, would indicate that under the government symbolized by that head, the life of the beast had become apparently extinct. This was the case when the empire was subverted. In the succession of the previous forms of government, the empire itself was not in any particular peril. They gave place, each to its successor, without any subversion of the government. But when the seventh head ceased to exercise sovereignty, the beast itself was apparently dead. The wound, however, did not prove mortal. The beast still lived. Its sovereignty was perpetuated by the decemregal governments; which constituted the eighth form of government--symbolized by the beast that was, is not, and yet is again in existence and will continue till the day of perdition, 17:11; 19:20.

They worshipped the dragon and beast, by regarding the latter as a continuation of the former power, and regarding the sovereign power of Rome as unparalleled and invincible--as is shown by the questions: "Who is like unto the beast? Who is able to make war with him?" Those combined governments were regarded by their subjects with wonder and veneration. Says Mr. Lord: "The serfs and common people, sunk for ages to the most degraded vassalage, revered the monarchs, the various ranks of nobles, and their armed followers, as a superior race, while poets and historians celebrated their warlike exploits, and philosophers and priests justified their usurpations, and eulogized the wisdom and benignity of their rule."

The Mouth of the Beast.

"And there was given to him a mouth speaking great things and revilings; and power was given to him to make war forty-two months. And he opened his mouth in reviling against God, to revile his name, and his tabernacle, and those who dwell in heaven. And it was given to him to make war with the saints, and to overcome them: and power was given him over every tribe, and people, and tongue, and nation. And all, who dwell on the earth, will worship him, whose names are not written in the book of life of the slain Lamb, from the foundation of the world. If any one hath an ear, let him hear. If any one leadeth into captivity, he will go into captivity: if any one killeth by the sword, he must be killed with the sword. Here is the patience and the faith of the saints."--Rev. 13:5-10.

The mouth of the beast, must symbolize the agency by which utterance is given to the great things and blasphemies which are spoken by it. Its likeness to the mouth of the lion, shows its resemblance to the Babylonian worship of the dead. Moses was "not eloquent,"--he was "slow of speech and of a slow tongue," and the Lord said to him, Aaron "shall be thy spokesman unto the people: and he shall be, even he shall be to thee instead of a mouth," Ex. 4:10, 16. As Aaron was a mouth to Moses, so did the Papacy become a mouth-piece for the Roman kingdoms. It was the agency by which the people were taught; and through which utterance was given to the blasphemies of the beast. It fills a place analogous to that of the image afterwards symbolized, which also had like power to speak blasphemies. See p. 188.

The beast had power to continue to utter blasphemies by the mouth given to it, forty-two months. This identifies the mouth with that of the "little horn" (Dan. 7:25), of which it was said, "He shall speak great words against the Most High, and think to change times and laws: and they shall be given into his hand until a time and times and the dividing of time"--i.e. 1260 prophetic days.

1. This mouth uttered blasphemy against God by claiming to be Christ's vicegerent--usurping the prerogatives of the Almighty. The Pope claimed that he was "Judge, as God's Vicar, and could himself be judged by none." In A. D. 799, a Roman council declined to hear accusations against the Pope, declaring that "he who was Judge of all men, was above being judged by any other than himself." Febroni wrote of the Pope: "He is the Prince of princes and Lord of lords. He is, as it were, a God on earth. He is above right, superior to law, superior to the canons. He can do all things against right, and without right. He is able to free from obligation in matters of

positive right, without any cause, and they who are so released are safe in respect to God." Assuming such prerogatives, and the power to forgive sins, the Holy name of God was blasphemed.

2. He blasphemed the tabernacle of God by "exalting himself above all that is called God, or that is worshipped; so that he as God sitteth in the temple of God, showing himself that he is God," 2 Thess. 2:2. The Pope claimed to be the head of the church and that from himself was derived the authority of all bishops and other clergy. He usurped the powers in the church, which only Christ, its Supreme Head and Lawgiver can exercise.

3. Those in heaven were blasphemed, by the ascription to them of the attributes and prerogatives of God; and by representing them as being well pleased with the bestowal on them of divine honors. Saint-worship by the Papists and demon-worship by the Pagans are alike. They both ascribe the same attributes to the spirits of the departed,--all the gods of the heathen being the ghosts of their departed heroes. A revival of this blasphemy, is subsequently symbolized by the frog-like spirits which emerge from the mouths of the beast, the dragon, and false prophet, 16:13,--see p. 255.

In connection with and in obedience to this mouth, the beast warred with the saints, and overcame them. Dissenters from the Papacy were subjected to unheard of cruelties and persecutions. And they whose names were not written in the book of life, sustained their rulers in these oppressive acts. In paying more deference to the edicts of government than to the requirements of Jehovah, they blasphemously bestowed on the beast an homage which was due only to God.

The revelator being shown what was to be endured by the saints during a long period of oppression, now receives an annunciation to which all were to listen,--all who had ears to hear. It was the announcement, that "if any one leadeth into captivity, he will go into captivity: if any one killeth with the sword, he must be killed with the sword." Most commentators have considered this as applicable to the fate of the wild beast,--that its end was to be effected by the sword and captivity, as it had in the same way tyrannized over the saints. Mr. Lord offers some reasons for supposing that it was a caution to the saints not to resist with the sword the attacks of enemies, nor to retaliate by making captives of the subjects of the beast who should fall into their power. He says:

"The prediction that he who led into captivity should himself become a captive, and he that slew with the sword be himself slain, had a signal fulfilment in the slaughter and vassalage of all those who attempted to deliver themselves by force from the religious tyranny of the European monarchs.

"The Albigenses were nearly exterminated by the cruel armies against which they attempted to defend themselves, and the small number that remained after the devastation of their fields, the conflagration of their cities, and the promiscuous slaughters to which they were subjected, were either forced to conform to the Catholic church, or driven into other lands. The Waldenses perished in far greater numbers by the sword, in their struggles for preservation and freedom, than by the fires of martyrdom; and sunk, after their contests, to a still more hopeless vassalage to their persecutors. The resort to the sword by the Bohemians and the Huguenots of France, to defend their religious freedom, resulted, after vast slaughters, in their defeat and helpless subjection to the tyranny from which they endeavored to extricate themselves. And the Protestants of Switzerland, Germany, Holland, Denmark, Sweden, and Great Britain, who succeeded in delivering themselves from the dominion of their ancient tyrants, instead of securing thereby their religious liberty, only placed themselves, by the nationalization of their churches, under the tyranny of Protestant rulers in place of Catholics."--Exp. of Apoc. p. 384.

In this was to be exhibited the patience and faith of the saints, who, amid all their persecutions, made a wonderful manifestation of these. Of the many thousands put to death, or subjected to satanic cruelties for their faith, only a very few apostatized. Says Mr. Lord:

"Of those who, under the insupportable agonies and distraction of the scourge and the rack, recanted, or promised a recantation, a large proportion immediately on being released from the sufferings which had overcome them, abjured their retractions, re-professed with redoubled energy the faith of Christ, and met without faltering the hideous death to which they were immediately hurried. Such is their uniform history in whatever age they fell, or to whatever nation or rank they belonged."--Exp. of Apoc., p. 385.

If there was no other evidence of their constancy, faith, and patience, the horrid instruments of torture which were resorted to to terrify them, testify to their adherence to their principles, which required such engines for their subversion.

The end of this beast, will be effected by his being cast alive into the lake of fire and brimstone, when the Lord shall make war with him, 19:20. This is also the end of Daniel's fourth beast, whose body is to be given to the burning flame (Dan. 7:11), and of the scarlet-colored beast on which the woman was seated, which is to go into perdition, 17:8.

The Two-Horned Beast.

"And I saw another wild beast ascending out of the earth, and he had two horns like a lamb, and he spoke like a dragon. And he exerciseth all the power of the first wild beast, in his sight, and causeth the earth and those, who dwell in it, to worship the first wild beast, whose deadly wound was healed. And he performeth great signs, so that he causeth fire to come down from heaven into the earth in the sight of men. And he deceiveth those, who dwell on the earth, by means of the signs which it was given him to perform in the sight of the wild beast; saying to those, who dwell on the earth, that they should make an image to the wild beast, that had the wound by a sword, and did live."--Rev. 13:11-14.

The coming up of another beast must symbolize the rise of another government. As the two-horned beast exercises its power before ({~GREEK SMALL LETTER EPSILON~}{~GREEK SMALL LETTER NU~}{~GREEK SMALL LETTER OMEGA~}{~GREEK SMALL LETTER PI~}{~GREEK SMALL LETTER IOTA~}{~GREEK SMALL LETTER OMICRON~}{~GREEK SMALL LETTER NU~}) i.e. in the presence, of the first beast, it is a contemporary power, and must necessarily symbolize a kingdom outside of the territory of the ten-horned beast. Within that territory it would be one of the horns of that beast; but a separate beast requires a separate territory. As it arises out of the earth, while it is outside of the territory occupied by the ten kingdoms, it must exist within that occupied by the former Roman empire, and commence its existence during a period of settled government.

All the forms of Roman government symbolized by the dragon, were also symbolized by the wild beast; and as the deadly wound of the former was healed in the latter, the two constitute one beast. As that is called the "first beast," the rise of the kingdom symbolized by the two-horned beast must have been subsequent to the commencement of the Roman empire. And as it caused those who dwell on the earth to worship that beast after its deadly wound was healed, it must have arisen anterior to the healing of that wound; and, consequently, before the succession of the ten kingdoms to the sovereignty of Rome, with which it held an intimate relation.

The only kingdom which has arisen within the geographical locality, and at the epoch required by these conditions of the symbol, is the Eastern Roman empire; which, consequently, is the government represented by the two-horned beast.

The imperial heads of Rome date from the battle of Actium, B. C. 31; but the Eastern empire was not commenced, till A. D. 324, when Constantine removed the seat of empire from Rome to Constantinople. Rome was, previous to that removal, the undisputed queen of nations, and Constantine was without a rival. Why he should abandon Rome, the citadel and throne of the Caesars, for an obscure corner of Thrace, has never been satisfactorily explained. Says Dr. Croly: "The change of government to Constantinople still perplexes the historian. It was an act in direct repugnance to the whole course of the ancient prejudices."

The indifference with which Constantine viewed the country of the Caesars, was regarded by Gibbon as the cause of removal.

He transferred the customs and forms of the Roman government, and there exercised all the powers of the empire,--the Italians still obeying the edicts which he condescended to address from Constantinople to the Senate and people of Rome. The western division continued dependent on the eastern head, till the death of Theodosius, A. D. 395. His two sons, Arcadius and Honorius, "were saluted by the unanimous consent of mankind, as the lawful emperors of the East, and of the West,"--the European boundary being "not very different from that which separates the Germans from the Turks."--Gibbon, v. 2, p. 199. Gibbon calls this "the final and permanent division of the Roman empire." But its existence as a beast more properly dates from the removal of Constantine.

Its two horns like a lamb, must symbolize two divisions of the kingdom. These may be contemporary, like those symbolized by the ten horns (17:12), or successive, like the two horns of the ram, Dan. 8:3, 20. From the history of the Eastern empire, the latter is the more probable; and its historical resemblance to the government symbolized by the ram, may be the reason of the comparison to "horns like a lamb." As Persia was a government outside of Media, and succeeded to its sovereignty, so did the kingdom of the Turks originate outside of the Eastern empire, and at length come in, occupy its territory, and succeed to its sovereignty, A. D. 1253. With this view, the horns would symbolize the kings of Eastern Rome and of Turkey. See pp. 99-104.

Its dragon-like speech shows it to be a blasphemous, persecuting power, like that which persecuted the woman, 12:17. Though the Greek empire claimed to be Christian, a successor of Constantine, Julian the Apostate, renounced Christianity, endeavored to restore the Pagan service in Constantinople, and "declared himself the implacable enemy of Christ." He assumed the character of Supreme Pontiff, and thus placed himself at the head of the Pagan worship. He labored incessantly to restore and propagate those dragonic rites, and even thought to disprove the predictions of Christ by rebuilding the temple of Jerusalem. "He affected to pity the unhappy Christians, as mistaken in the most important object of their lives; but his pity was degraded by contempt, his contempt was embittered by hatred; and the sentiments of Julian were expressed in a style of sarcastic wit which inflicts a deep and deadly wound whenever it issues from the mouth of a sovereign." And he intimated that they might have occasion "to dread, not only confiscation and exile, but fire and the sword."--Gibbon.

The successors of Julian, though Christian in name, issued cruel and tyrannical edicts. Valens embraced Arianism, and bitterly persecuted the Orthodox party. Justinian established Catholicism by arms. Theodosius proscribed Paganism by the infliction of severe penalties. Marcian and Leo "enforced, with arms and edicts, the symbols of their faith," and it was declared that "the decrees of the synod of Chalcedon might be lawfully supported, even with blood." And after the accession of the Mohammedan power, religious intolerance towards dissenting creeds was still more rigidly enforced.

The Eastern empire exercised all the power of the Western. The original organization of its government was the same, and it had the same titles and prerogatives. Gibbon says of Julian: "The spirit of his administration, and his regard for the place of his nativity, induced him to confer on the senate of Constantinople the same honors, privileges, and authority which were still enjoyed by the senate of ancient Rome."

It caused worship to be bestowed on the first beast, by extending to the Latin rulers that aid which enabled them to perpetuate their system of tyranny, to legislate over the laws and subjects of Jehovah, and to claim the obedience which only God can demand. The arms of Justinian, both in the East and West, caused the Roman name to be respected, and its favor sought for.

The wonders to be performed by it, may be as yet involved in some obscurity. But by these it is identified as the power which afterwards became the seat of the False Prophet. When the "beast" is taken, "the false prophet that wrought miracles before him, with which he deceived them that had the mark of the beast, and them that worshipped his image," is cast with him "into a lake of fire burning with brimstone," 19:20. This identifies the two-horned beast as the Mohammedan kingdom. It also proves that the Romanic Turkish government will continue till the Second Advent.

Among the wonders it would perform, making fire come down from heaven is specified. John does not intimate that he saw, in vision, fire thus descend. The fact is spoken of; and therefore it is not necessarily symbolic, but may refer to literal fire. Gibbon, in speaking of "the novelty, the terrors, and the real efficacy of the Greek fire," for which the Eastern empire was so famous, says:

"The important secret of compounding and directing this artificial flame was imparted by Callinicus, a native of Heliopolis, in Syria, who deserted from the service of the caliph to that of the emperor. The skill of a chemist and engineer was equivalent to the succor of fleets and armies; and this discovery or improvement of the military art was fortunately reserved for the distressful period, when the degenerate Romans of the East were incapable of contending with the warlike enthusiasm and youthful vigor of the Saracens. The historian who presumes to analyze this extraordinary composition, should suspect his own ignorance and that of his Byzantine guides, so prone to the marvellous, so careless, and, in this instance, so jealous of the truth. From their obscure, and perhaps fallacious hints, it should seem that the principal ingredient of the Greek fire was the naphtha, or liquid bitumen, a light, tenacious, and inflammable oil, which springs from the earth, and catches fire as soon as it comes in contact with the air. The naphtha was mingled, I know not by what methods, or in what proportions, with sulphur, and with the pitch that is extracted from evergreen firs. From this mixture, which produced a thick smoke and a loud explosion, proceeded a fierce and obstinate flame, which not only rose in perpendicular ascent, but likewise burned with equal vehemence in descent or lateral progress; instead of being extinguished, it was nourished and quickened by the element of water; and sand, urine, or vinegar, were the only remedies that could damp the fury of this powerful agent, which was justly denominated by the Greeks, the liquid, or maritime fire. For the annoyance of the enemy, it was employed with equal effect by sea and land, in battles or in sieges. It was either poured from the rampart in large boilers, or launched in red-hot balls of stone and iron, or darted in arrows and javelins, twisted round with flax and tow, which had deeply imbibed the inflammable oil; sometimes it was deposited in fire-ships, the victims and instruments of a more ample revenge, and was most commonly blown through long tubes of copper, which were planted on the prow of a galley, and fancifully shaped into the mouths of savage monsters, that seemed to vomit a stream of liquid and consuming fire. This important art was preserved at Constantinople, as the palladium of the state; the galleys and artillery might occasionally be lent to the allies of Rome; but the composition on the Greek fire was concealed with the most jealous scruple, and the terror of the enemies was increased and prolonged by their ignorance and surprise. In the treatise of the administration of the empire, the royal author suggests the answers and excuses that might best elude the indiscreet curiosity and importunate demands of the barbarians. They should be told that the mystery of the Greek fire had been revealed by an angel to the first and greatest of the Constantines, with a sacred injunction, that this gift of heaven, this peculiar blessing of the Romans should never be communicated to any foreign nation; that the prince and subject were alike bound to religious silence under the temporal and spiritual penalties of treason and sacrilege; and that the impious attempt would provoke the sudden and supernatural vengeance of the God of the Christians. By these precautions the secret was confined, above four hundred years, to the Romans of the East; and at the end of the eleventh century, the Pisans, to whom every sea and every art were familiar, suffered the effects, without understanding the composition, of the Greek fire. It was at length either discovered or stolen by the Mohammedans; and, in the holy wars of Syria and Egypt, they retorted an invention, contrived against themselves, on the heads of the Christians. A knight, who despised the swords and lances of the Saracens, relates, with heartfelt sincerity, his own fears and those of his companions, at the sight and sound of the mischievous engine that discharged a torrent of the Greek fire, the feu Gregeois, as it is styled by the more early of the French writers. It came flying through the air, says Joinville, like a winged long-tailed dragon, about the thickness of a hogshead, with the report of thunder, and the velocity of lightning; and the darkness of night was dispelled by this deadly illumination."--Hist. Rome, vol. III., pp. 465-467.

Its use is thus described by the same author, when the Greeks turned its power against the Saracens, at the siege of Constantinople, A. D. 718:

"The Greeks would gladly have ransomed their religion and empire, by a fine or assessment of a piece of gold on the head of each inhabitant of the city; but the liberal offer was rejected with disdain, and the presumption of Moslemah was exalted by the speedy approach and invincible force of the natives of Egypt and Syria. They are said to have amounted to eighteen hundred ships: the number betrays their inconsiderable size; and of the twenty stout and capacious vessels, whose magnitude impeded their progress, each was manned with no more than one hundred heavy-armed soldiers. This huge armada proceeded on a smooth sea and with a gentle gale, towards the mouth of the Bosphorus; the surface of the strait was over-shadowed, in the language of the Greeks, with a moving forest, and the same fatal night had been fixed by the Saracen chief for a general assault by sea and land. To allure the confidence of the enemy, the emperor had thrown aside the chain that usually guarded the entrance of the harbor: but while they hesitated whether they should seize the opportunity or apprehend the snare, the ministers of destruction were at hand. The fireships of the Greeks were launched against them: the Arabs, their arms and vessels, were involved in the same flames, the disorderly fugitives were dashed against each other, or overwhelmed in the waves; and I no longer find a vestige of the fleet, that had threatened to extirpate the Roman name."--Ib., p. 464.

It deceiveth them that dwell on the earth by its miracles. This deception resulted in the creation of:

The Image of the Beast.

"And it was given to him to give breath to the image of the wild beast, that the image of the wild beast should even speak, and to cause, that as many as would not worship the image of the wild beast, should be killed. And he causeth all, the small and the great, and the rich and the poor, and the free and the bond, to receive a mark on their right hand, or on their forehead. And that no one might buy or sell, but he, who had the mark, the name of the wild beast, or the number of his name."--Rev. 13:15-18.

This new creation is not another beast, but the image of one. An image is only the likeness of something. As the beast symbolizes a political power, its image must symbolize some analogous power of a different nature; and this likeness can only be found in a religious government.

1. The beast which received its death-wound (v. 14), was the form of government to which the image was made, i.e., the imperial. Of this the Roman hierarchy was a perfect counterpart. It was an ecclesiastical government, coextensive in its authority with the political power of the empire. And, like the officers of the civil, there was a regular gradation of rank in the subordinates of the religious government. The head of the former was an emperor, chosen by an electoral college,--the senators of Rome.(3) The head of the latter was a Pope, chosen in a similar manner by the college of Cardinals,--the ecclesiastical senators of the religious empire. Each of those bodies constituted the highest deliberative and legislative body in its respective government. The empire had its governors of provinces, appointed by the imperial head; and the spiritual rule of the church was, in like manner, sustained by diocesan bishops who, in their respective provinces, were governors in spiritual matters and creatures of the Pope. Subordinate offices in the state and church, also, singularly corresponded.

2. The religious customs of the empire, as well as its political, were likewise imitated by the papacy. Rome deified her heroes; the papacy canonized her saints. The ghosts of the departed were the gods of the heathen; and the papists supplicate the dead. The Pagans burned incense to their gods; the Papists burn incense in their religious ceremonies. The ancient heathen sprinkled themselves with "holy water;" the Papists use the same material in a similar manner. Lactantius says of the Pagans, they "light up candles to God as if he lived in the dark; and do they not deserve to pass for madmen who offer lamps to the author and giver of light?" This custom is imitated by the Papists in the use of wax candles on their altars.

The ancient Romans prostrated themselves before images of wood and stone; and Jerome tells us that "by idols were to be understood the images of the dead." In Catholic Rome, worshippers prostrated themselves before images of departed saints. The old Roman Pantheon, which was dedicated by Agrippa "to Jove, and all the gods," was re-consecrated by Pope Boniface IV., about A. D. 610, "to the blessed Virgin and all the saints." As in the old pagan temple, any stranger could find the god of his own country; so in its re-consecrated state, each country could find its patron saint. Other temples were changed and re-consecrated in the same manner. The ancient statue of Jupiter stands now as the statue of St. Peter. The pagans had their vestal virgins; the Papists their nuns.

Dr. Middleton, who visited Rome in 1729, says:

"Nothing, I found, concurred so much with my original intention of conversing with the ancients; or so much helped my imagination, to find myself wandering about in old heathen Rome, as to observe and attend to their religious worship; all whose ceremonies appear plainly to have been copied from the rituals of primitive Paganism: as if handed down by an uninterrupted succession from the priests of old, to the priests of new Rome, whilst each of them readily explained, and called to mind some passages of a classic author, where the same ceremony was described, as transacted in the same form and manner, and in the same place where I now saw it executed before my eyes."--Dowl. Hist. of Rom., p. 114.

Says Mr. Lord:

"After a struggle of more than four centuries, the ecclesiastics of all the hierarchies in the empire were united in one vast organization, with the pontiff as their supreme legislative and judicial head, and a single ecclesiastical government was established over the whole Roman church, after the model of the civil government of the ancient empire under Constantine and his successors. It is, accordingly, denominated by Catholics themselves a monarchy. 'All Catholic doctors agree in this, that the ecclesiastical government committed to men by God is a monarchy.'--Bellarmini de Rom. Pont., lib. i., c. v. Bellarmine devotes his first book 'of the Pontiff' to prove that such is and ought to be its government. 'If the monarchical is the best form of government, as we have shown, and it is certain that the church of God instituted by Christ its head, who is supremely wise, ought to be governed in the best manner, who can deny that its rule ought to be monarchical?'--Ib., i., c. ix., p. 527.

"The canonists are accustomed, accordingly, to denominate the Pope a king.

"The pontiffs were as absolutely the legislative and judicial head of this ecclesiastical kingdom, as the emperors from Constantine to Augustulus were of the civil empire, and imposed whatever laws they pleased on subordinate ecclesiastics and on the church by decrees, in the same manner as those emperors enacted laws by edicts. The decrees, bulls of canonization, sentences, charters, and other legislative and judicial acts of the pontiffs, from Gregory VII., in 1073, to Benedict XIV., in 1757, collected in the Bullarium Magnum, fill nineteen folios. Many others are contained in the decretals and councils.

"They appointed to all ecclesiastical offices throughout the empire, as the Christian emperors appointed to all civil and military offices in their dominions.

"They exacted oaths of fidelity from all whom they advanced to important offices; as the emperors exacted engagements of fidelity from their civil magistrates.

"They established courts in which all violations of their laws were tried, and a tribunal at the capital for the decision of appeals. There were gradations of rank in the hierarchy, like those of the magistrates of the civil empire. The hierarchies, as nationalized by Constantine, were formed in each patriarchate, after the model of the civil government in the provinces. The hierarchy of the western kingdoms, under the Pope, was formed after that pattern; having archbishops or metropolitans at the head of the clergy of each nation, or large district, and bishops, abbots, and a long catalogue of subordinate ranks, under each metropolitan.

"They levied taxes for their support on ecclesiastics and laics.

"They inflicted ecclesiastical penalties on the violators of their laws; exclusion from communion, suspension from office, deposition, excommunication, and a sentence of eternal death."--Exp. of Apoc., pp.

429-432.

These, with many other striking resemblances, demonstrate that the Roman hierarchy, in all its great features, was a counterpart to imperial Rome--an image of, and belonging to, the seven-headed, ten-horned monster, whose deadly wound was healed.

Life was to be given to this image by the two-horned beast. The papal hierarchy is created when its supremacy over other churches is declared and sustained; and the power by which this is done, is that which gives life to it. This was done, according to the following history, by the Eastern empire.

The power of the papacy, symbolized by the image, had been predicted in Daniel under the symbol of "a Little Horn," that came up among the previous "ten horns," before whom "there were three of the first horns plucked up by the roots: and behold, in this horn were eyes like the eyes of man, and a mouth speaking great things," Dan. 7:8. These horns were thus explained to Daniel: "The fourth beast shall be the fourth kingdom upon earth, which shall be diverse from all kingdoms, and shall devour the whole earth, and shall tread it down, and break it in pieces. And the ten horns out of this kingdom are ten kings that shall arise: and another shall arise after them; and he shall be diverse from the first, and he shall subdue three kings. And he shall speak great words against the Most High, and shall wear out the saints of the Most High, and think to change times and laws: and they shall be given into his hand until a time and times and the dividing of time. But the judgment shall sit, and they shall take away his dominion to consume and to destroy it unto the end. And the kingdom and dominion, and the greatness of the kingdom under the whole heaven, shall be given to the people of the saints of the Most High, whose kingdom is an everlasting kingdom, and all dominions shall serve and obey him." Ib. vs. 23-27.

When Paul spoke of the second coming of Christ, in his first epistle to the Thessalonians, they understood that it was an event then imminent. The apostle, in his second epistle, corrects this impression, by referring to the foregoing prediction in Daniel, which must be previously fulfilled. He assures them that "the day of Christ" "shall not come, except there be" an apostasy, or "a falling away first, and that Man of Sin," or the lawless one, "be revealed, the son of perdition; who opposeth and exalteth himself above all that is called God, or that is worshipped; so that he, as God, sitteth in the temple of God, showing himself that he is God. Remember ye not, that when I was yet with you, I told you these things? And now ye know what withholdeth that he might be revealed in his time. For the mystery of iniquity doth already work: only he who now letteth will let, until he be taken out of the way. And then shall that Wicked be revealed, whom the Lord shall consume with the spirit of his mouth, and shall destroy with the brightness of his coming," 2 Thess. 2:2-8.

The uniform application of these predictions to the Papacy, by Protestant writers, renders it unnecessary to argue this point. That power began early to be manifested, but its full development was "let," i.e., hindered, by the continuance of the Western empire, which had to be taken out of its way. Tertullian, near the close of the second century, in expounding those words, says: "Who can this be but the Roman state, the division of which into ten kingdoms will bring on Antichrist?" And he gives as a reason why the Christians of his time prayed for the Roman empire: that the greatest calamity hanging over the world was retarded by the continuance of it. Cyril of Jerusalem in the fourth century applied the passage in the same manner, and says:

"Thus the predicted Antichrist will come when the times of the Roman empire shall be fulfilled, and the consummation of the world shall approach. Ten kings of the Romans shall arise together, in different places indeed, but they shall reign at the same time. Among these the eleventh is Antichrist, who, by magical and wicked artifice, shall seize the Roman power." A large number of the ancient fathers interpreted this text in the same manner.

In A. D. 257, 1260 years before the time of Luther, Stephen, Bishop of Rome, began to act the pope in good earnest,--excommunicating those who dissented from the doctrines of Rome.

In 312, 1260 years before the massacre of St. Bartholomew in 1572, Constantine became Emperor of Rome, embraced Christianity, and terminated the last and bloodiest of the Pagan persecutions--that of Diocletian, which had continued ten years. Constantine undertook to remodel the church, in conformity to the government of the state, and the unhallowed union of the two resulted in the dignities of patriarchs, exarchs, archbishops, canons, prebendaries, &c., which he endowed with wealth and worldly honors.

While paganism was superseded by Christianity under Constantine, its ceremonies were not suppressed. The senate was still pagan; and "the title, the ensigns, and the prerogatives of Sovereign Pontiff, which had been instituted by Numa, and assumed by Augustus, were accepted, without hesitation, by seven Christian emperors."--Gibbon, v. 2, p. 183. Gratian became emperor, A. D. 376, and was the first who refused the pontifical robe. In 378, he invested Theodosius with the Empire of the East; under their rule paganism was "wholly extirpated," and the senate was suddenly converted.--Ib. That which hindered was thus taken out of the way. In 378, also, Gratian refusing the office, Damasus, the Bishop of Rome, was "declared Pontifix Maximus,"(4) and made "the sole judge in religious matters." All who would not adhere to the religion "professed by the Pontiff Damasus, and by Peter, Bishop of Alexandria," were declared heretics.-- Gibbon, v. 2, p. 156. Damasus, by virtue of his power, introduced the worship of the saints, and of Mary, "the mother of God,"--excommunicating those who dissented. Thus the apostasy, by adopting the gods of the heathen, and the name of the heathen pontiff, began to be set up, and the excommunicated church disappeared in the wilderness.

In the ninth century a document was produced, which claimed to be a deed of gift from Constantine to the Pope, dated A. D. 324, ceding him the city of Rome and all Italy, with the crown, the mitre, &c.; but the forgery of this has been fully exposed. With the removal of the capital of the world to Constantinople, the empire began to decline; but the church augmented as fast. A provisional synod at Sardica, in A. D. 344, and a decree of the Emperor Valentinian III., in 445, had acknowledged the Bishop of Rome as the primate of the five patriarchs, and as the last tribunal of appeal from the other bishops; but the edicts of the Pope were often disregarded and opposed, and he continued subject to the civil power till the subversion of the Western empire by Odoacer, King of the Heruli, in A. D. 476.

The ten kingdoms which had arisen on the ruins of the Western empire (p. 169), had nearly all embraced Christianity, corrupted by Arianism. And the barbarians transferred to their Christian instructors, the profound submission and reverence which they were accustomed to yield to the teachers of paganism,--many of the rites and ceremonies of which had been incorporated into the Catholic service. Ecclesiastical courts were established, in which were tried all questions relating to character, office, or property of the clergy; and thus they became nearly independent of the civil judges.

The Heruli, which was the first of the ten horns plucked up, were conquered by the Ostrogoths, in A. D. 493, when all Italy submitted to Theodoric. He fixed his capital at Ravenna, which left the Pope the only Prince of Rome; and the Romans, for protection, were forced to pay more deference to him.

About A. D. 500, two Popes were simultaneously elected, when Theodoric gave the papal chair to Symmachus. Gross crimes being alleged against him by the defeated party, the king summoned a council in A. D. 503 to investigate the charges; and he was acquitted. The other party being dissatisfied, Ennodius, Bishop Ticonum, drew up an apology for the Pope and council, in which, for the first time, the Pope was styled a "Judge in the place of God, and Vicegerent of the Most High;" and "subject to no earthly tribunal." Thus did the Lawless One attempt, "as God," to "sit in the temple of God."

In A. D. 533, Justinian, Emperor at Constantinople, being about to attack the Vandals in Africa, and wishing first to settle the religious disputes of his capital in which he felt a great interest, he submitted the controversy to the primate of Rome. To induce a decision in his own favor, or to give force to it, he acknowledged the Bishop of Rome the Chief of the whole Ecclesiastical body of the empire; and thus addressed him, in a letter sent by two distinguished prelates:--

"Justinian, pious, fortunate, renowned, triumphant emperor, consul, &c., to John, the most holy Archbishop of our city of Rome, and patriarch.

"Rendering honor to the Apostolic chair, and to your Holiness, as has been always and is our wish, and honoring your blessedness as a father; we have hastened to bring to the knowledge of your Holiness all matters relating to the state of the churches. It having been at all times our great desire to preserve the unity of your Apostolic chair, and the constitution of the holy churches of God which has obtained hitherto, and still obtains.

"Therefore we have made no delay in subjecting and uniting to your Holiness all the priests of the whole East.

"For this reason we have thought fit to bring to your notice the present matters of disturbance; though they are manifest and unquestionable, and always firmly held and declared by the whole priesthood according to the doctrine of your Apostolic chair. For we cannot suffer that anything which relates to the state of the Church, however manifest and unquestionable, should be moved, without the knowledge of your Holiness, who are The Head of all the Holy Churches, for in all things, as we have already declared, we are anxious to increase the honor and authority of your Apostolic chair."

Says Dr. Croly:--

"The emperor's letter must have been sent before the 25th of March, 533. For, in his letter of that date to Epiphanius he speaks of its having been already despatched, and repeats his decision, that all affairs touching the church shall be referred to the Pope, 'head of all bishops, and the true and effective corrector of heretics.'

"In the same month of the following year, 534, the Pope returned an answer repeating the language of the emperor, applauding his homage to the See, and adopting the titles of the imperial mandate. He observes that, among the virtues of Justinian, 'one shines as a star, his reverence for the Apostolic chair, to which he has subjected and united all the churches, it being truly the head of all; and was testified by the rules of the fathers, the laws of the princes, and the declarations of the emperor's piety.'

"The authenticity of the title receives unanswerable proof from the edicts in the 'Novell?' of the Justinian code.

"The preamble of the 9th states that 'as the elder Rome was the founder of the laws, so was it not to be questioned that in her was the supremacy of the pontificate.'

"The 131st, on the ecclesiastical titles and privileges, chapter II. states: 'We therefore decree that the most holy Pope of the elder Rome is the first of all the priesthood, and that the most blessed archbishop of Constantinople, the new Rome, shall hold the second rank after the holy Apostolic chair of the elder Rome.'

"The supremacy of the Pope had by those mandates and edicts received the fullest sanction that could be given by the authority of the master of the Roman world. However worthless the motives, the act was done, authentic and unquestionable, sanctioned by all the forms of state, and never abrogated,--the act of the first potentate in the world. If the supremacy over the church of God had been for man to give, it might have been given by the unrivalled sovereignty of Justinian.

"From this era the church of Rome dates the earthly acknowledgment of her claim. Its heavenly authority is referred to the remoter source of the apostles."--Apoc., pp. 14-16, 30, 31.

The war against the Vandals was vigorously prosecuted by Belisarius, Justinian's general, and resulted in their conquest the same year. Thus was the second of the first ten divisions of the empire subjugated: the second horn was plucked up.

Rome was still in possession of an Arian monarch, who was the bitter enemy of the Catholic church. Intelligence of the success of Belisarius in Africa reached the emperor, Dec. 16th, A. D. 533. "Impatient to abolish the temporal and spiritual tyranny of the Vandals, he proceeded, without delay, to the full establishment of the Catholic church."--Gibbon, Harpers' ed., v. 3, p. 67. Belisarius proceeded to the conquest of Italy, which he effected, and marched on to Rome. Only 4000 soldiers were stationed for its defence; and they could not oppose the wishes of the Romans, who voluntarily submitted. Seized with a momentary enthusiasm, "they furiously exclaimed that the apostolic throne should no longer be profaned by the triumph or toleration of Arianism; that the tombs of the Caesars should no longer be trampled on by the savages of the north; and without reflecting that Italy must sink into a province of Constantinople, they fondly hailed the restoration of a Roman emperor as a new era of freedom and prosperity. The deputies of the Pope and clergy, of the senate and people, invited the lieutenant of Justinian to accept their voluntary allegiance, and to enter the city." Thus was "the city, after sixty years' servitude delivered from the yoke of the barbarians," Dec. 10, A. D. 536. And "the Catholics prepared to celebrate, without a rival, the approaching festival of the nativity of Christ."--Ib. p. 80.

In the winter, the Ostrogoths made preparations, and besieged Rome with an army of 150,000 fighting men. Pope Sylverius was suspected of treachery, and on proof that he had communicated with the enemy, he was banished by Belisarius. At the emperor's command, the clergy of Rome proceeded to the choice of a new bishop, and elected "deacon Virgilius, who had purchased the papal throne by a bribe of two hundred pounds of gold."--Ib. p. 85. As he had obtained the papal seat by fraud, it was claimed that he was not the lawful Pope; but in A. D. 538, he was owned as such by the 5th General Council, and the whole Christian world.--See Bowers' Hist. Popes, v. 2, p. 374. In March of this year (538),--after "one year and nine days"--the Ostrogoths raised the siege of Rome, and burned their tents--one-third of their number having perished under its walls. The arms of Justinian triumphed, and the Catholic hierarchy was established. The third horn had been plucked up by the fall of the third of the first ten divisions of Rome.

The Bishop of Constantinople did not submit willingly to the Primacy of Rome. On the death of Justinian, the supremacy of the Pope was utterly denied; and, in A. D. 588, John, Bishop of Constantinople, himself assumed the coveted title of "Universal Bishop." The Roman bishop, Gregory the Great, indignant at this usurpation, denounced him as a "usurper, aiming at supremacy over the whole church," and declared that whoever claims such supremacy "has the pride and character of Antichrist."

Boniface succeeded to the Roman See, and in the following year, A. D. 606, only two years after Gregory's death, applied to Phocas,--who had ascended the throne of Constantinople by the murder of the Emperor Mauritius,--for the same blasphemous title, with the privilege of continuing it to his successors. His request was granted, the Eastern Bishop was forbidden its use, and the Primate of Rome was again acknowledged as "Universal Bishop," and the unrivalled "Head of all the churches." This title has been worn by all the succeeding Popes; "but the highest authority," says Dr. Croly, "among the civilians and annalists of Rome, spurn the idea that Phocas was the founder of the supremacy of Rome. They ascend to Justinian as the only legitimate source, and rightly date the title from the memorable year 533."--Apoc. p. 117.

In A. D. 730, Emperor Leo issued an edict for the destruction of all images used in religious worship. From that time the Pope scorned his authority, and acted in defiance of the emperor's will, who found himself unable to compel the Pope to obey the edict.

The Papacy thus defied all human authority; but did not as yet attempt the exercise of political power.

In A. D. 756, Pepin, the usurper of the crown of France, compelled the King of Lombardy to cede the exarchate of Ravenna to the Pope, "to be forever held and possessed by St. Peter and his lawful successors in the See of Rome." The Pope had now become a temporal prince, and one of the kings of the earth. In A. D. 774, Charlemagne, the successor of Pepin, confirmed the former gift, and in addition, subjugated the Lombards, and annexed a large portion of their kingdom and the Duchy of Rome to the Roman See. In A. D. 817, Louis the Pious, granted "St. Peter's patrimony" to the Pope and his successors, "in their own right, principality, and dominion, unto the end of the world." Hence, as a temporal prince, the Pope wears a triple crown.

In A. D. 800, Charlemagne was solemnly crowned and proclaimed emperor by the Pope, having reduced under his sway nearly the whole of Europe. From this time the Popes claimed superiority to all kings and emperors, received homage from them, and exercised all the rights of sovereignty; but they were nominally dependent on the Emperors of the West till A. D. 1278, when the Emperor Rudolph released the people of the Papal States from all allegiance they might still owe to the imperial crown. This act was confirmed by the electors and princes of the empire. The Popes, in the greatness of their power, crowned and uncrowned kings at their pleasure, absolved subjects from all allegiance to their rulers, excommunicated whoever they would, and compelled secular princes to put to death heretics.

In A. D. 1294, Boniface VIII. became Pope. From his accession Hallam dates the decline of the Papacy, which, for "more than two centuries, had been on throne of the earth, and reigned despot of the world."--Dowling. This was 1260 years from the death of Peter,--the earliest time from which they can date. His bull of excommunication against Philip of France, being disregarded by that monarch, who adroitly made the Pope his prisoner, his rage brought on a fever, which caused his death. Only a few succeeding pontiffs claimed, and none attempted to enforce, the prerogatives exercised by the preceding Popes. For seventy years the successors of Boniface resided at Avignon, in France, and paid great deference to the monarch of that country. After this was the Western schism, which divided the church for forty years,--two rival Popes claiming the mitre, and thundering out their anathemas against each other. These events greatly weakened the Papacy. About this time appeared Wickliffe and Huss, and Jerome of Prague; and still later, in 1517, Martin Luther, in opposition to the Papal pretensions, published his Thesis against Indulgences, 1260 years from the time of the arrogance of Pope Stephen.

In A. D. 1572, 1260 years from the removal of Constantine from Rome to Constantinople, occurred the bloody massacre of St. Bartholomew, when in one day 5000 Protestants were murdered in Paris, and in the same proportion in other parts of France. The persecutions of the Papists continued till near the close of the last century; and as late as November, 1781, a woman was burned alive by the Inquisition in Spain.

In 1793, 1260 years from Justinian's letter to the Pope, the Papal church, with all religion, was entirely suppressed in France. And in 1798, which was the same length of time from the establishment of the papacy, by the conquest of the Ostrogoths,--the plucking up of the last of the three horns in 538, Gen. Berthier entered Rome, compelled the Pope to flee, and terminated the Papal government.

The temporal power was afterwards restored; but in 1848, twelve hundred and sixty years from 588 when John assumed the title of Universal Bishop, the Pope again fled from his throne. Two years subsequently, he was again restored.

"Flacius, in his 'Catalogue of Witnesses,' represented the twelve hundred and sixty days as having commenced in 606;" and Scott, and several others, reckon them from the same epoch.

4. The image had power to speak. It thus filled the office of the "mouth," which was given to the ten-horned beast (v. 5), which synchronizes with the view taken of that appendage, p. 172.

5. It should cause the infliction of death on those who should refuse to worship. The worship it would exact, is doubtless of the kind bestowed on the wild beast, 13:4. The Papal hierarchy claimed to be infallible and invincible, and to have power to bind and loose on earth and in heaven; those who refused to recognize its claims, if incorrigible, were punished with death.

The Image was not to put to death, but would cause them to be killed. The symbolization corresponds with the fulfilment in this particular. The ecclesiastical officials punished rebellious subjects, by delivering them over to the civil arm; which punished heretics according to the will of the Papacy. "Lucius III. and Innocent III. by formal decrees required them to be seized, condemned, and delivered by the civil magistrates, to be capitally punished; and enjoined the princes and magistrates to execute on them the sentences denounced by the canon and civil laws."--Lord's Exp. of Apoc., p. 434. This is substantiated by Bellarmini and other writers. Civil rulers, who refused to enforce the decrees of the councils, were anathematized, excommunicated, and often deprived of their political power. When the Papacy has been reminded of the numbers killed and otherwise punished for alleged heresy, she has replied that the civil power, and not the church, has done this! She, however, has caused the kings of the earth to execute her wishes.

6. The image would cause all to receive the mark of the Beast. A mark is a token of recognition. Slaves, soldiers, and the devotees of various gods, were thus identified on their hands or foreheads, both before and after the time of St. John--slaves by the name of the Emperor on their forehead, and soldiers by his name on their hand. Mr. Elliott proves this by quotations from Valerius, Maximus, Ælian, Ambrose, and others. The devotees of particular gods gained admittance to the secret meetings of the worshippers of their respective deity, by a mark by which they identified each other. At the present day the Hindoos are marked on the forehead by the hieroglyphic of the god they are consecrated to.

The mark of the beast, is its name, or the number of its name. The ancients often used numbers to indicate names. "Among the Pagans, the Egyptian mystics spoke of Mercury, or Thouth, under the number 1218, because the Greek letters composing the name Thouth, when estimated according to their numerical value, together made up that number. By others, Jupiter was invoked under the mystical number 717; because the letters of {~GREEK CAPITAL LETTER ETA WITH DASIA~} {~GREEK CAPITAL LETTER ALPHA~}{~GREEK CAPITAL LETTER RHO~}{~GREEK CAPITAL LETTER CHI~}{~GREEK CAPITAL LETTER ETA~}, the beginning, or first origin, which was a characteristic title of the supreme deity worshipped as Jupiter, made up that number: and Apollo under the number 608, as being that of {~GREEK SMALL LETTER ETA~} {~GREEK SMALL LETTER UPSILON~}{~GREEK SMALL LETTER FINAL SIGMA~}, or {~GREEK SMALL LETTER UPSILON~}{~GREEK SMALL LETTER ETA~}{~GREEK SMALL LETTER FINAL SIGMA~}, words expressing certain solar attributes. Again, the pseudo-Christian or semi-pagan Gnostics, from St. John's time downwards, affixed to their gems and amulets, of which multitudes remain even to the present day, the mystic word {~GREEK SMALL LETTER SIGMA~}{~GREEK SMALL LETTER BETA~}{~GREEK SMALL LETTER RHO~}{~GREEK SMALL LETTER ALPHA~}{~GREEK SMALL LETTER SIGMA~}{~GREEK SMALL LETTER ALPHA~}{~GREEK SMALL LETTER XI~}, or {~GREEK SMALL LETTER ALPHA~}{~GREEK SMALL LETTER BETA~}{~GREEK SMALL LETTER RHO~}{~GREEK SMALL LETTER ALPHA~}{~GREEK SMALL LETTER XI~}{~GREEK SMALL LETTER ALPHA~}{~GREEK SMALL LETTER FINAL SIGMA~}, under the idea of some magic virtue attaching to its number 365, as being that of the days of the annual solar circle; and equal moreover with that of {~GREEK CAPITAL LETTER MU~}{~GREEK SMALL LETTER EPSILON~}{~GREEK SMALL LETTER IOTA~}{~GREEK SMALL LETTER THETA~}{~GREEK SMALL LETTER RHO~}{~GREEK SMALL LETTER ALPHA~}{~GREEK SMALL LETTER FINAL SIGMA~}, or Mithras, the Magian name for the sun, whom they identified also with Christ. Once more, the Christian fathers themselves fell into the same fancies, and doctrine of mysteriousness in certain verbal numbers. For example, both Barnabas and Clement of Alexandria speak of the virtue of the number 318 as being that of {~GREEK CAPITAL LETTER IOTA~}{~GREEK CAPITAL LETTER ETA~}{~GREEK CAPITAL LETTER TAU~} the common abbreviation for Jesus crucified; and partly ascribe to its magical virtue the victory which Abraham gained with his 318 servants over the Canaanitish kings. Similarly Tertullian refers the victory of Gideon, with his 300 men, to the circumstance of that being the precise number of {~GREEK CAPITAL LETTER TAU~}, the sign of the cross. In the name of Adam, St. Cyprian discerned a mysterious numeral affinity to certain characteristics in the life and history of the second Adam, Jesus Christ. Irenæus notes the remarkable number 888 of the name {~GREEK CAPITAL LETTER IOTA~}{~GREEK SMALL LETTER ETA~}{~GREEK SMALL LETTER SIGMA~}{~GREEK SMALL LETTER OMICRON~}{~GREEK SMALL LETTER UPSILON~}{~GREEK SMALL LETTER FINAL SIGMA~}, Jesus. And in the pseudo-Sibylline verses, written by Christians about the end, probably, of the second century, and consequently not long after Irenæus, we find enigmas proposed of precisely the same characters as that in the text;--the number being given, and the name required."--Elliott's Hor?Apoc., vol. iii., pp. 204-6.

The "number of the beast" is indicated in the text by the Greek letters "{~GREEK SMALL LETTER CHI~}{~GREEK SMALL LETTER XI~} {~GREEK SMALL LETTER FINAL SIGMA~}" which were severally used to represent the numbers 600, 60 and 6, making 666. As the name of the beast is equivalent to this number, the letters in it will represent numbers which amount to six hundred threescore and six.

After the division of the Roman empire, the western kingdom adopted for itself the name of the Latin kingdom; and its subdivisions were called the Latin kingdoms. The church connected with those kingdoms was also emphatically called the Latin church. Says Dr. More: "They Latinize everything. Mass, prayers, hymns, litanies, canons, decretals, bulls, are conceived in Latin. The Papal councils speak in Latin. Women pray in Latin. The Scriptures are read in no other language under the Papacy than Latin. In short, all things are Latin." The Council of Trent declared the Latin Vulgate to be the only authentic version of the Scriptures; and their doctors have preferred it to the Hebrew and Greek text, written by prophets and apostles.

This Latin kingdom is the only one that ever corresponded to the characteristics of the beast. And its name--Latinos in the Greek, and Romiith in the Hebrew--is equivalent to the required number.

"The Greek and Hebrew letters composing the words {~HEBREW LETTER RESH~}{~HEBREW LETTER VAV~}{~HEBREW LETTER MEM~}{~HEBREW LETTER YOD~}{~HEBREW LETTER YOD~} {~HEBREW LETTER TAV~}, Romiith--{~HEBREW LETTER RESH~} {~HEBREW LETTER MEM~}{~HEBREW LETTER AYIN~} {~HEBREW LETTER NUN~}{~HEBREW LETTER VAV~}{~HEBREW LETTER SHIN~}, Romanus--{~GREEK SMALL LETTER LAMDA~} {~GREEK SMALL LETTER ALPHA~}{~GREEK SMALL LETTER TAU~}{~GREEK SMALL LETTER EPSILON~}{~GREEK SMALL LETTER IOTA~}{~GREEK SMALL LETTER NU~}{~GREEK SMALL

LETTER OMICRON~}{~GREEK SMALL LETTER FINAL SIGMA~}, Latinos, each of them making in numerals exactly 666, plainly point out not only his name, and the number of his name, but also the mark of his name; as for example:

in {~HEBREW LETTER RESH~} {~HEBREW LETTER VAV~} {~HEBREW LETTER MEM~} {~HEBREW LETTER YOD~} {~HEBREW LETTER YOD~} {~HEBREW LETTER TAV~} Romiith; so likewise 400 10 10 40 6 200 = 666 {~HEBREW LETTER RESH~} {~HEBREW LETTER MEM~} {~HEBREW LETTER AYIN~} {~HEBREW LETTER NUN~} {~HEBREW LETTER VAV~} {~HEBREW LETTER SHIN~} Romanus; and also 300 6 50 70 40 200 = 666 the Greek {~GREEK SMALL LETTER LAMDA~} {~GREEK SMALL LETTER ALPHA~} {~GREEK SMALL LETTER TAU~} {~GREEK SMALL LETTER EPSILON~} {~GREEK SMALL LETTER IOTA~} {~GREEK SMALL LETTER NU~} {~GREEK SMALL LETTER OMICRON~} {~GREEK SMALL LETTER FINAL SIGMA~} Latinos, 30 1 300 5 10 50 70 200 = 666.

in each of which the exact mark is contained.

"It therefore evidently appears, that each name is both a mark and a number; a mark, when viewed as made up of so many letters, therefore called the mark of his name; a number, when viewed as made up of so many numerals, then called the number of his name. But when considered merely as a name, derived from Romiith, a Roman, or Romulus, the founder of Rome, a name common among men, it may then be properly called the mark, or number of a man."--Fleming's Rise and Fall of Papacy.

To receive the mark of the beast, would be an acknowledgment of subjection to it. The connection of the beast and its image was so intimate, that submission to the one, was virtual submission to the other. To submit to the rites of the church modelled after the wild beast, to profess its faith, and to honor its authority, would be a reception of its mark. And all persons were compelled to do this, and give evidence of submission to its authority on the peril of their lives.

7. Those who should refuse the mark of the beast, were to be prohibited from buying and selling. The Lateran Council under Pope Alexander II., passed an act forbidding any to harbor heretics in their houses or to trade with them. The Synod of Tours passed a law that no one should assist them, "no, not so much as to exercise commerce with them in selling or buying."(5)--Elliott. In 1179, the third Lateran Council sentenced certain heretics, "their defenders and harborers, to an anathema, and forbid, under an anathema, that any should presume to keep them in their house, or on their lands, sustain them, or transact any business with them."--Lord. "It was just the same fearful penalty of interdict from buying and selling, traffic and intercourse, that had been inculcated long before by the Pagan Dragon's representative Diocletian, against the early Christians."--Elliott.

So exact a correspondence between the wild beast and the Western kingdoms, the two-horned beast and the Eastern empire, and the image to the wild beast and the Roman Hierarchy, makes the symbolization of this chapter very intelligible. These three agencies will severally continue till the end of the world. The latter will be destroyed by the brightness of Christ's coming (2 Thess. 2:8), and the two former will then be taken and "cast alive into the lake of fire," 19:20.

The vision would have been defective without a representation of the end of those who refuse to worship the beast, or its image, or to receive their mark, and who, although warred against and overcome by the beast, should maintain their integrity to Christ. Accordingly the revelator has a view of:

The Redeemed on Mount Zion.

"And I looked, and behold a lamb stood on the mount Zion, and with him a hundred and forty-four thousand, having his name and the name of his Father written on their foreheads. And I heard a voice from heaven, like the voice of many waters, and like the voice of loud thunder: and the voice which I heard was like that of harpers playing with their harps: and they sung as it were a new song before the throne, and before the four living beings, and the elders: and no one could learn the song except the hundred and forty-four thousand, who were redeemed from the earth. These are they, who were not defiled with women; for they are virgins. These are they who follow the Lamb wherever he goeth. These were redeemed from among men, the first fruit to God and to the Lamb. And in their mouth no lie was found for they are faultless."--Rev. 14:1-5.

The Lamb is shown by the connection to be Christ,--here called by one of his metaphorical names.

The Mount Zion, doubtless, symbolizes the place where, in the regeneration, the Lord will reign with his saints--i.e. in the new earth. "The Lord shall reign over them in Mount Zion," Micah 4:7.--"And they sung a new song, saying, Thou art worthy to take the book, and to open the seals thereof: for thou wast slain, and hast redeemed us to God by thy blood out of every kindred and tongue, and people, and nation, and hast made us kings and priests: and we shall reign on the earth," 5:9,10.--"And I saw a new heavens and a new earth: for the first heaven and the first earth were passed away.... And I heard a great voice out of heaven, saying, Behold the tabernacle of God is with men, and he will dwell with them, and they shall, be his people, and God himself shall be with them and be their God," 21:1-3.

The names of Mount Zion, and Jerusalem, were both used to denote the city which the Lord chose above all the goodly places of earth to put his name there. It is proper to designate the heavenly city, the new Jerusalem, by all the names which were applied to the old. The king is to be set upon the holy hill of Zion--"Walk about Zion, and go round about her: tell the towers thereof. Mark ye well her bulwarks, consider her palaces," Psa. 48:12, 13. "When the Lord shall build up Zion, he shall appear in glory," Ib. 102:16. "For the Lord hath chosen Zion; he hath desired it for his habitation. This is my rest forever; here will I dwell; for I have desired it," Ib. 132:13, 14. "For the Lord shall comfort Zion: he will comfort all her waste places; and he will make her wilderness like Eden, and her desert like the garden of the Lord; and joy and gladness shall be found therein, thanksgiving and the voice of melody.... Therefore the redeemed of the Lord shall return and come with singing unto Zion; and everlasting joy shall be upon their head: they shall obtain gladness and joy, and sorrow and mourning shall flee away." Isa. 51:3-11. "Awake, awake, put on thy strength, O Zion; put on thy beautiful garments, O Jerusalem, the holy city; for henceforth there shall no more come into thee the uncircumcised and the unclean.... How beautiful on the mountains are the feet of him that bringeth good tidings, that publisheth peace; that bringeth good tidings of good, that publisheth salvation; that saith unto Zion, 'Thy God reigneth!' Thy watchmen shall lift up the voice; with the voice together shall they sing: for they shall see eye to eye when the Lord shall bring again Zion. Break forth into joy, sing together, ye waste places of Jerusalem: for the Lord hath comforted his people, he hath redeemed Jerusalem." Ib. 52:1-9. "And the Redeemer shall come to Zion, and unto them that turn from transgression in Jacob, saith the Lord." Ib. 59:20.

The standing of the Lamb on Mount Zion, symbolizes an epoch when Christ shall assume a corresponding relation to his people. He there appears in person; and "when Christ who is your life, shall appear, then shall ye also appear with him in glory," Col. 3:4. It will not be till he shall have judged "the quick and the dead at his appearing," (2 Tim. 4:1), that "the redeemed from among men" will "follow the Lamb whithersoever he goeth."

The 144,000, who are with Christ, correspond with the number which are sealed, "of all the tribes of the children of Israel," (7:4); and they are doubtless the same persons, who, under the sixth seal, are designated, among all denominations of Christians, by the mark of the living God. They are there shown to be the godly, who shall be alive on the earth at Christ's coming and shall then be changed, and, with the risen dead, caught up to meet him in the air.

The sealing process there symbolized, is here shown to be the inscribing of the Father's name on their foreheads. The subjects of the beast and its image, receive its mark; but the children of God and the Lamb, are designated instead, by the name of the Father.

The voice from heaven as the voice of many waters, with the voice of harpers, is the singing of the new song which none but the 144,000 could learn. Those who are translated at Christ's coming, will be favored above all, save two, who will have lived on the earth, insomuch as they will have been redeemed from the earth without being subjected to death.

These sing in the presence of the four living creatures and the elders, who symbolize those who also are redeemed from among men and will reign on the earth, 5:8-10. Consequently those must symbolize the resurrected dead, with whom the 144,000 will be ushered into the Lord's presence, 1 Thess. 4:16, 17. The two bodies of the redeemed, are therefore both represented with the Lord on Mount Zion.

Their not being defiled with women, probably implies that they were not guilty of idolatry, which is represented by that figure, Ezek. 16:15. They had not submitted to the wiles of the woman seated on the scarlet-colored beast, (17:3); had not worshipped the beast or its image (14:9), and had been true to their Divine Sovereign.

They follow the Lamb whithersoever he goeth. All the redeemed will doubtless thus follow the Lamb, for of all the "great multitude which no man could number, of all nations and kindreds, and people, and tongues," who stood before the throne and before the Lamb, clothed "with white robes, and palms in their hands," (7:9)--it was said: "The Lamb which is in the midst of the throne shall feed them, and shall lead them unto living fountains of water," 7:17.

Those who are redeemed from among men, are called the "first fruits unto God and to the Lamb." They are not necessarily first fruits of the redeemed, to distinguish them from others of the redeemed, but are first fruits of the race: "Of his own will begat he us with the word of truth, that we should be a kind of first fruits of his creatures," James 1:18. By his resurrection from the dead, Christ became "the first fruits of them that slept," 1 Cor. 15:20. And at his coming there is to be a "first resurrection" (20:6), when the bodies of the saints will "be fashioned like unto his glorious body" (Phil. 3:21), and thus become the first fruits with their risen Head. Those who come up at the second resurrection will not attain to that beatific state.

They are faultless, and without guile. They are not perfect by reason of any inherent goodness in themselves; for "all we like sheep have gone astray ... and the Lord laid on him the iniquity of us all," Isa. 53:6. The redeemed church will be faultless, because its members will be sanctified and cleansed by the blood of Christ. Such will constitute "a glorious church, not having spot, or wrinkle, or any such thing ... holy and without blemish," Eph. 5:27. While "the nations of them which are saved shall walk in the light" of the New Jerusalem, and shall "bring their glory and honor into it," there "shall in no wise enter into it anything that defileth, neither whatsoever worketh abomination, or maketh a lie: but they which are written in the Lamb's book of life," 21:24-27.

"There awaiteth at the end Such a home, and such a Friend, Such a crown, and such a throne, Such a harp of heavenly tone, Such companions, such employ, Such a world of hallowed joy!"--Bunyan.

The Angel of the Everlasting Gospel.

"And I saw another angel flying in the midst of heaven, having the everlasting good news to preach to those dwelling on the earth, and to every nation, and tribe, and tongue, and people, saying with a loud voice, Fear God and give glory to him; for the hour of his judgment is come: and worship him who made the heaven, and the earth, and the sea, and fountains of water!"--Rev. 14:6, 7.

The era symbolized by the flight of this angel, has been applied, by different writers to the epoch of the Reformation, to that of modern missions, &c. The view here taken, is that it synchronizes with the preaching of the gospel to the Gentiles.

The angel flying through the midst of heaven, doubtless symbolizes a body of men conspicuous for their position, energetic in their movements, extensive in their operations, and urgent in their proclamation,--whose teachings correspond with this announcement of the angel.

The message they bear is that of the everlasting gospel {~GREEK SMALL LETTER EPSILON~}{~GREEK SMALL LETTER UPSILON~}

{~GREEK SMALL LETTER ALPHA~}{~GREEK SMALL LETTER GAMMA~}{~GREEK SMALL LETTER GAMMA~}{~GREEK SMALL LETTER EPSILON~}{~GREEK SMALL LETTER LAMDA~}{~GREEK SMALL LETTER IOTA~}{~GREEK SMALL LETTER OMICRON~}{~GREEK SMALL LETTER NU~}, (evangelion)--which is, literally, the good news, the glad tidings; that which brings "life and immortality to light," 2 Tim. 1:10. It is a message which foreshadows the resurrection and coming judgment at Christ's appearing; and is therefore called "the gospel of the kingdom," (Matt. 4:23);--the good news of the glorious kingdom of the Son of God.

It is the preaching of the everlasting gospel which is thus symbolized. It is no new gospel; for, "the Scripture foreseeing that God would justify the heathen through faith, preached before the gospel unto Abraham,--saying: In thee shall all nations be blessed," Gal. 3:8. And not Abraham alone, but all the fathers "did eat the same spiritual meat, and did all drink the same spiritual drink: for they drank of that spiritual Rock that followed them: and that rock was Christ," 1 Cor. 10:3, 4. Of this gospel the Jewish nation and a few proselytes, were for ages the sole recipients. "Unto them were committed the oracles of God." Rom. 3:2. To them pertained "the adoption, and the glory, and the covenants, and the giving of the law, and the service of God, and the promises," Rom. 9:4. But the time had been foretold when the Gentiles should come to their light, and kings to the brightness of their rising, Isa. 60:3.

With the coming of Christ, and his rejection of that nation, the gospel, was no longer to be confined within its former narrow limits. The Savior said to his disciples: "Go ye therefore and teach all nations, baptizing them in the name of the Father, and of the Son, and of the Holy Ghost; teaching them to observe all things whatsoever I have commanded you: and lo, I am with you alway, even unto the end of the world," Matt. 28:19, 20. "Go ye into all the world and preach the gospel to every creature. He that believeth and is baptized shall be saved; but he that believeth not shall be damned," Mark 16:15, 16. "Then opened he their understanding that they might understand the Scriptures, and he said unto them, Thus it is written, and thus it behoved Christ to suffer, to rise from the dead the third day: and that repentance and remission of sins should be preached in his name among all nations, beginning at Jerusalem," Luke 24:45-47.

The fulfilment of those predictions and commands could not be more beautifully and appropriately symbolized, than by an angel flying "in the midst of heaven having the everlasting gospel to preach unto them that dwell on the earth, and to every nation, and kindred, and tongue, and people." It could be no other gospel: for Paul testified: "Though we, or an angel from heaven, preach any other gospel unto you than that which we have preached unto you, let him be accursed. As we said before, so say I now again, If any man preach any other gospel unto you than that ye have received, let him be accursed," Gal. 1:8, 9.

In accordance with the divine command, to preach the gospel to all the nations, beginning at Jerusalem, the apostles began their mission; and when the Jews rejected their message, they turned to the Gentiles, and went everywhere preaching the word "according to the revelation of the mystery, which was kept secret since the world began, but now is made manifest, and by the scriptures of the prophets, according to the commandment of the everlasting God, made known to all nations for the obedience of faith," Rom. 16:25, 26.

The first converts to the faith, comprised "Parthians, and Medes, and Elamites, and the dwellers in Mesopotamia, and in Judea, and Cappadocia, in Pontus, and Asia, Phrygia, and Pamphylia, in Egypt, and in the parts of Libya about Cyrene, and strangers of Rome, Jews and proselytes, Cretes and Arabians," Acts 2:9-12. When the Jews contradicted and blasphemed, "Paul and Barnabas waxed bold, and said, It was necessary that the word of God should first have been spoken to you: but seeing ye put it from you, and judge yourselves unworthy of everlasting life, lo, we turn to the Gentiles," Acts 13:46. Afterwards Paul, in writing to the Colossians, refers to the gospel as that "which was preached to every creature which is under heaven," Col. 1:23.

This gospel was to be preached to those who dwell on the earth, and also to all nations. The symbolic earth of the Apocalypse, being generally admitted to be the Roman empire under a quiet government, its fulfilment would require an early introduction of the gospel there. Accordingly we find, within thirty years after the crucifixion of Christ, a flourishing church existing in the metropolis of the Roman empire, to which Paul addressed one of his most able letters. In it, he thanks God that their "faith is spoken of throughout all the world," Rom. 1:8. The apostle had then "fully preached the gospel of Christ" from Jerusalem "round about [the coast of the Mediterranean] unto Illyricum," (Rom. 16:19);--a country on the Adriatic, or Gulf of Venice. He afterwards visited Rome, and is supposed to have preached the gospel as far west as Spain. The apostles spread Christianity throughout the Roman empire. Palestine, Syria, Natolia, Greece, the islands of the Mediterranean, Italy, and the northern coast of Africa, contained societies of Christians in the first century. In the second century societies existed, and Christ was worshipped, among the Germans, Spaniards, French, Celts, and Britons, and many other nations in Europe, and almost throughout the whole east. In the fourth century Christianity had become the prevailing religion of the empire.

In later times the gospel which began to be preached at Jerusalem, has been extended to more distant countries, and is still finding its way to every tribe and people that have not before heard its joyful sound. Thus has the light of the gospel nearly encircled the globe, having been, in one age or another, proclaimed in every known country--fulfilling the words of the Saviour: "And this gospel of the kingdom shall be preached in all the world, for a witness unto all nations; and then shall the end come," Matt. 24:14. "And the gospel must first be published among all nations," Mark 13:10. It would not follow from these predictions that it must be preached at the same time to all nations, any more than the light of day shines on all parts of the earth at once: but all must have been illumined by it before the end.

In accordance with this view, those who are finally redeemed to God "out of every kindred, and tongue, and people, and nation" (5:9), are those who will "have washed their robes and made them white in the blood of the Lamb" (7:14), in consequence of this universal extension of the gospel.

The command to fear and give glory to God, and to worship the Creator of all things implies that it was to be proclaimed to worshippers of false gods, and was not a mere proclamation addressed to actual Christians. The Gentiles to whom the apostles preached were actual worshippers of such, and needed to be taught the worship of the true God. While Paul was at Athens, his spirit was stirred within him when he saw the city wholly given to idolatry. "Then Paul stood in the midst of Mars hill, and said, Ye men of Athens, I perceive that in all things ye are too superstitious. For as I passed by, and beheld your devotions, I found an altar with this inscription: TO THE UNKNOWN GOD. Whom therefore ye ignorantly worship, him declare I unto you. God that made the world and all things therein, seeing that he is the Lord of heaven and earth, dwelleth not in temples made with hands," Acts 17:22-24. "Ye know that ye were Gentiles, carried away unto these dumb idols, even as ye were led," 1 Cor. 12:2. "For they themselves show us of what manner of entering in we had unto you, and how ye turned to God from idols, to serve the living and true God: and to wait for his Son from heaven, whom he raised from the dead, even Jesus, which delivered us from the wrath to come," 1 Thess. 1:9, 10.

The great motive, to be held forth to induce men to turn from the worship of idols to that of God, was the certainty of the approaching judgment. In accordance with this, the apostles make constant references to it. The Corinthians are exhorted to "come behind in no gift; waiting for the coming of our Lord Jesus Christ: who shall also confirm you unto the end, that ye may be blameless in the day of our Lord Jesus Christ," 1 Cor. 1:7, 8. As Paul "reasoned of righteousness, temperance, and judgment to come, Felix trembled," Acts 24:25. He said to the impenitent Romans, that they were "treasuring up to themselves wrath against the day of wrath, and revelation of the righteous judgment of God," Rom. 2:5. The first things which were presented in all their teachings were "the foundation of repentance from dead works, and of faith toward God, of the doctrine of baptisms, and of laying on of hands, and of resurrection of the dead, and of eternal judgment," Heb. 6:1, 2. Thus "Enoch also, the seventh from Adam, prophesied of these, saying, Behold the Lord cometh with ten thousand of his saints," Jude 14, 15.

As Christ was to judge the world "at his appearing and kingdom" (2 Tim.

4:1), a reference to his coming always involved a consideration of the hour of his judgment; and his appearing was a great incentive to holiness. "For our conversation is in heaven, from whence also we look for the Saviour, the Lord Jesus Christ," Phil. 3:20. And "when Christ, who is our life, shall appear, then shall ye also appear with him in glory," Col. 3:4. "For what is our hope, or joy, or crown of rejoicing? Are not even ye in the presence of our Lord Jesus Christ at his coming?" 1 Thess. 2:19. "To the end he may establish your hearts unblamable in holiness before God, even our Father, at the coming of our Lord Jesus Christ with all his saints," Ib. 3:13. "For if we believe that Jesus died and rose again, even so them also which sleep in Jesus will God bring with him. For this we say unto you by the word of the Lord, that we which are alive and remain unto the coming of the Lord shall not prevent them which are asleep. For the Lord himself shall descend from heaven with a shout, with the voice of the archangel, and with the trump of God: and the dead in Christ shall rise first: Then we which are alive and remain shall be caught up together with them in the clouds, to meet the Lord in the air: and so shall we ever be with the Lord," Ib. 4:14-17. "And to you who are troubled, rest with us, when the Lord Jesus shall be revealed from heaven with his mighty angels, in flaming fire taking vengeance on them that know not God, and that obey not the gospel of our Lord Jesus Christ," 2 Thess. 1:7, 8.

Not only the apostles, but their successors, in succeeding ages, have constantly made reference to the judgment, as the motive to holiness. Beginning in the days of the apostles, the same gospel has been continued by a succession of men to the present time; and those who are now preaching, or who support those who so preach the everlasting gospel, in connection with the warning of approaching judgment, must be regarded as belonging to the same body of men symbolized by the angel flying in the midst of heaven.

Commencing in the apostolic age, sections of the globe were evangelized-- in Asia and Africa, that have never received the gospel since, either under the reformers or by modern missionaries. But beginning with the dispensation of the gospel to the Gentiles, its fulfilment is found in China, in Tartary, in Japan, in Egypt, and Ethiopia, and in lands so remote that no one can say it has not been almost universally promulgated.

The Angel announcing the Fall of Babylon.

"And another angel, a second, followed, saying, She is fallen! Babylon the great is fallen! She made all nations drink of the wine of the wrath of her fornication!"--Rev. 14:8.

This angel, like the former, must symbolize a body of religious teachers. The former resulted in the spread of Christianity. This announces the fall of a corrupt hierarchy.

Babylon being regarded as a symbol of the Roman church, her fall must be understood to be her loss of power, as mistress of the kings of the earth; and synchronizes with her displacement from her position on the beast, as symbolized in the 17th chapter. The epoch of her fall, and consequently of the flight of this angel, is that of the Reformation, when the corruptions of the Papal See were first exposed, and it was denounced as the Apocalyptic harlot. The argument for this application is given in the exposition of Rev. 18:1, which is a repetition of the symbol here given, p. 300.

The Wrath-denouncing Angel.

"And another angel, a third, followed them, saying with a loud voice, If any one worship the wild beast and his image, and receive his mark on his forehead, or on his hand, even he will drink of the wine of the wrath of God, which is poured out unmingled into the cup of his wrath; and he will be tormented with fire and brimstone in the presence of the holy angels and in the presence of the Lamb: and the smoke of their torment ascendeth for ever and ever: and they have no rest day or night, who worship the wild beast and his image, and whoever receiveth the mark of his name!"--Rev. 14:9-11.

The cry of this angel synchronizes with the "voice from heaven" (18:4), and follows the discovery of the corruptions of Romanism.--See the exposition of that Scripture, p. 307.

The worship of the beast consisted in a regard for it, equivalent to saying, "Who is like unto the beast? and, Who is able to make war with him?" 13:4. To worship, is to manifest homage and respect. To worship any inferior object, is to bestow on it the confidence and affection which is due only to God. It is to trust in it, as invincible, able to protect, and infallible in judgment. Thus to regard any civil or ecclesiastical organization, is to substitute it for Him, by whom the powers that be are ordained (Rom. 13:1), who giveth the kingdom to whomsoever he will (Dan. 4:17), and by whom alone, kings reign, and princes decree justice, Prov. 8:15.

Whenever any civil or ecclesiastical enactment conflicts with the requisitions of Jehovah, that power is worshipped, which is obeyed in preference to the other: "Know ye not that to whom ye yield yourselves servants to obey, his servants ye are whom ye obey?" Rom. 6:16. The worship of God is incompatible with obedience to any power which compels a violation of His laws. Due obedience to government is commanded, when no question of conscience is involved. When it is, no forcible resistance to the execution of the law is permitted; but while God is obeyed, the penalty of the law is to be meekly endured.

The early Christians chose death, rather than to deny their Saviour at the command of Jewish Sanhedrim or Roman emperor. When Peter and John were commanded "not to speak at all, nor teach in the name of Jesus," their answer was, "Whether it be right in the sight of God to hearken unto you more than unto God, judge ye; for we cannot but speak the things which we have seen and heard," Acts 4:19, 20. In like manner, the Christians living at the epoch of this angel, were to be similarly tried, which is implied in the command, not to worship.

So soon as the reformers were placed in direct conflict with the Church of Rome, her anathemas were hurled against all who assented not to her mummeries. And the power of the civil arm was also brought into exercise to compel obedience to her commands. Those who maintained their integrity, did so in opposition to the requirements of the church and state; while those who submitted to the state as invincible, or to the church as infallible, extended to the beast or its image that homage and regard which was due to God. They thus acknowledged themselves the servants of him whom they obeyed, and subjected themselves to the wrath of God.

The smoke of their torment ascendeth up for ever and ever, and they have no rest, day nor night, who worship the beast and his image. While the righteous enter into rest, the wicked are like the troubled sea which cannot rest, whose waters cast up mire and dirt, Isa. 57:20.

The Harvest of the Earth.

"Here is the patience of the saints: here are those who keep the commandments of God, and the faith of Jesus. And I heard a voice from heaven, saying, Write, Happy the dead who die in the Lord, from henceforth! Yea, saith the Spirit, that they may rest from their toils; and their works go with them. And I looked, and behold, a white cloud, and one was seated on the cloud like the Son of man, having on his head a golden crown, and in his hand a sharp sickle. And another angel came out of the temple, crying with a loud voice to him seated on the cloud, Thrust forth thy sickle and reap: for the hour is come for thee to reap; for the harvest of the earth is ripe. And he, who sat on the cloud, cast his sickle on the earth; and the earth was reaped."--Rev. 14:12-16.

The announcement that here are they who keep the commandments of God, implies that, at the epoch symbolized, they are to be the subjects of special notice. By the voice from heaven, they are shown to include all of the dead who have died in the Lord; and their being blessed from thenceforth, indicates that they will at that epoch enter upon their eternal reward.

The "rest" of the righteous, is at the advent of Christ:--"To you who are troubled, rest with us when the Lord Jesus shall be revealed from heaven," 2 Thess. 1:6. "There remaineth a rest for the people of God," Heb. 4:9.

On hearing the voice from heaven, the revelator looked, and beheld on a cloud "one like the Son of man." In Ezek. 1:26, "the likeness as the appearance of a man," upon "the likeness of the throne," is explained to be "the appearance of the likeness of the glory of the Lord." In Dan. 7:13, "one like the Son of man," who comes to the Ancient of days, is evidently a symbol of Christ. In Rev. 1:13, "one like unto the Son of man," is the one who was alive, was dead, and is alive forevermore. The same symbol repeated, must here also be a representative of Christ.

His position on a cloud, indicates the arrival of the period when he is to be manifested in mid-heaven: "Behold he cometh with clouds; and every eye shall see him," 1:7. "One like the Son of man came with the clouds of heaven, and came to the Ancient of days, and they brought him near before him. And there was given him dominion and glory and a kingdom, that all people, nations, and languages should serve him," Dan. 7:13, 14. "And they shall see the Son of man coming in the clouds of heaven, with power and great glory. And he shall send his angels, with a great sound of a trumpet, and they shall gather together his elect from the four winds, from one end of heaven to the other," Matt. 24:30, 31.

The epoch of this manifestation, according to the above, is that of the last trump, the second advent, and the first resurrection. "At the last trump ... the dead shall be raised incorruptible, and we shall be changed," 1 Cor. 15:52. "For the Lord himself shall descend from heaven with a shout, with the voice of the archangel, and with the trump of God; and the dead in Christ shall rise first; then we which are alive and remain, shall be caught up together with them in the clouds, to meet the Lord in the air," 1 Thess. 4:16, 17.

His "golden crown" indicates that he is now to take to himself his great power, and to reign, "when the kingdoms of this world become our Lord's and his Christ's," 11:15, 17. Crowns are symbols of sovereignty. As such, they respectively denoted the periods, when the forms of government, symbolized by the heads of the beast (12:3) and its horns (13:1), bore rule. Now the diadem is to be transferred from them, to encircle the brow of earth's rightful Sovereign.

The sharp sickle in his hand, indicates that the time of harvest has arrived; and the act of reaping, the gathering of the harvest. There are two gatherings symbolized, corresponding to the two classes of persons who are to be gathered. "The dead in Christ shall rise first," and will be "caught up to meet the Lord in the air," before the wicked are gathered, 1 Thess. 4:16, 17. "I will come again, and receive you unto myself," said the Saviour, John 14:5. The Lord of the harvest directs its gathering, but effects it by the instrumentality of angels: "He shall send his angels, and shall gather together his elect from the four winds, from the uttermost part of the earth, to the uttermost part of heaven," Mark 13:27. When thus gathered, they are caught up to meet the Lord in the air, where the Lord of the harvest sits. This is the separation of the righteous and wicked, who were to "grow together till the harvest," which, says the Saviour, "is the end of the world," Matt. 13:39.

Mr. Lord suggests, that it is inconsistent with the dignity of Christ, to be notified by an angel when to begin his work; and therefore dissents from the application of the symbol to him. It may not, however, be necessary to consider the cry of the angel, as one of command. The angel may be a messenger from the Ancient of days, announcing the epoch of the resurrection. Or he may symbolize a body of men, who will be ardently praying for the return of the nobleman to take his kingdom.

The harvest is spoken of in distinction from the gathering of the vine, and in contrast with it. Men harvest what they prize,--their grain and fruits. They do not harvest briers and thorns. They cut or reap both; but the act of reaping is not expressive of the destiny of what is reaped. This is indicated by the disposition made, and the terms applied; the one is gathered into the garner of the Lord; but the other is given to the consuming fire.

The righteous being caught up to meet the Lord at his coming, the destruction of the wicked, which must precede the regeneration of the earth and descent of the saints, is next symbolized.

The Reaping of the Vine.

"And another angel came out of the temple in heaven, he also having a sharp sickle. And another angel came out from the altar, who had power over the fire, and called with a loud shout to him who had the sharp sickle, saying, Thrust in thy sharp sickle, and cut off the clusters of the vine of the earth; for its grapes are ripe. And the angel cast in his sickle into the earth, and cut off the vine of the earth, and cast it into the great wine-press of the wrath of God. And the wine-press was trodden without the city, and blood came out of the wine-press, even to the bridles of the horses, for the distance of one thousand six hundred furlongs."--Rev. 14:17-20.

The wicked also are gathered by the instrumentality of angels: said the Saviour, "As therefore the tares are gathered and burned in the fire; so shall it be in the end of this world. The Son of man shall send forth his angels, and they shall gather out of his kingdom all things that offend, and them which do iniquity; and shall cast them into a furnace of fire: there shall be wailing and gnashing of teeth," Matt. 13:40-42. In the parable of the tares, the Saviour said, "Let both grow together until the harvest: and in the time of harvest I will say to the reapers, Gather ye together first the tares, and bind them in bundles to burn them: but gather the wheat into my barn." Thus the tares were to be gathered first--not before the righteous are gathered, but before the wheat is placed in the garner: the new earth being the garner where the righteous are finally to be gathered, they cannot be placed there till the wicked have been gathered out. "Then shall the righteous shine forth as the sun in the kingdom of their Father. Who hath ears to hear, let him hear," Matt. 13:30, 43.

The disposition of the vine, its being trodden down, and the great presence of blood flowing, symbolize the awful judgments to overtake the wicked, after the escape of the righteous, when they are gathered into bundles and burned. Thus Isaiah prophesied: "Who is this that cometh from Edom, with dyed garments from Bozrah? this that is glorious in his apparel, travelling in the greatness of his strength? I that speak in righteousness, mighty to save. Wherefore art thou red in thine apparel, and thy garments like him that treadeth in the wine-vat? I have trodden the wine-press alone: and of the people there was none with me: for I will tread them in mine anger, and trample them in my fury, and their blood shall be sprinkled upon my garments, and I will stain all my raiment. For the day of vengeance is in my heart, and the year of my redeemed is come," Isa. 63:1-4.

Before the destruction of the old world by the deluge, Noah was secure in the ark. Before the destruction of Sodom, Lot is removed to a place of safety. So before the destruction of the vine of the earth, the righteous are caught up to the Lord in the air, where they are symbolized, in the following chapter, as:

The Victors on the Sea of Glass.

"And I saw another sign in heaven, great and wonderful, seven angels having the seven last plagues; for by these, the wrath of God is completed. And I saw as it were a transparent sea mingled with fire; and those who had obtained the victory over the wild beast, and over his image, and over the number of his name, standing on the transparent sea, having harps of God. And they sing the song of Moses the servant of God, and the song of the Lamb, saying, Great and wonderful are thy works, O Lord God Almighty; just and true are thy ways, king of nations! Who should not fear thee, O Lord, and glorify thy name? for thou only art holy; for all nations will come and worship before thee; for thy judgments are manifested." Rev. 15:1-4.

This appears to close the vision commencing with the sixth verse of the 14th chapter, and to be independent of the remaining portion of the 15th chapter.

These "seven angels," in the subsequent vision, discharge the contents of the vials of God's wrath; but the epoch here presented is evidently subsequent to that fulfilment; for the imitation of the "Song of Moses," must follow the infliction of the judgments which call forth that song of rejoicing. They had here completed the wrath of God, the manner of which act is subsequently shown in a separate vision.

The "sea of glass," must represent an elevation above the earth. For those stationed there had gotten the victory over the beast and his image, had escaped the wrath to be poured on those who worshipped those powers (14:9), had been gathered when the harvest of the earth was reaped (14:16), being then caught up to meet the Lord in the air (1 Thess. 4:17), and now, the clusters of the vine of the earth having been gathered and cast into the wine-press of the wrath of God (14:19), they rejoice above the fires of earth, witnesses of the manifestations of God's judgments. They have come out of all their tribulations, and evidently synchronize with the palm-bearing multitude (Rev. 7:9), the hundred and forty-four thousand on Mount Zion (14:1), and the multitude in heaven who sing Alleluia over the judgment of the great harlot, 19:1.

"The song of Moses," was that sung by the Israelites when the Egyptians had perished in the waters of the Red Sea, and they were safely encamped on its further shore. The Lord had triumphed gloriously over the enemies of Israel, had buried the horse and his rider in the sea, and was about to plant his people in the mountain of his inheritance,--in the place which he had made for them to dwell in,--in the sanctuary which he had established, Ex. 15:1-21. The analogy requires that when this corresponding song is sung, the ransomed of the Lord shall have correspondingly witnessed the overthrow of the adversaries of Jehovah, and shall themselves have escaped from the perils of the many waters which had threatened to engulf them.

The judgments of God being manifested on the nations of the ungodly, there are none remaining, only "the nations of them which are saved," 21:24. As these will all walk in the light of the new Jerusalem, those on the sea of glass may well sing:

"Great and marvellous are thy works, Lord God Almighty! Just and true are thy ways, thou King of saints! Who shall not fear thee, O Lord, and glorify thy name? For thou only art Holy: For all nations shall come and worship before thee; For thy judgments are made manifest."

In accordance with the foregoing view, this synchronizes with the "new song" sung by those who are redeemed from every nation, kindred, tongue and people (5:9), who are afterwards seen standing with the Lamb on Mount Zion, 14:3.

The Angels with the Seven Vials.

"And after this, I looked, and the temple of the tabernacle of the testimony in heaven was opened; and the seven angels came out of the temple, having the seven plagues, clothed in pure white linen, and girded around the breasts with golden girdles. And one of the four living beings gave to the seven angels, seven golden bowls filled with the wrath of God, who liveth for ever and ever. And the temple was filled with smoke from the glory of God, and from his power, and no one was able to enter the temple till the seven plagues of the seven angels were completed." Rev. 15:5-8.

"And I heard a loud voice out of the temple saying, to the seven angels, Depart, and pour out the bowls of the wrath of God on the earth." Rev. 16:1.

"The temple of the tabernacle of the testimony in heaven," must symbolize heaven itself. It corresponds with the tabernacle "after the second veil,"-- called "the holiest of all," where the tables of the covenant were deposited by the command of Moses, Heb. 9:1-5. There, the "cherubims of glory" over-shadowed the mercy-seat,--a type of the presence-chamber of the Almighty. Consequently, when it is symbolized as being opened in heaven, the angels who come out are divinely commissioned executors of God's purposes.

The "seven angels," are the ministers of the divine vengeance,--the rectitude of their character and the dignity of their office, being symbolized by their "white robes" and "golden girdles."

The period of time symbolized by the pouring out of the vials, must be anterior to the second advent; for in the analogous instances of God's judgments, he visits his enemies with plagues previous to the deliverance of his children. Thus were the ancient Egyptians visited, before the Israelites escaped from their power, Ex. 5-11.

The deliverance of the vials to the angels by one of the four "living creatures," indicates that the intelligences in the divine presence, which are thus symbolized, are cognizant of God's design, and acquiesce in his purpose to visit the subjects of his wrath with these plagues.

By these being called "the vials of God's wrath," we learn that their infliction is not corrective, but judicial;--that they are not agents of mercy, but of vengeance.

The filling of the temple with the smoke of God's glory, to the exclusion of all persons during the pouring out of the vials, shows that during that period, there will be no intercession with God for him to refrain from the execution of the purposes thus symbolized. They are inevitable; and there will be no supplication for their suspension. When Moses had finished the type of the "Holiest of all," a "cloud covered the tent of the congregation, and the glory of the Lord filled the tabernacle. And Moses was not able to enter into the tent of the congregation, because the cloud abode thereon, and the glory of the Lord filled the tabernacle," Ex. 40:34, 35. It was only when Moses could enter the tabernacle, that he could there commune with God face to face, Ex. 33:9, 11.

The voice from the temple to the seven angels, shows that the acts commanded are the subjects of divine appointment,--the angels simply designating the commencement of the several judgments.

The First Vial.

"And the first went away, and poured out his bowl on the earth; and there came an evil and sore ulcer on the men who had the mark of the beast, and on those worshipping his image." Rev. 16:2.

The "earth," in the Apocalypse, symbolizes a quiet and settled government (13:11), in distinction from one politically agitated, which is symbolized by waters, 13:1; 17:15.

Those who receive the contents of the first vial, being the worshippers of the "beast" and its "image" (13:15), it is certain that the governments on which it is poured, are subservient to the church of Rome and within the boundaries of the ten kingdoms.

The effect of the vial is "a noisome and grievous sore;" and the only things analogous, are mental maladies. Therefore the results symbolized must be noxious principles and opinions, which fill the mind with rancor and hate,-- producing strife, alienation and contention.

The epoch here symbolized, in the very unanimous opinion of most judicious writers, corresponds with the commencement of the agitations which preceded the outbreak of the first French revolution, about A. D. 1785. Commencing in France, and extending with more or less virulence throughout the ten kingdoms, there was excited an intense uneasiness of the people respecting their relation to their rulers. They regarded themselves as insupportably oppressed and degraded, and were exasperated to madness against their respective governments. This, under the next vial, resulted in the overthrow of the French monarchy, and in attempted revolutions in other kingdoms.

The Second Vial.

"And the second angel poured out his bowl on the sea; and it became like the blood of a dead person; and every living creature in the sea died." Rev. 16:8.

The first vial having excited political agitations in previously quiet governments, they are now more fitly symbolized by the "sea" than by the "earth." And on such the second vial is poured.

As the sea symbolizes a people agitated and disquieted, the living things in it, must symbolize those who live on and are sustained by the people. Consequently, the waters becoming blood, and the death of the things living in the waters, symbolize the shedding of the blood of the people, and the slaughter, by them, of their rulers and superiors.

The epoch symbolized, would therefore correspond with the actual outbreak of the French revolution, to which the agitations produced by the previous vial had goaded on the excited people. In their riots and insurrections, history records the destruction of large numbers of the populace; and these exterminated the members of the royal family, and all persons of rank and influence. A million of people, according to Alison, perished in the civil war of La Vendee alone; and thousands of the nobility and persons of distinction were ruthlessly slaughtered throughout France, whose rivers were discolored with the blood of the slain.

The Third Vial.

"And the third poured out his bowl on the rivers and on the fountains of waters; and they became blood. And I heard the angel of the waters say, Thou art righteous, O Thou, who art, and wast holy, because thou hast inflicted these judgments; for they have poured out the blood of saints and prophets, and thou hast given them blood to drink: they are worthy! And I heard one from the altar, saying, Even so, Lord God Almighty, true and righteous are thy judgments!" Rev. 16:4-7.

Mr. Lord justly remarks that "Rivers and fountains of waters, are to a sea, what smaller exterior communities and nations are to a great central people." As the French nation was the sea, the "rivers and fountains" symbolize contiguous or more remote communities surrounding it. These are said to have become blood, without its being specified that the living things in them perished, as in the sea. Accordingly, while the greater portion of Europe continued, with little interruption, for twenty years from 1792, to be deluged with war and bloodshed, the nobles and rulers of the other nations were not exterminated, as in France.

The nations thus overwhelmed with blood, were those which had sanctioned the shedding of the blood of the saints; consequently their retribution was just.

The Fourth Vial.

"And the fourth angel poured out his vial on the sun; and it was given him to burn men with fire. And men were burned with great heat, and reviled the name of God, who had power over these plagues; and they repented not to give him glory." Rev. 16:8, 9.

The influence of the sun on the earth and sea, is analogous to that of a government on the subjects of its rule. As the right degree of light and heat is conducive to vegetation, and the excessive action of the sun's rays will scorch and destroy; so a genial government is a blessing to the people, while its arbitrary and tyrannical acts are often insupportably oppressive.

With the overthrow of the French monarchy under the second vial, there arose new rulers in France, who usurped despotic powers, and subjected the governed to most oppressive exactions. The rich were impoverished, the nation was robbed, the business of the country was paralyzed, the obnoxious were slain, every species of misery and wickedness abounded, the males were subjected to military conscription, and hundreds of thousands of them were sent to subjugate surrounding nations. The countries they invaded were also devastated, and oppressed, and robbed by impoverishing taxations. These continued, though in a milder form, under the imperial rule, and all parts of the Roman earth felt the scorching effects of the devouring heat of French usurpation. But when Napoleon passed beyond the boundaries of the Roman empire, he was met and driven back by the snow and frost of the Almighty.

Notwithstanding the oppressions to which the people were subjected, and the exactions under which they groaned, they made no recognition of God's sovereignty. They saw not that this chastisement was from Him. They did not deprecate his wrath, nor acknowledge his righteousness, but still continued to be infidels and apostates. They continued to blaspheme the name of God, who had power over these plagues, and repented not to give him glory.

The Fifth Vial.

"And the fifth angel poured out his bowl on the throne of the wild beast; and his kingdom was darkened; and they gnawed their tongues through pain, and reviled the God of heaven, because of their pains and their ulcers, and repented not of their deeds" Rev. 16:10, 11.

The beast, here spoken of, is the same seven-headed, ten-horned wild beast that ascended out of the sea (Rev. 13:1), symbolizing the Roman empire in its divided form. Consequently the seat or throne of the beast would be the ruling power which exercised and controlled the government of these kingdoms. Just previous to this epoch, Napoleon had reached the summit of his power; and the subversion of his throne, with the restoration of the Bourbon dynasty in 1814 and 1815, is evidently here symbolized. Napoleon had become the idol of France, which worshipped at the shrine of his glory. With his fall, their sun was stricken from its firmament, and the kingdom was darkened.

The change being effected by foreign arms, the chagrin and mortification of his adherents was natural and expected. They were filled with pain and anguish at this termination of all their hopes. The re-imposition on them of the Bourbon line, revived all their former hatred towards their rulers and sense of oppression, symbolized by the ulcers of the first vial. They continued still a nation of infidels, performing the same works of blasphemy against God; and again and again have they risen in rebellion against their government.

The Sixth Vial.

"And the sixth poured out his bowl on the great river, the Euphrates; and its water was dried up, that the way of the kings from the rising of the sun might be prepared." Rev. 16:12.

This symbol resembles a like prediction respecting ancient Babylon: "A drought is upon her waters, and they shall be dried up," (Jer. 50:38); and "I will dry up her sea, and make her springs dry," Jer. 51:36. Ancient Babylon was situated on the river Euphrates, which contributed to the wealth and greatness of the city, and was a means of its defence. The kings of Media and Persia, from the east of Babylon, subjugated it by diverting from the city the waters of the river, and entering by its unprotected bed. The turning of the waters into other channels, fulfilled the prediction that it should be dried up.

Waters, when used as a symbol, are explained to be "peoples, nations," &c., Rev. 17:15. In the 17th chapter of the Apocalypse, the angel informs the revelator that he will show him "the judgment of the great harlot who sitteth on many waters," (17:1); which implies that he had already seen a vision to that effect. He is then shown a woman on a scarlet-colored beast (v. 3), who is spoken of as sitting "on many waters" (v. 1), and on seven mountains (v. 10), and who is affirmed to be the "great city, which reigneth over the kings of the earth," v. 18. Under the seventh vial, the "great city," which is "great Babylon," is divided into three parts (16:19); and the inference is, that the harlot and ancient Babylon are analogous symbols of the same organized agency; and, that the city was here exhibited on the great river Euphrates.

As a woman clothed with sunbeams and crowned with stars (Rev. 12:1), and a city illuminated with the glory of God (Rev. 21:10), are each symbols of the true church, corresponding symbols of opposite moral characteristics are appropriate representatives of a corrupt and apostate church. As Jerusalem was the seat of the ancient church, so was Babylon the seat of her oppressors. The former is addressed as a woman, and told to put on her "beautiful garments," (Isa. 52:1); and Babylon is called the "daughter of the Chaldeans," and "the lady of kingdoms," (Isa. 47:5): so that a woman, and a city of corresponding character, may, interchangeably, symbolize the same object. Consequently, the "Babylon," and the "harlot" of the Apocalypse, both symbolize the corrupt Roman hierarchy.

Ancient Babylon is described as a harlot, and is addressed as one who "dwellest upon many waters, abundant in treasures," (Jer. 51:13); whose end was to come by her waters being dried up, 51:36. That city sustained a relation to the waters on which it was situated, analogous to that held by the Roman Catholic church to the people who support and defend her pretensions. Their alienation and withdrawal from her support, must therefore be symbolized by the drying up of the great river Euphrates, which becomes diverted into other channels. This is now apparently being fulfilled in the marked alienation of feeling from the church of Rome, which is evident throughout the ten kingdoms. During the last twenty years, the hold of that community on the affection of her supporters in Europe, has been constantly becoming weaker and weaker. Infidel principles have been extensively propagated. Her cathedrals have been comparatively deserted; and her existence has been endured more as a matter of expediency than of affection. At the present moment, probably, the mass of the people have little confidence in her pretensions; but it will require a more marked withdrawal from her support than has yet been witnessed, to fulfil, in all its significance, the meaning conveyed in the symbol.

The "kings of the east," whose way is to be thus prepared, are doubtless her enemies, who, having produced the desired alienation from her support, will take advantage of her defenceless position, and hasten her ruin; as the kings of Media and Persia, in like manner, subjugated old Babylon.

Under the operation of the sixth vial, and, according to the fulfilment of the preceding symbols, corresponding with the present time, are to be developed:

The Unclean Spirits.

"And I saw three unclean spirits like frogs come out of the mouth of the dragon, and out of the mouth of the wild beast, and out of the mouth of the false prophet. For they are spirits of demons, performing signs, that go forth to the kings of the whole world, to gather them to the battle of that great day of God Almighty." Rev. 16:13, 14.

The "dragon," "beast," and "false prophet," being regarded as symbols: the first, of the Roman empire previous to its subversion by the northern barbarians; the second of the ten kingdoms which subsequently arose; and the third, of the eastern Roman empire--now the Mohamedan power; the mouths of each, from which the frog-like spirits emerge, are next to be considered.

To the wild beast was given "a mouth, speaking great things and blasphemies," the power of which was "to continue forty and two months," Rev. 13:5. The agreement of this with the corresponding appendages of Daniel's "little horn" (Dan. 7:8), makes it evident that a "mouth" is a symbol of an ecclesiastical organization existing in a political one,--that it symbolizes the agency by which the people are taught, and is representative of ecclesiastics, who are the mouthpiece of the nation in all matters of faith and worship, p. 172.

The religion of Rome imperial, when symbolized by the dragon, was Paganism; that of the ten kingdoms, was the Papacy; and that of the eastern empire, is Mohammedanism. From these three, then, emerge the "unclean spirits." Diverse as their origin appears, they have no marked individual peculiarities. Being alike in their characteristics, they must symbolize some common agency:--a combination of religious teachers, whose views harmonize in a system of belief common to Paganism, Catholicism, and Mohammedanism.

The character of these teachers, is shown by the declaration that "they are the spirits of devils working miracles."

There are two words rendered devils in the New Testament, viz.: {~GREEK SMALL LETTER DELTA~}{~GREEK SMALL LETTER ALPHA~}{~GREEK SMALL LETTER IOTA~}{~GREEK SMALL LETTER MU~}{~GREEK SMALL LETTER OMICRON~}{~GREEK SMALL LETTER NU~}{~GREEK SMALL LETTER IOTA~}{~GREEK SMALL LETTER OMICRON~}{~GREEK SMALL LETTER NU~} (daimonion) or {~GREEK SMALL LETTER DELTA~}{~GREEK SMALL LETTER ALPHA~}{~GREEK SMALL LETTER IOTA~}{~GREEK SMALL LETTER MU~}{~GREEK SMALL LETTER OMEGA~}{~GREEK SMALL LETTER NU~} (daimoon), and {~GREEK SMALL LETTER DELTA~}{~GREEK SMALL LETTER IOTA~}{~GREEK SMALL LETTER ALPHA~}{~GREEK SMALL LETTER BETA~}{~GREEK SMALL LETTER OMICRON~}{~GREEK SMALL LETTER LAMDA~}{~GREEK SMALL LETTER OMICRON~}{~GREEK SMALL LETTER FINAL SIGMA~} (diabolus). The latter signifies the Devil, or Satan, who is the same as Beelzebub the prince of the demons, Matt. 12:25. He it was by whom Jesus was tempted in the wilderness, (Matt. 4:1-11); who sowed the tares in the field, (Matt, 13:39); and for whom, with his angels, the final punishment for the wicked is prepared, Matt. 25:41.

The word here, is daimoon. It is used, in different forms, sixty-five times by our Lord and his apostles; and on no occasion do they hint that they use the word in a sense different from its then accepted signification; to learn which, recourse must be had to the testimony of the Pagan, Jewish, and Christian writers of those times.(6)

HESIOD taught that, "The spirits of departed mortals become demons when separated from their earthly bodies;" and PLUTARCH, that "The demons of the Greeks were the ghosts and genii of departed men." "All Pagan antiquity affirms," says Dr. CAMPBELL, "that from Titan and Saturn, the poetic progeny of Coelus and Terra, down to Æsculapius, Proteus, and Minos, all their divinities were the ghosts of dead men; and were so regarded by the most erudite of the Pagans themselves."

Among the Pagans, the term demon, as often represented a good as an evil spirit; but among the Jews, it generally, if not universally, denoted an unclean, malign, or wicked spirit. Thus JOSEPHUS says: "Demons are the spirits of wicked men." PHILO says that "The souls of dead men are called demons." "The notion," says Dr. LARDNER, "of demons, or the souls of dead men, having power over living men, was universally prevalent among the heathen of these times [the first two centuries], and believed by many Christians." JUSTIN MARTYR speaks of "those who are seized by the souls of the dead, whom we call demons and madmen." Ignatius quotes the words of Christ to Peter thus: "Handle me and see; for I am not a daimoon asomaton,--a disembodied demon,"--i.e. a spirit without a body.

The foregoing is evidence of the New Testament signification of the word daimoon, here improperly rendered devils,--spirits of which, the frog-like agencies are affirmed to be.

Demon worship is a characteristic of the three religions referred to. As already shown, all Pagans regarded their gods as the ghosts of dead men; and the Bible speaks of them as devils, i.e. demons. Moses says of them, "Even their sons and their daughters they have burnt in the fire to their gods," (Deut. 12:31); while the Psalmist affirms that "they sacrificed their sons and their daughters unto devils," Ps. 106:37. "They sacrificed unto devils, not to God; to gods whom they knew not, to new gods that came newly up," Deut. 32:17. Jeroboam "ordained him priests for the high places, and for the devils," 2 Chron. 11:15. "The things which the Gentiles sacrifice, they sacrifice to devils, and not to God: and I would not that ye should have fellowship with devils. Ye cannot drink the cup of the Lord and the cup of devils; ye cannot be partakers of the Lord's table, and of the table of devils,"--i.e. of demons.

Of the same kind are the gods of the heathen now. In the Youth's Day-Spring, for June, a missionary describing the alarm and grief of the Africans on the Gaboon river, at the near prospect of a death in their village, says: "The room was filled with women, who were weeping in the most piteous manner, and calling on the spirits of their fathers and of others who were dead, and upon all spirits in whom they believe, Ologo, Njembi, Abambo, and Mbwini, to save the man from death. These spirits could not help them, but they knew of none mightier, and so called on them." Mr. White, a Wesleyan missionary, says: "There is a class of people in New Zealand, called Eruku, or priests. These men pretend to have intercourse with departed spirits, ... by which they are able to kill by incantation any person on whom their anger may fall." The Sandwich Islanders, when they found that Christians supposed they worshipped the images of their gods, were much amused, and said "We are not such fools." They used the idol as an aid to fix their minds on their divinity. Some of them supposed their divinity was a spirit residing in their idol.

The Mohammedans, while they recognize God, are also "taught by the Koran to believe the existence of an intermediate order of creatures, which they call Jin, or genii;" some of which are supposed to be good and others bad, and capable of communicating with men, and rewarding or punishing them. The 72d chapter of the Koran consists of a pretended communication from the genii to Mohammed. They are made to say: "There are some among us who are upright, and there are some among us who are otherwise;" and speaking of men: "If they tread in the way of truth, we will surely water them with abundance of rain," i.e. will grant them plenty of good things. Thus they are recognized as dispensers of good. They bear a striking resemblance to the spirits which now pretend to communicate with men! All who are familiar with Arabian romances know how frequently genii, fairies, &c., figure as agents in the execution of wonderful exploits.

The Romanists also pretend to communicate with demons,--i.e. with departed spirits. They deify the Virgin Mary, and supplicate the intercessions of many departed saints; and some they supplicate, whose claim to saintship is somewhat equivocal. Their teachings in this particular, Protestants generally recognize as the subject of the following prediction: "Now the Spirit speaketh expressly that in the latter times some shall depart from the faith, giving heed to seducing spirits, and doctrines of devils,"-- demons, 1 Tim. 4:1.

Demon-worship being common to Paganism, Mohammedanism, and Popery, when the frog-like agency emerges from them, the conditions of the symbol seem to require that it shall originate with, but shall pass beyond and outside the influence of those religions. The agency thus symbolized, was to "go forth unto the kings of the earth, and of the whole world." Its fulfilment requires a wonderful and an alarming increase of those who teach and believe these doctrines; and as they are to work miracles, whereby the world will be deceived, their teachings are to be accompanied by extraordinary phenomena, which will be unexplainable by any of the known laws of science. The spirits of the departed are to be recognized by them as authoritative teachers, who are to be reverenced and obeyed. They will be regarded as communicating with mortals, as unveiling the hidden things of the invisible state, and as performing acts requiring the exercise of physical power. The former are evident from the analogy which exists between this and demon-worship; and the latter, from the ascription to them of miraculous acts.

The existence of demoniacal intelligences, capable of communicating with and acting on mortals, appears to be in accordance with the teachings of the Saviour and apostles. Demoniacal possessions are clearly distinguished from all diseases; and demons are shown, by the admissions of the New Testament, to be actual intelligences, capable of physical power. When the fame of Christ "went throughout all Syria, they brought unto him all sick people that were taken with divers diseases and torments, and those which were possessed with devils, and those which were lunatic, and those which had the palsy; and he healed them," Matt. 4:24. "When the unclean spirit is gone out of a man, he walketh through dry places, seeking rest, and findeth none. Then he saith, I will return into my house from whence I came out; and when he is come, he findeth it empty, swept, and garnished. Then goeth he, and taketh with himself seven other spirits more wicked than himself, and they enter in and dwell there: and the last state of that man is worse than the first," Matt. 12:43-45. "And as they went out, behold they brought to him a dumb man possessed with a devil.(7) And when the devil was cast out, the dumb spake; and the multitudes marvelled, saying, It was never so seen in Israel. But the Pharisees said, He casteth out devils,(8) through the prince of the devils," Matt. 9:32-34. "And when they were come to the multitude, there came to him a certain man kneeling down to him, and saying, Lord, have mercy on my son; for he is lunatic, and sore vexed, for oft-times he falleth into the fire, and oft into the water. And I brought him to thy disciples, and they could not cure him. Then Jesus answered and said, O faithless and perverse generation, how long shall I be with you? how long shall I suffer you? Bring him hither to me. And Jesus rebuked the devil, and he departed out of him; and the child was cured from that very hour," Matt. 17:14-18. "And there was in their synagogue a man with an unclean spirit: and he cried out, saying, Let us alone; what have we to do with thee, thou Jesus of Nazareth? art thou come to destroy us? I know thee who thou art, the Holy One of God. And Jesus rebuked him, saying, Hold thy peace, and come out of him. And when the unclean spirit had torn him, and cried with a loud voice, he came out of him. And they were all amazed, insomuch that they questioned among themselves, What thing is this? what new doctrine is this? for with what authority commandeth he even the unclean spirits, and they do obey him!" Mark 1:23-27. "And when he was come out of the ship, immediately there met him out of the tombs a man with an unclean spirit, who had his dwelling among the tombs; and no man could bind him, no, not with chains: because that he had been often bound with fetters and chains, and the chains had been plucked asunder by him, and the fetters broken in pieces: neither could any man tame him. And always, night and day, he was in the mountains, and in the tombs, crying, and cutting himself with stones. But when he saw Jesus afar off, he ran and worshipped him, and cried with a loud voice, and said, What have I to do with thee, Jesus, thou Son of the Most High God! I adjure thee, by God, that thou torment me not. (For he said unto him, Come out of the man, thou unclean spirit.) And he asked him, What is thy name? And he answered, saying, My name is Legion: for we are many. And he besought him much that he would not send them away

171

out of the country. Now there was nigh unto the mountains a great herd of swine feeding. And all the devils besought him, saying, Send us into the swine, that we may enter into them. And forthwith Jesus gave them leave. And the unclean spirits went out, and entered into the swine; and the herd ran violently down a steep place into the sea (they were about two thousand), and were choked in the sea," Mark 5:2-13.

In all these instances, the demons are recognized as actual intelligences, performing given acts. Without the admission of this, it will be difficult to explain the meaning of a large class of scriptures. It cannot for a moment be supposed that the inspired writers would be permitted to use language which should directly mislead the common mind.

Among the miracles which the apostles wrought, "unclean spirits, crying with a loud voice, came out of many possessed with them, and many taken with palsies, and that were lame, were healed," Acts 8:7. "And God wrought special miracles by the hands of Paul: so that from his body were brought unto the sick handkerchiefs, or aprons, and the diseases departed from them, and the evil spirits went out of them. Then certain of the vagabond Jews, exorcists, took upon them to call over them which had evil spirits, the name of the Lord Jesus, saying, We adjure you by Jesus whom Paul preacheth. And there were seven sons of one Sceva, a Jew, and chief of the priests, who did so. And the evil spirit answered and said, Jesus I know, and Paul I know; but who are ye? And the man in whom the evil spirit was, leaped on them, and overcame them, and prevailed against them, so that they fled out of that house naked and wounded. And many that believed, came and confessed, and showed their deeds. Many of them also which used curious arts, brought their books together, and burned them before all men: and they counted the price of them, and found it fifty thousand pieces of silver," Acts 19:11-16, 18, 19.

The necromancy, divination, and witchcraft, forbidden in the Old Testament and practised by the heathen of those times, were all of a similar character. A necromancer was one who had, or pretended to have communication with the dead,--who sought "for the living to the dead,"(9) Isa. 8:19. They practised divination in divers ways, but usually admitted their dependence on familiar spirits,--the spirits of the departed,--demons. "The king of Babylon stood at the parting of the way, at the head of the two ways, to use divination; he made his arrows bright, he consulted with images, he looked in the liver. At his right hand was the divination for Jerusalem, to appoint captains, to open the mouth in the slaughter, to lift up the voice with shouting, to appoint battering-rams against the gates, to cast a mount, and to build a fort. And it shall be unto them as false divination in their sight, to them that have sworn oaths: but he will call to remembrance the iniquity, that they may be taken," Ezek. 21:21-23. They observed times, i.e. they regarded some as lucky, and others as unlucky times for the commencement of any work,--recognizing distinctions which God had not made. The heathen divinities were regarded as more propitious at some times than others. It is enumerated among the sins of Manasseh, that he "made his sons pass through the fire, and observed times, and used enchantments, and dealt with familiar spirits and wizards," 2 Kings 21:6.

They practised various arts, whereby they thought to protect themselves from evil, and to pry into the secrets of futurity. Because of these things, ancient Babylon was suddenly overwhelmed,--"for the multitude of thy sorceries, and for the great abundance of thine enchantments." These could not save, as they supposed. Therefore God said to them: "Stand now with thine enchantments, and with the multitude of thy sorceries, wherein thou hast labored from thy youth; if so be thou shalt be able to profit, if so be thou mayest prevail. Thou art wearied in the multitude of thy counsels. Let now the astrologers, the star-gazers, the monthly prognosticators, stand up, and save thee from these things that shall come upon thee," Isa. 47:12, 13. All these practices were forbidden by God, who said: "Neither shall ye use enchantments, nor observe times," Lev. 19:26.

Those who consulted with familiar spirits were termed wizards and witches,--the practice of which was also expressly forbidden. To make witchcraft a mere pretence, is to impute to Jehovah the making of laws against pretences and nonentities. To suppose that he would legislate against, and inflict capital punishment, because of mere pretences, is incredible! God said to Moses, "Thou shalt not suffer a witch to live," Ex. 22:18. And to the Jews he said, "Regard not them that have familiar spirits, neither seek after wizards, to be defiled by them: I am the Lord your God," Lev. 19:31. "And the soul that turneth after such as have familiar spirits, and after wizards, to go a whoring after them, I will even set my face against that soul, and will cut him off from among his people." "A man, also, or a woman, that hath a familiar spirit, or that is a wizard, shall surely be put to death: they shall stone them with stones: their blood shall be upon them," Lev. 20:6,27. When Egypt was to be destroyed, they were left to "seek to the idols, and to charmers, and to them that have familiar spirits, and to wizards," Isa. 19:3.

The manner in which the familiar spirit spoke, was by "peeping," "muttering," whispering out of the dust, &c. God said to Ariel, "And thou shalt be brought down, and shalt speak out of the ground, and thy speech shall be low out of the dust, and thy voice shall be as of one that hath a familiar spirit, out of the ground, and thy speech shall whisper out of the dust," Isa. 29:4. "And when they shall say unto you, Seek unto them that have familiar spirits, and unto wizards that peep, and that mutter: (should not a people seek unto their God? for the living to the dead!) to the law and to the testimony: if they speak not according to this word, it is because there is no light in them," Isa. 8:19, 20.

Saul had put away those that had familiar spirits, and the wizards, out of the land; but when he "inquired of the Lord, the Lord answered him not, neither by dreams, nor by Urim, nor by prophets. Then said Saul unto his servants, Seek a woman that hath a familiar spirit, that I may go to her, and inquire of her. And his servants said to him, Behold, there is a woman that hath a familiar spirit at En-dor. And Saul disguised himself, and put on other raiment, and he went, and two men with him, and they came to the woman by night: and he said, I pray thee divine unto me by the familiar spirit, and bring me him up whom I shall name unto thee. And the woman said unto him, Behold, thou knowest what Saul hath done, how he hath cut off those that have familiar spirits, and the wizards out of the land; wherefore, then, layest thou a snare for my life, to cause me to die? And Saul sware unto her by the Lord, saying, As the Lord liveth, there shall no punishment happen to thee for this thing. Then said the woman, Whom shall I bring up to thee? And he said, Bring me up Samuel. And when the woman saw Samuel she cried with a loud voice: and the woman spake to Saul, saying, Why hast thou deceived me? for thou art Saul. And the king said unto her, Be not afraid: for what sawest thou? And the woman said unto Saul, I saw gods ascending out of the earth. And he said unto her, What form is he of? And she said, An old man cometh up; and he is covered with a mantle. And Saul perceived that it was Samuel, and he stooped with his face to the ground, and bowed himself. And Samuel said to Saul, Why hast thou disquieted me, to bring me up? And Saul answered, I am sore distressed; for the Philistines make war against me, and God is departed from me, and answereth me no more, neither by prophets, nor by dreams: therefore I have called thee, that thou mayest make known unto me what I shall do. Then said Samuel, Wherefore then dost thou ask of me, seeing the Lord is departed from thee, and is become thine enemy? And the Lord hath done to him, as he spake by me: for the Lord hath rent the kingdom out of thine hand, and given it to thy neighbor, even to David: because thou obeyedst not the voice of the Lord, nor executedest his fierce wrath upon Amelek, therefore hath the Lord done this thing unto thee this day. Moreover, the Lord will also deliver Israel with thee into the hand of the Philistines: and to-morrow shalt thou and thy sons be with me: the Lord also shall deliver the host of Israel into the hand of the Philistines. Then Saul fell straightway all along on the earth, and was sore afraid, because of the words of Samuel: and there was no strength in him," 1 Sam. 28:6-20.

Micaiah "saw the Lord sitting on his throne, and all the host of heaven standing by him on his right hand and on his left. And the Lord said, Who shall persuade Ahab, that he may go up and fall at Ramoth-gilead? And one said on this manner, and another said on that manner. And there came forth a spirit, and stood before the Lord, and said, I will persuade him. And the Lord said unto him, Wherewith? And he said, I will go forth, and I will be a lying spirit in the mouth of all his prophets. And he said, Thou shalt persuade him, and prevail also: go forth, and do so. Now therefore, behold, the Lord hath put a lying spirit in the mouth of all these thy prophets, and the Lord hath spoken evil concerning thee," 1 Kings 22:19-23.

When Paul was in the house of Lydia, he says, "It came to pass, as we went to prayer, a certain damsel possessed with a spirit of divination, met us, which brought her masters much gain by her soothsaying: the same followed Paul and us, and cried, saying, These men are the servants of the most high God, which show unto us the way of salvation. And this she did many days. But Paul, being grieved, turned and said to the spirit, I command thee in the name of Jesus Christ to come out of her. And he came out the same hour," Acts 16:16-18.

By sorcery, enchantment, &c., they performed wonders, or miracles, either real or pretended. "There was a certain man called Simon, which beforetime in the same city used sorcery, and bewitched the people of Samaria, giving out that himself was some great one: to whom they all gave heed, from the least to the greatest, saying, This man is the great power of God. And to him they had regard, because that of long time he had bewitched them with sorceries," Acts 8:9-11. When "Aaron cast down his rod before Pharaoh, and before his servants, and it became a serpent, then Pharaoh also called the wise men, and the sorcerers: now the magicians of Egypt they also did in like manner with their enchantments. For they cast down every man his rod, and they became serpents: but Aaron's rod swallowed up their rods," Ex. 7:10-12. When Aaron turned the water of the river to blood, "the magicians did so with their enchantments," v. 22. In like manner they "brought up frogs upon the land of Egypt," 8:7. But when Aaron changed the dust to lice, the magicians attempted the same with their enchantments, "but they could not," Ex. 8:18. These sorcerers who withstood Moses, we learn by Paul, were "Jannes and Jambres," 2 Tim. 3:8. They belonged to an ancient profession in Egypt; for, when Pharaoh dreamed his dreams, he first "sent and called for all the magicians of Egypt, and all the wise men thereof: and Pharaoh told them his dreams; but there was none that could interpret them unto Pharaoh," Gen. 41:8. In like manner Nebuchadnezzar "commanded to call the magicians, and the astrologers, and the sorcerers, and the Chaldeans, for to show the king his dreams. So they came, and stood before the king," Dan. 2:2.

These things were practised to some extent in Judah, but were all put away by Josiah. "Moreover, the workers with familiar spirits, and the wizards, and the images, and the idols, and all the abominations that were spied in the land of Judah and in Jerusalem, did Josiah put away, that he might perform the words of the law which were written in the book that Hilkiah the priest found in the house of the Lord," 2 Kings 23:24.

The acts and influences of demoniacal agencies are apparent from the foregoing; and the symbolization under the sixth seal, seems to indicate a revival of those teachings and manifestations at the present time. Within a few years, the curiosity of the community has been excited, and large numbers of persons greatly interested, in various phenomena, known as Mesmerism, Animal-Magnetism, Clairvoyance, Pathetism, Neurology, Psychology, Biology, Electro-Biology, &c. &c. Similar manifestations have been before exhibited, but not in modern times to the extent now witnessed. These were regarded as harmless phenomena and independent of any supernatural agency, till audible sounds were heard communicating intelligible responses. Then the claim was set up that these are caused by departed spirits.

These sounds were first heard near Rochester, New York, in 1847; and, at the present time (1852), they are affirmed to exist in hundreds of places in this country, and other sections of the globe. They are audible raps, the cause of which, aside from the hypothesis of spiritual agency, has never been satisfactorily accounted for. By these raps, unimpeached and credible witnesses testify that correct answers have been given to questions, the facts respecting which were known to no one at the time of answering. Since then, furniture has been seen to move about the room, and other wonders, or miracles, been performed, by invisible agency, at the command of mediums to attending spirits,--i.e. to demons. Mediums have written on paper, as they profess, involuntarily, lengthy communications, in poetry and prose, the subjects of which they claim to have been ignorant of, while the pen they held was moved independent of their own will. These exhibitions have been attested by hundreds of credible witnesses.

By such manifestations large numbers of persons have given their adherence to these real or pretended agencies as truthful and reliable intelligences; whose responses they receive with the same credence that we do the revelations of scripture. "Circles" are extensively formed, who have sittings, at stated times, to receive communications from the spirits of the departed; and these are enforced by miracles, audible sounds, the exercise of physical power, &c.

The reality and the credibility of these agencies are separate questions. Their reality is shown by their identity with similar manifestations of former times. The Bible affirms the existence of such: "For we wrestle not against flesh and blood, but against principalities, against powers, against the rulers of the darkness of this world, against spiritual wickedness in high places;" or "wicked spirits" in "heavenly places," as the margin reads, Eph. 6:12.

1. The familiar spirits of old responded in a manner similar to these. They did "peep" and "mutter;" their speech was low out of the dust; they spoke out of the ground, and whispered; or, as in the margin, did "peep" or "chirp" out of the dust. These "rap" and mutter. They respond from beneath chairs, tables and floors.

2. They exercised similar physical powers. They threw down and tare the persons they possessed. They turned the swine into the sea, &c. These claim that chairs and tables, are lifted and moved at will by an invisible agency.

3. They made similar pretensions to credibility. Simon Magus gave out "that himself was some great one;" and these, that they utter divine truths.

4. Similar regard was bestowed on those, which is claimed for these. To Simon "they all gave heed, from the least to the greatest, saying, This man is the great power of God." Yet "he had bewitched them with sorceries." Similar claims by, and regard for these modern pretenders to the same art, do not relieve them from the suspicion of a like agency. "For such are false apostles, deceitful workers, transforming themselves into the apostles of Christ. And no marvel; for Satan himself is transformed into an angel of light. Therefore, it is no great thing if his ministers also be transformed as the ministers of righteousness: whose end shall be according to their works," 2 Cor. 11:13-15.

5. Both have given utterance to some truths. The legion of demons who

were cast out of the man into a herd of swine, acknowledged Jesus to be "the Son of the Most High God;" and the pythonic spirit which so grieved Paul, declared the apostles to be "the servants of the Most High God, which show unto us the way of salvation." Such communications with the invisible world being forbidden, their credibility is disproved.

They claim that spirits of the departed are brought into direct and intelligent communication with the living, who desire to interrogate them. What more was claimed by the necromancers of old? Said Saul to the woman of Endor: "Divine unto me by the familiar spirit, and bring me him up whom I shall name unto thee," 1 Sam. 28:8.

They claim that not all, but only those persons are mediums who are peculiarly susceptible to spiritual influences. Wherein, then, admitting their claims, do the "mediums" differ from those of old, who divined by a familiar spirit?

Their responses are frequently disproved by facts; and themselves admit the existence of unreliable spirits, which communicate like them. They give contradictory responses, and mutually criminate each other; but their reality is not disproved by any discrepancy, or want of truthfulness in their responses; for if they are spirits, none but unclean spirits would respond in a forbidden manner.

These spirits are to be discredited, because they preach a different gospel from that preached by Paul, who says: "I marvel that ye are so soon removed from him that called you into the grace of Christ, unto another gospel: which is not another; but there be some that trouble you, and would pervert the gospel of Christ. But though we, or an angel from heaven, preach any other gospel unto you than that ye have received, let him be accursed," Gal. 1:6-9. "If any man love not the Lord Jesus Christ, let him be Anathema, Maran-atha." 1 Cor. 16:22. Said John, "Beloved, believe not every spirit, but try the spirits whether they are of God: because many false prophets are gone out into the world," 1 John 4:1. Also Isaiah said, "And when they shall say unto you, Seek unto them that have familiar spirits, and unto wizards that peep, and that mutter: should not a people seek unto their

God? To the law and to the testimony: if they speak not according to this word, it is because there is no light in them," Isa. 8:19, 20.

Because of these practices, the nations were driven out from before the children of Israel. And with the miracles to be wrought, the frog-like spirits are to go forth to "the whole world to gather them to the battle of that great day of God Almighty."

In the time of Abraham, "the iniquity of the Amorites was not yet full," (Gen. 15:16); but in four hundred years they had practised all the abominations for which they were to be destroyed, and the practice of which God has expressly forbidden. He said to Israel, in the wilderness, "When thou art come into the land which the Lord thy God giveth thee, thou shalt not learn to do after the abominations of those nation. There shall not be found among you any one that maketh his son or his daughter to pass through the fire, or that useth divination, or an observer of times, or an enchanter, or a witch, or a charmer, or a consulter with familiar spirits, or a wizard, or a necromancer. For all that do these things are an abomination unto the Lord: and because of these abominations the Lord thy God doth drive them out from before thee. Thou shalt be perfect with the Lord thy God. For these nations, which thou shalt possess, hearkened unto observers of times, and unto diviners: but as for thee, the Lord thy God hath not suffered thee so to do," Deut. 18:9-14.

Similar pernicious practices and dangerous heresies, are to prepare the way for the final destruction of the nations who reject the claims of Jehovah. Peter declares that "there shall be false teachers among you, who privily shall bring in damnable heresies, even denying the Lord that bought them, and bring upon themselves swift destruction. And many shall follow their pernicious ways; by reason of whom the way of truth shall be evil spoken of. And through covetousness shall they with feigned words make merchandise of you: whose judgment now of a long time lingereth not, and their damnation slumbereth not," 2 Pet. 2:1-3. And Paul says of that wicked: "Whose coming is after the working of Satan, with all power, and signs, and lying wonders, and with all deceivableness of unrighteousness in them that perish; because they received not the love of the truth, that they might be saved. And for this cause God shall send them strong delusion, that they should believe a lie: that they might be damned who believed not the truth, but had pleasure in unrighteousness," 2 Thess. 2:9-12.

"The battle of that great day of God Almighty," it would seem, must commence by a conflict of opinions. Mind will war with mind, and puny man will stoutly contend against the truths of the Almighty. In this revival of demon-worship, the old gods of the heathen are to be set up against the claims of Jehovah. His declarations are to be made to give place to "doctrines of demons." The teachings of God and of these spirits are to be brought into direct conflict.

The followers of the spirits have baptized their new theological dogmas, "The Harmonial Philosophy," of which Reason is the final umpire. Revelation no longer speaks to them in tones of authority. From the Bible, it is claimed, "the seal of infallibility must be broken away, before a new light and beauty can enliven and embellish the mystical disclosures of any seer, prophet, or evangelist." So writes Andrew Jackson Davis, the Poughkeepsie seer, one of the leaders of this new school, who complains that "owing to the dogmatism of infallibility, the Bible is taught now-a-days as it was nearly four centuries ago."--Review of Dr. Bushnell, p. 10.

The Scriptures are, with those of his faith, only "the paper and ink relics of Christianity," (Ib., p. 21); which they regard as "a foundation as impermanent as the changeful sand" (Ib. p. 24), and not adapted "to the wants or requirements of the nineteenth century," Ib. p. 26. They reject Him, whom they style "the cruel and capricious God generally worshipped by the Bible Christians," Ib. p. 47. "The Jewish God," says Davis, "is cruel, capricious and tyrannical," whose "kingdom is more despotic, and more contracted in principle, than the present government of the Russian empire," Ib. p. 61. He adds, "The Old Testament idea of a Deity is the outgrowth of the despotic stage of human mental development," and "a superannuated monotheistic conception," Ib. p. 62. In their opinion, "the developments of republicanism, and of mental happiness among men, depend very much upon the absence of these dogmatical compilations, or fossil relics, of an old Hebrew and Chaldean theology," Ib. p. 70. With them "the Bible account of creation is a very interesting myth,--mainly a plagiarism from the early traditions and cosmological doctrines of the ancient Persians and Chaldeans;" and, instead of being "a divine revelation of truth," is "a pagan relic, which should no more command serious respect than the ancient doctrines of Fetichism," Ib. p. 90.

These "Harmonial Philosophers" are antagonistic to the teachings of Jehovah in nearly all their theological notions. They scout the idea that any actual evil exists in the universe. They deny the existence of the devil, and of evil spirits. "Everything," says Davis, "is forever progressing in goodness and perfection," Ib. p. 180. The salvation of all men, is with them as certain as the operation of fixed laws. They recognize no Saviour and no atonement in their system of faith. The teachings of spirits, and "a certain organization of labor, capital and talent," they fancy, "will effect the desired cure" for all actual or supposed ills, Ib. p. 178. They recognize no responsibility in the sinner, but attribute his wrong-doings to ignorance and accident; and their laws of right, are the dictates of their own wisdom.

Their system is essentially Pantheistic, all things being regarded by them as a part and parcel of Deity. They argue that "every object which has an existence in the universe must be in its nature good and pure, on the principle that the effect must partake of the nature of the cause, and the stream must be the corresponding emanation of the fountain from which it flows."--Elements of Spiritual Philosophy, p. 55. They teach that human spirits are "formed primarily from the animating essences that pervade the creation,--which essences," they say, "are the breath and presence of the Divinity;" and hence they argue, "that there are no spirits which are intrinsically evil in their nature, and none which do not present in their inward depths the reflection of divine purity," Ib. p. 56. Going still further, they claim that there is no existing "source of positive evil," "no principle of this nature in the human spirit," and that consequently "there can be no evil designs to emanate from such a source," Ib. p. 60.

These assertions are put forth authoritatively; for the "Elements of Spiritual Philosophy" are attested by witnesses to be "written by Spirits of the Sixth Circle, R. P. Ambler, Medium." And if they are met by the declarations written by those who spake as they were moved by the Holy Ghost, they reply: "The Christian who deifies his Bible is as much an idolater as the heathen who burns his incense before his household image. It is surely attributing to the book what the Pagan attributes to his image."--Shekinah, April No., p. 251. Christianity, they denominate, "learned scepticism, baptized in the name of Jesus," &c., Ib., p. 301. Thus are they warring against the word of God, and placing themselves in direct conflict with the Almighty.

This warfare is not only avowed to be against the God of the Bible, but is recognized by themselves as the last great conflict previous to the millennium. They regard this subject as "the great question of the age, which is destined to convulse and divide Protestantism, and around which all other religious controversies must necessarily revolve."--Davis' Review of Bushnell, page 3. The millennium which is to be thus ushered in, they regard as a period when "every one that desires will be able to hold direct intercourse and conversation with the spirit world."--Spiritual Tel., Vol. 1, No. 1. Says Davis: "The thunders of a stupendous reformation are soon to issue from the now open mouth of the Protestant church. The supernatural faith," i.e. a belief in the authenticity of Scripture, "will be shaken, as a reed in the tempest. New channels will be formed for the inflowing of new truths, and then a long-promised era will steal upon the religious and political world."--Review of Bushnell, p. 187.

In another place he says: "You may be assured of the truth of this approaching crisis. The world must recognize it, because it will be accompanied with war; for politics are inseparably connected, all over the world, with religious systems. Religion will develop reason; but politics will impel the masses to unsheath the sword, and to stain the bosom of Nature with blood! Friends of progress! be not discouraged; for the FINAL CRISIS must come; then the strange interregnum," Ib. p. 217. "Protestantism as now constructed will first decay; because it is to be divided into two,--the smallest party will go back into Catholicism; the other will go forward into Rationalism. And then, after a succession of eventful years, a political revolution will hurl the Catholic superstructure to the earth, and the prismatic bow of promise will span the heavens. The children of earth will then be comparatively free and happy! for the millennial epoch will have arrived; and there will be something like a realization of peace on earth, and good will toward all men!" Ib. p. 221.

Such are their delusive hopes, while setting themselves against the Lord, and against his Anointed. The Bible teaches that multitudes will be deceived by them, and, if it were possible, some of the elect; and hence:

The Admonition.

"Behold, I come like a thief. Happy is he who watcheth, and keepeth his garments, lest he walk naked, and they see his shame." Rev. 16:15.

"The day of the Lord will come as a thief in the night; in which the heavens shall pass away with a great noise, and the elements shall melt with fervent heat," 2 Pet. 3:10. The Saviour said to his disciples: "Watch, therefore; for ye know not what hour your Lord doth come," Matt. 24:42. Says Paul: "Yourselves know perfectly that the day of the Lord so cometh as a thief in the night; for when they shall say, peace and safety, then sudden destruction cometh, ... and they shall not escape; but ye, brethren, are not in darkness that that day should overtake you as a thief," 1 Thess. 5:1-6.

Thus will the day of the Lord come, as a thief, on those who are careless and indifferent to its approach; but it will not thus overtake those who watch, and keep their garments. Because so many will be deceived by the strange performances of the spirits of demons, and their miracles so delude the multitude, Christ's coming will be to them sudden and unexpected. Therefore the greater necessity for watchfulness. While this is a predicted means for lulling the world to sleep, it is given to the Christian as an indication of the near coming of Christ, whose advent synchronizes with the outpouring of the seventh vial. The blessing pronounced on those who watch, is an intimation that the people of God will be expecting Christ's advent, while others will be taken by surprise: "unto them that look for him shall he appear the second time without sin unto salvation," Heb. 9:28. "For the grace of God that bringeth salvation hath appeared to all men, teaching us, that denying ungodliness, and worldly lusts, we should live soberly, righteously, and godly, in this present world; looking for that blessed hope, and the glorious appearing of the great God, and our Saviour Jesus Christ," Titus 2:11-13.

Those who keep their garments, are those who have not "defiled" them with sin, (3:4); they will walk with Christ in white, being worthy; "for the fine linen" in which they are to be arrayed "is the righteousness of saints," 19:8. To be destitute of this, is to be unclothed; and hence the Saviour says: "I counsel thee to buy of me ... white raiment, that thou mayest be clothed, and that the shame of thy nakedness do not appear," 3:18. The intimation is clear, that to be deceived by the unclean spirits, is to lose those robes of righteousness, and to be found naked at Christ's appearing.

The Success of the Spirits.

"And they gathered them into a place called in Hebrew Armageddon." Rev. 16:16.

Before the coming of the Lord, and as a preparation for that event, the nations are to be thus gathered. Armageddon is the name of a valley at the foot of Mount Megiddo, famous for its bloody slaughters. It fitly symbolizes the final gathering of the nations. The enemies of God will marshal for the final conflict. The powers of darkness will fancy themselves on the verge of victory; and then will be poured out:

The Seventh Vial.

"And the seventh poured out his bowl on the air; and there came a loud voice from the temple [of heaven], from the throne, saying, It is done! And there were lightnings, and voices, and thunders; and there was a great earthquake, such as was not since men were on the earth, so mighty and so great an earthquake. And the great city became three parts, and the cities of the nations fell: and great Babylon was remembered before God, to give to her the cup of the wine of his furious wrath. And every island fled, and the mountains were no more. And vast hail, weighing a talent, fell from heaven on men; and men reviled God because of the plague of the hail; for the plague thereof was exceedingly great." Rev. 16:17-21.

The atmosphere is not limited, like a river, or portion of the earth, to a given locality, but encircles the globe. Consequently the effect of the vial poured out on the air, would be universal, and not local like the effects of the previous vials. The air is the region of storms. These symbolize the expression of conflicting opinions, and violent outbursts of passion; which may be the commencement of that "great battle," for the preparation of which the unclean spirits went forth under the sixth vial, to gather the people, and which terminates by the slaying of the remnant with the sword of the Lord, 19:21.

An earthquake is a symbol of a political revolution. As this is to be greater than all preceding ones, it must extend to all nations. It is during the earthquake, that the cities fall and the mountains and islands flee away. This commotion evidently synchronizes with the "time of trouble, such as never was since there was a nation even to that same time," when God's "people shall be delivered, every one that shall be found written in the book," Dan. 12:1.

"It is done," is a declaration indicating the completion of the work symbolized. It marks the termination of the events of the seventh vial, which are described in the verses following:

"The great city" is "Babylon," (14:8); which "reigneth over the kings of the earth," (17:8); and which John had seen sitting "upon many waters," 17:1. This was doubtless seen when he saw the waters of the symbolic Euphrates being dried up, 16:12. Babylon, being a symbol of the Roman hierarchy, its triple division indicates a like division of the church of Rome, not geographical, but under different leaders, previous to its destruction.

"The cities of the nations," must symbolize other hierarchies, analogous to that of Rome, of which there are the Greek church, in Russia and Greece, the Arminian and Syrian churches, and other corrupt nationalized establishments. All such will become disconnected, like Babylon, with the governments by which they are sustained.

"Great Babylon" then comes into remembrance to drink the cup of the wine of the fierceness of God's wrath. Because her sins have reached unto heaven, "God hath remembered her iniquities," 18:5. This synchronizes with her destruction, symbolized in Rev. 18:8-23. As the Papacy continues till Christ's coming (Dan. 7:21, and 2 Thess. 2:3-8), this epoch must synchronize with that event, when he comes to receive his chosen ones.

With the destruction of Babylon, occurs the subversion of all national authority. As ecclesiastical hierarchies are symbolized by cities, the "mountains" and "islands" on which they are situated must symbolize the larger and smaller governments; and their removal from their places, their subversion in the great moral "earthquake" which is to overwhelm them. This synchronizes with the sixth seal, when they are all "removed out of their places," (6:14); and it leaves the inhabitants of earth in a state of anarchy. It is at this time that the kings and great men of the earth become aware that the great day of God's wrath is come, 6:15-17. With this time of trouble, comes the deliverance of God's people, (Dan. 12:1); who shall be caught up together "to meet the Lord in the air," 1 Thess. 4:17. To them the Lord has said, "Thou shalt not be afraid for the terror by night; nor for the arrow that flieth by day; nor for the pestilence that walketh in darkness; nor for the destruction that wasteth at noon-day. A thousand shall fall at thy side, and ten thousand at thy right hand; but it shall not come nigh thee. Only with thine eyes shalt thou behold and see the reward of the wicked. Because thou hast made the Lord which is my refuge, even the Most High, thy habitation," Ps. 91:5-9.

The removal of the saints leaves the wicked exposed to the vengeance of God's wrath, of which a terrific hail-storm on their defenceless heads, is an expressive symbol. The Lord said, by Isaiah: "Judgment also will I lay to the line, and righteousness to the plummet: and the hail shall sweep away the refuge of lies, and the waters shall overflow the hiding-place. And your covenant with death shall be disannulled, and your agreement with hell shall not stand; when the overflowing scourge shall pass through, then ye shall be trodden down by it. From the time that it goeth forth it shall take you: for morning by morning shall it pass over, by day and by night: and it shall be a vexation only to understand the report. For the bed is shorter than that a man can stretch himself on it: and the covering narrower than that he can wrap himself in it. For the Lord shall rise up as in Mount Perazim, he shall be wroth as in the valley of Gibeon, that he may do his work, his strange work; and bring to pass his act, his strange act. Now therefore be ye not mockers, lest your bands be made strong: for I have heard from the Lord God of hosts a consumption even determined upon the whole earth," Isa. 28:17-22.

This must synchronize with the final conflict, (symbolized in Rev. 19:19-21): also with the casting of the vine of the earth into the wine-press of God's wrath (14:19), and terminates the battle of "Armageddon,"--the "battle of that great day of God Almighty," 16:14.

The Judgment of the Harlot.

"And one of the seven angels, who had the seven bowls, came and talked with me, saying, Come here; I will show thee the judgment of the great harlot who sitteth on many waters; with whom the kings of the earth have committed fornication, and the inhabitants of the earth have been made drunk with the wine of her fornication." Rev. 17:1, 2.

The Roman hierarchy had been frequently referred to in the preceding visions; but an institution, so interwoven with the history of the nations, required a more full and minute symbolization.

The subject of this vision is announced to the revelator, by one of the angels who had the seven vials;--very probably, the seventh. The harlot is identified as one "that sitteth upon many waters." Ancient Babylon was thus addressed: "O thou that dwellest upon many waters, abundant in treasures, thine end is come, and the measure of thy covetousness," Jer. 51:13. She is also described as "The well-favored harlot, the mistress of witchcrafts, that selleth nations through her whoredoms, and families through her witchcrafts," Nahum 3:4. Therefore the harlot whose judgment is to be more minutely shown, is the city of the previous vision, which received the cup of the wine of God's wrath (16:19), and which probably was shown to John on the waters of the Euphrates, (16:12); for the reference indicates that she had been thus previously exhibited,--the waters on which she was seated, being the people, nations, &c., which sustained and defended her idolatries, 17:15. In the vision now to be shown John, the Roman hierarchy is symbolized by Babylon; but it is first exhibited as:

A Woman on a Scarlet-Colored Beast.

"And he carried me away in spirit into a desert: and I saw a woman seated on a crimson-colored wild beast, full of names of reviling, having seven heads and ten horns. And the woman was arrayed in purple and crimson, and decked with gold and precious stones and pearls, having a golden cup in her hand full of abominations and the impurities of her fornication; and on her forehead a name was written, A SECRET: BABYLON, THE GREAT, THE MOTHER OF THE HARLOTS AND THE ABOMINATIONS OF THE EARTH. And I saw the woman drunken with the blood of the saints, and with the blood of the witnesses of Jesus; and when I saw her I wondered greatly." Rev. 17:3-6.

"And the angel said to me, Why dost thou wonder? I will tell thee the secret of the woman, and of the wild beast that carrieth her, which hath the seven heads and the ten horns. The wild beast which thou didst see, was, and is not, and will ascend out of the abyss, and go into destruction; and those who dwell on the earth will wonder, (whose names were not written in the book of life from the foundation of the world,) as they behold the wild beast that was and is not, and will be. And here is the mind having wisdom. The seven heads are seven mountains, on which the woman sitteth, and they are seven kings: five are fallen, and one is and the other is not yet come; and when he cometh he must remain a little while. And the wild beast that was, and is not, even he is the eighth, and is of the seven, and goeth into destruction. And the ten horns which thou didst see are ten kings, who have not yet received a kingdom; but they receive power as kings, one hour, with the wild beast. These have one mind, and will give their power and strength to the wild beast. These will make war with the Lamb, and the Lamb will overcome them; for he is Lord of lords, and King of kings; and those with him are called, and chosen, and faithful." Rev. 17:7-14.

"And he saith to me, The waters which thou didst see, where the harlot sitteth, are peoples, and crowds, and nations, and tongues. And the ten horns which thou didst see, and the wild beast, these will hate the harlot, and will make her desolate and naked, and will eat her flesh, and burn her up with fire. For God hath put it into their hearts to perform his purpose, and to agree, and give their kingdom to the wild beast, until the words of God shall be fulfilled. And the woman whom thou didst see is the great city, which reigneth over the kings of the earth." Rev. 17:15-18.

That the woman and city symbolize the same, is shown by the declaration that she is that great city, which reigneth over the kings of the earth, v. 18. She is also thus indicated by the name of "Babylon," on her forehead, and the golden cup in her hand: "Babylon hath been a golden cup in the Lord's hand, that made all the earth drunken: the nations have drunken of her wine; therefore are the nations mad," Jer. 51:7. In like manner has the church of Rome intoxicated the nations.

"The scarlet-colored beast" on which the woman is seated, is evidently the same beast that John saw "rise out of the sea, having seven heads, and ten horns," 13:1. The Roman empire had been symbolized by "a great red dragon," which also had seven heads and ten horns. In that vision, crowns were on the heads of the beast, (12:3); which indicated that Rome, during the period thus represented, existed under the forms of government symbolized by the heads. These heads, the angel affirms, are the seven mountains on which the woman sitteth, (v. 9); and also that they are seven kings (v. 10), or forms of government. Mountains also symbolize governments, (16:20); and as the heads and mountains are the same, they must alike symbolize the seven forms of government under which Rome existed previous to its subversion by the northern barbarians,--viz.: 1, the kingly; 2, consular; 3, dictatorial; 4, decemviral; 5, tribunitial; 6, pagan-imperial; and 7, Christian-imperial. At the time of the explanation of this vision to John, the "five" first-named forms had passed away; or, as the angel says, had "fallen," v. 10. One then was:--Rome then existed under its pagan-imperial, or sixth head. The other, the Christian-imperial, had not then come; but after it came, and had continued for a time, the Roman empire was subverted by the irruptions of northern barbarians. Thus "the beast was;" and then, was not for a season. But afterwards it emerged again from the sea (13:1), under an "eight" form, which was of the previous seven, 17:11. When it reappears, its crowns are not upon its heads, but encircle its horns, (13:1); indicating that those governments have the ascendency, which are symbolized by the "ten horns;" and which, according to the angel, are "ten kings," which had not received their kingdom at the time of the vision, v. 12. These were to be kings in "one," or the same hour with the beast, and must therefore be contemporary kingdoms, while the forms symbolized by the heads, are evidently successive. They constitute the government of Rome, in its eighth, or decem-regal form; and symbolize the ten kingdoms which arose after and out of the subversion of imperial Rome. Under this form, the beast goes into perdition, (v. 11):--they continue under various combinations, till the end of the world, when they will war with and be overcome by the Lamb (v. 14), in the great battle of Armageddon, 19:19-21.

The ten contemporary kingdoms have one mind, (v. 13): they perpetuate the kingdom of the beast, by adopting similar laws, pursuing the same line of policy, and assuming the same powers that the empire exercised.

The "names of blasphemy" which cover the beast, symbolize its arrogating the right to dictate in matters of faith and religious worship, and to punish those who dissent from its creed. The Roman hierarchy was supported by legal enactments against heretics in all of the ten kingdoms. Those who dissented from the church were delivered over to the power of the civil arm, which punished by imprisonment, confiscation of goods, bodily torture, and death. The exercise of such power, was a blasphemous usurpation of the prerogatives of Christ, and an assumption of authority over the legislation of God.

On this beast the woman is seated. As its rider, she guides it, and is sustained by it. She is its directing power; and while she is thus seated, there is no reference to crowns encircling either heads or horns. All rule for a time is subservient to her control. Thus were the ten kingdoms obedient to the Roman hierarchy,--sustaining, and being controlled by it. She crowned their kings, and dethroned them at her pleasure. The religion of the church was enforced by the sword of the state; and thus did the kings of the earth commit fornication with her,--the idolatries of the church being sanctioned by them.

The superb attire of the woman, and the costly gems with which she is decked, denote the wealth, luxury, and regal splendor of the hierarchy which she symbolizes. The cup, and its abominations in her hand, denote the false doctrines with which she would seduce the nations. Her names describe her nature, and identify her with Babylon; and her intoxication with blood, indicates her blood-thirsty, persecuting character, and the delight with which she would exult over the slaughter of the saints.

The Roman hierarchy was not, however, always to retain her supremacy over the nations. She was in due time to fall from the position symbolized by the woman seated on the beast; and the kings of the earth were to hate and burn with fire, her whom they had recognized as their mistress, and to whose control they had submitted. The governments which have sustained her pretensions, were to cast her off contemptuously. This has been in progress of fulfilment from the days of Martin Luther, since which her control of the ten kingdoms has been only limited and partial. Many of her ecclesiastical estates have been confiscated, and she has been deprived of her prerogatives in many countries. There may, perhaps, be hereafter a more complete fulfilment of this prediction. It is symbolized in the following chapter, by:

The Fall of Babylon.

"And after this, I saw another angel descending from heaven, having great power; and the earth was enlightened by his glory. And he cried with a mighty voice, saying, She is fallen: Babylon the great is fallen, and is become a dwelling of demons, and a prison of every unclean spirit, and a prison of every unclean and hateful bird, for all the nations have drunk of the wine of the fury of her fornication, and the kings of the earth have committed fornication with her, and the merchants of the earth have become rich through the abundance of her luxury." Rev. 18:1-3.

This announcement of the fall of the city, synchronizes with the same symbolization in the 14th chapter: "And there followed another angel, saying, Babylon is fallen, is fallen, that great city, because she made all nations drink of the wine of the wrath of her fornication," 14:8. The angel, proclaiming her fall, doubtless symbolizes a body of men, who shall give utterance to corresponding declarations.

The epoch of this utterance is shown by the identity of this angel with that of Rev. 10:1-3. They thus correspond: They both descend from heaven: the one is a mighty angel, and the other has great power; the one is enveloped with a robe of cloud, his head is arched with the rainbow, his face is like the sun, and his feet like fire, and he stands on both earth and sea; the other is so glorified, and occupies a position so conspicuous, that the earth is enlightened with his glory; and the one cries "with a loud voice as when a lion roareth," while the other cries "mighty with a strong voice." Thus their position, manner and conspicuousness, are alike. What was uttered by the angel of the tenth chapter, is not revealed; but the fall of Babylon being announced in the eighteenth, it follows that it was the subject of the angel's utterance in the tenth.

As the messenger of the tenth chapter appears subsequent to the sixth, and before the seventh trumpet; and as, after this epoch, there were to be prophesyings "again, before many peoples, and nations, and tongues, and kings" (10:11), it follows that the time then symbolized must be at an epoch anterior to the end of the world. A corresponding reason--namely, the command to come out of Babylon, and the fulfilment of her plagues and sorrows, which are to intervene between the cry of the angel announcing her fall and the time of her actual destruction--proves that the mighty angel of the 18th of Revelation must also be at an epoch having a considerable period between it and the end.

It follows, that when John saw the angel of the eighteenth chapter, and "the earth was lightened with his glory," it did not symbolize a literal but a moral light,--the light of truth. And as the enlightening of the earth by its promulgation, pre-supposes a previous state of corresponding moral darkness, it must, as in the tenth chapter, symbolize an epoch, prominent in the history of the world, as a time when the darkness of ignorance, error and superstition, began rapidly to disappear before the spread of the light of truth and knowledge.

These considerations point to the epoch of the REFORMATION, when the midnight darkness of the dark ages began to be scattered before the uprising and onward progress of truth and knowledge. Then appeared a body of religious teachers, aided by the newly discovered art of printing, who so brought the Scriptures out from their obscurity, opposed the pretensions of the Papal hierarchy, and, by the clear teachings of the word, so secured the spread of gospel light and liberty, that they might appropriately be symbolized by an angel coming down from heaven, and enlightening the earth with his glory. The descent from heaven would symbolize the heavenly origin of the doctrines promulgated. His mighty power, and the strong voice with which he proclaimed his cry, would symbolize the greatness and earnestness of the movement, and the mighty results to be effected by it. This symbolization, twice given, could only be fulfilled by some great and mighty movement, like the Reformation.

The fall of Babylon is distinct from and anterior to its destruction, and must correspond with the fall of the woman from her position on the beast;--she is no longer to be the director of, and to be sustained by, the civil power. The cry of the angel, announcing her fall, as Mr. Elliot remarks, seems to be anticipative, and not retrospective. The denunciations of the Papacy by the reformers were of a character to fulfil this symbolization.

The year 1300, during the pontificate of Boniface VIII., may be regarded as marking the highest eminence to which the Papal power ever attained. From this period the dominion of the Roman Pontiffs appeared to be gradually undermined. Twenty-four years after this date, John Wickliffe was born, who, together with his followers, made more vigorous attacks upon Babylon itself. Some of these declared Rome to be mystical Babylon, and the Pope and church there to be Antichrist. These heralds announced the fall of mystical Babylon, as the ancient prophets had done that of literal Babylon, long before the event.--Jer. 51:7, 8. Antichrist and Babylon are identified in prophecy. In 1518, Luther first suspected their application to the Papacy; and, writing to his friend Link, on sending him a copy of the acts just published of the conference at Augsburg, he says: "My pen is ready to give birth to things much greater. I know not myself whence these thoughts come to me. I will send you what I write, that you may see if I have well conjectured in believing that the Antichrist of whom St. Paul speaks now reigns in the court of Rome."

At first, Luther and his companions sought only the reformation of that church. They had no idea of dissolving their own connection with it. But when the thunders of the Vatican were hurled at them, and they found themselves excommunicated as heretics, they came to the conclusion that the church of Rome was the Babylon of the Apocalypse. Immediately upon this conviction, they began to cry, "Babylon is fallen!"

In 1520 appeared a famous book, by Luther, on the "Babylonish Captivity of the Church," in which he attacked Rome with great skill and courage. In Switzerland and England the reformers considered themselves as fulfilling this message of the Apocalyptic angel. Elliot says, "They seized on this very prophecy for application; and, for the first time, upon grounds of evidence sound and tenable, concluded on the fact of progress having been made up to it, in the evolution of the great mundane drama, and on their own chronological place being already far advanced under the sixth trumpet, and in near expectancy of the seventh trumpet, of the Apocalyptic prophecy."

These denunciations against Mystic Babylon, and protestations against all her idolatrous ceremonies and superstitious appendages, were given, by the great body of the reformers, within the very bounds of her empire. They resulted in her loss of power, and of control over the princes of Europe. In 1526, the other monarchs becoming jealous of the power of Charles V., Emperor of Germany, "Pope Clement VII. placed himself at the head of a league of the principal states of Italy against him; but their ill-directed efforts were productive of new misfortunes. Rome was taken by storm, by the troops of the constable, sacked, and the Pope himself made prisoner. Charles V. publicly disavowed the proceedings of the constable, went into mourning with his court, and carried his hypocrisy so far as to order prayers for the deliverance of the Pope. On restoring the holy father to liberty, he demanded a ransom of four hundred thousand crowns of gold, but was satisfied with a quarter of that sum."--Ency. Am., v. 3. p. 76.

All the Protestant princes of Germany denied the assumptions of the Pope; and the powers of western and northern Europe, one after another, denied their allegiance to him. In 1798, Pius VI. was taken prisoner by the French, under Gen. Berthier, and died in exile. When Berthier entered Rome, many of the cardinals "fled from the city on the wings of terror;" but those who remained "were disposed still to uphold the authority of the Pontiff." Finally, however, "with melancholy voice, they pronounced their absolute renunciation of the temporal government."--Life of Pius VI. His successor resumed his position. But in 1848 Pius IX. fled from his own subjects, and was only restored by French arms. Thus gradually the Babylonish woman became unseated, and fell from her position on the beast; and, instead of guiding and directing the civil power, now only exists by sufferance. As a city, also, her supremacy was gone. Being no longer the mistress of the nations, or the ruling city, the Papal See is in the condition of ancient Babylon when becoming a dependency of the Medes and Persians.

After the fall of ancient Babylon, it became gradually more and more deserted, until there was a literal fulfilment of the words of Isaiah: "Wild beasts of the desert shall lie there; and their houses shall be full of doleful creatures; and owls shall dwell there, and satyrs shall dance there. And the wild beasts of the islands shall cry in their desolate houses, and dragons in their pleasant palaces," Isa. 13:21, 22. In like manner the apocalyptic Babylon, after her fall, and the withdrawal of Protestants from her communion, was to become the receptacle of corresponding spirits. Her members were to be more impious than before, and were to adhere more closely than ever to her idolatrous practices. The contrast between these and true Christians would also be more apparent from the separation which succeeds her fall, in obedience to:

The Voice From Heaven.

"And I heard another voice from heaven, saying, Come out of her, my people, that ye partake not of her sins, and that ye receive not of her plagues, for her sins have reached to heaven, and God hath remembered her iniquities! Reward her even as she rendered to you, and double to her according to her works, in the cup which she hath poured out, pour out double to her. By as much as she hath glorified herself, and lived luxuriously, so much torment and mourning give her; for she saith in her heart, I sit a queen, and am not a widow, and shall see no mourning. On this account, her plagues will come in one day, death, and mourning, and famine; and she will be burned up with fire; for strong is the Lord God, who judgeth her."--Rev. 18:4-8.

So long as the true character of the apostate church was unperceived, she would contain many good, as well as a multitude of bad members. The voice from heaven, indicates an epoch when there should be a widely extended and marked separation between these two classes. Till the time of that separation should be indicated, the children of God would be justified in continuing members of her communion; but not subsequently. The condition of Babylon, at the time of her fall, indicates that the separation must take place in near connection with that event; and the cry must synchronize with that of the third angel in Rev. 14:9,--which symbolized a body of men who should insist on such a separation from the Papacy as that here symbolized.

After the discovery that the church of Rome was the Babylon of the Apocalypse, the reformers began to call on the people of God to desert her communion; and the formation of the reformed churches was the consequence. This was preached wherever the Reformation extended, and has been continued to the present time. The Protestant churches have proclaimed connection with Romanism, an obstacle to salvation; and have called on its Christian members to come out from her abominations. Even the name "Protestant," was given because of their protestation against the corruptions of the Papal See.

After the fall of ancient Babylon, and before her destruction, the people were, in like manner, commanded to forsake her. Said Jeremiah: "Flee out of the midst of Babylon, and deliver every man his soul: be not cut off in her iniquity; for this is the time of the Lord's vengeance; he will render unto her a recompense. Babylon is suddenly fallen and destroyed: howl for her; take balm for her pain, if so be she may be healed. We would have healed Babylon, but she is not healed: forsake her, and let us go every one into his own country: for her judgment reacheth unto heaven, and is lifted up even to the skies," Jer. 51:6, 8, 9. And Isaiah said: "Go ye forth of Babylon, flee ye from the Chaldeans, with a voice of singing declare ye, tell this, utter it even to the end of the earth; say ye, The Lord hath redeemed his servant Jacob," Isa. 48:20. "Depart ye, depart ye, go ye out from thence, touch no unclean thing; go ye out of the midst of her; be ye clean, that bear the vessels of the Lord," Isa. 52:11.

Sins reaching to heaven, indicate great wickedness. Thus God said to Jonah: "Go to Nineveh, that great city, and cry against it; for their wickedness is come up before me," Jonah 1:2. And he said of old Babylon: "Her judgment reacheth unto heaven, and is lifted up even to the skies," Jer. 51:9.

The Destruction of Babylon.

"And the kings of the earth, who have committed fornication and lived luxuriously with her, will weep and wail for her, when they see the smoke of her burning, standing afar off through the fear of her torment, saying, Woe! woe! that great city, Babylon, that mighty city! for in one hour is thy judgment come! And the merchants of the earth will weep and mourn over her; for no one buyeth their merchandise any more; the merchandise of gold, and silver, and precious stones, and pearls, and fine linen, and purple, and silk, and crimson, and all thine wood, and all kinds of vessels of ivory, and all kinds of vessels of most precious wood, and of brass, and iron, and marble, and cinnamon, and fragrant ointment, and incense, and myrrh, and frankincense, and wine, and oil, and fine flour, and wheat, and beasts, and sheep, and horses, and chariots, and bodies, and souls of men. And the autumnal fruit of thine appetite's desire is departed from thee, and all things dainty and sumptuous are destroyed from thee, and thou wilt find them no more at all. The merchants of these things, who were enriched by her, will stand afar off, through the fear of her torment, weeping and mourning, saying, Woe! woe! that great city, that was clothed in fine linen, and purple, and crimson, and adorned with gold, and precious stones, and pearls! for in one hour such great wealth is destroyed. And every pilot, and every one sailing to any place, and sailors, and as many as trade by sea, stood afar off, and cried, when they saw the smoke of her burning, saying, What city is like the great city? And they cast dust on their heads, and cried out, weeping and mourning, saying, Woe! woe! the great city by which all who had ships on the sea, were made rich through her precious merchandise! for in one hour she is desolated." Rev. 18:9-20.

"Rejoice over her, O heaven, and ye saints and apostles and prophets; for God hath avenged you on her!" Rev. 18:20.

"And a strong angel took up a stone like a great mill-stone, and cast it into the sea, saying, Thus violently, will Babylon, the great city, be cast down, and be no more at all. And the voice of harpers, and musicians, and pipers, and trumpeters, will be heard no more at all in thee; and no craftsman, of any art, will be found any more in thee; and the sound of a mill-stone will be heard no more at all in thee; and the light of a lamp will shine no more at all in thee; and the voice of the bridegroom and the bride will be heard no more at all in thee; for thy merchants were the nobles of the earth; for by thy sorcery all nations were deceived. And in her was found the blood of prophets, and of saints, and of all those slain on the earth." Rev. 18:21-24.

The punishment of Babylon is proportioned to her wickedness, and is to be inflicted partially by the kings of the earth, and partially by other agencies. The kings were to hate, and burn her with fire, (17:16); and were also, when they should see the smoke of her burnings, to bewail and lament for her, 18:9. The former passage indicates their agency in her impoverishment, and has been fulfilled in the confiscation of her property in France and England, the spoliation of churches and religious houses, wherever the arms of Napoleon extended; the dethronement of the Pope, by Gen. Berthier, in 1798; the refusal of some of the powers to permit her to nominate, within their limits, the candidates for ecclesiastical preferment, &c. She is thus made to feel her widowhood,--her divorce from the secular arm,--and has mourned the loss of her most devoted children, who have forsaken her communion.

Her final destruction is, however, to be entire. She is totally to disappear, like the sinking of a millstone in the sea. She is to be utterly burned with fire; but the lamentation of the kings over her burning, indicates that her destruction is to be completed by other instrumentality than theirs. Probably the multitude are to be incensed against her, and will so manifest their hatred that the governments will neither join in it, nor attempt to resist it, for fear that the same torment will be inflicted on them, 18:10. But her existence is terminated by the brightness of Christ's coming, 2 Thess. 2:8. Her destruction precedes that of the kings of the earth, who mourn her end. The merchants of the earth, the captains, sailors, &c., symbolize those who bear a relation to the hierarchy, analogous to that sustained by such to a great commercial emporium. They are those who have the control of her preferments, benefices and revenues,--who traffic in her indulgences, and thereby become themselves enriched. And these articles of traffic are symbolized by the merchandise which, after her destruction, no man would buy.

The commerce of this ecclesiastical city, has been immense,--particularly in indulgences. The sale of these was reduced to a system, says D'Aubign? by "the celebrated and scandalous Tariff of Indulgences," which went through more than forty editions. The least delicate ears would be offended by an enumeration of all the horrors it contains. Incest, if not detected, was to cost five groats; and six, if it was known. There was a stated price for murder, infanticide, adultery, perjury, burglary, &c. Polygamy cost six ducats; sacrilege and perjury, nine; murder, eight; and witchcraft, two ducats.

The penances of various kinds which were imposed as a punishment for sin, might also be compounded for money.

Tetzel, one of Rome's travelling merchants, told the people of Germany that for "a quarter of a florin" they might "receive letters of indulgence," by means of which they might "introduce into paradise a divine and immortal soul, without its running any risk." Hist. Ref., pp. 56, 242.

He also said "Indulgences avail not only for the living but for the dead. With twelve groats you can deliver your father from purgatory." "At the very instant," said he, "that the money rattles at the bottom of the chest, the soul escapes from purgatory, and flies, liberated to heaven." This is but a specimen of her vile traffic.

Responding to the command, are heard the voices of much people in heaven,

Rejoicing Over Babylon's Destruction.

"And after this, I heard a loud voice of a mighty crowd in heaven, saying, Praise ye Jehovah! The salvation, and the glory, and the power of our God! For true and righteous are his judgments; for he hath judged the great harlot, who corrupted the earth with her fornication, and hath avenged the blood of his servants at her hand! And again they said, Praise ye Jehovah! And her smoke ascendeth for ever and ever. And the twenty-four elders and the four living beings fell down and worshipped God, who sat on the throne, saying, So be it! Praise ye Jehovah!" Rev. 19:1-4.

Daniel, in vision, saw the same persecuting power symbolized by a "Little Horn," having "eyes like the eyes of a man and a mouth speaking great things;" and he beheld, "and the same Horn made war with the saints, and prevailed against them, until the Ancient of days came, and judgment was given to the saints of the Most High, and the time came that the saints possessed the kingdom," Dan. 7:8, 21, 22. And Paul testified of "that Wicked" who was to be revealed, that he was the "Man of Sin," "whom the Lord shall consume with the spirit of his mouth, and shall destroy with the brightness of his coming," 2 Thess. 2:3-8. The destruction of that which was thus symbolized and predicted, must, consequently, be at the epoch of Christ's second coming and of the establishment of the kingdom of God.

It is also at the epoch anticipated by "the souls of them that were slain for the word of God and for the testimony which they held," who, from under the altar, on the opening of the "fifth seal," "cried with a loud voice, saying, How long, O Lord, holy and true, dost thou not judge and avenge our blood on them that dwell on the earth?" 6:9, 10. The epoch which they anticipated not having then arrived, "white robes were given unto every one of them;

and it was said unto them, that they should rest yet for a little season, until their fellow servants also, and their brethren that should be killed as they were, should be fulfilled" (6:11),--i.e., till their number should be filled up. As the destruction of that hierarchy, in which "was found the blood of prophets and of saints and of all that were slain upon the earth" (18:24), had just been symbolized (in the 18th chap.), and as these rejoicings are because God "hath judged the great whore which did corrupt the earth with her fornication, and hath avenged the blood of his servants at her hand" (19:2), it follows that the epoch here symbolized is that to which the saints were to wait, and that they are now to be crowned with their reward.

As the destruction of Babylon is a little anterior to that of the beast and false prophet (19:20), and is to be destroyed by the brightness of Christ's coming (2 Thess. 2:8), at a time when the kingdom is to be given to the saints of the Most High (Dan. 7:22), it explains how it is that the kingdom is set up in the days of the kings symbolized by the divided toes of Nebuchadnezzar's image: symbolic of the same as the horns of the beast in Dan. 7:7, 24, and Rev. 17:3, 12, 16; for "in the days of these kings shall the God of heaven set up a kingdom which shall never be destroyed, and the kingdom shall not be left to other people, but it shall break in pieces and consume all these kingdoms, and it shall stand forever," Dan. 2:44.

The kingdom is therefore commenced previous to the descent of the Lord to the earth, by the saints being caught up to meet him in the air. "For the Lord himself shall descend from heaven with a shout, with the voice of the archangel and the trump of God; and the dead in Christ shall rise first; then we which are alive and remain shall be caught up together with them in the clouds, to meet the Lord in the air: and so shall we ever be with the Lord," 1 Thess. 4:16, 17.

This epoch, then, is that of the sounding of the seventh trumpet; for "in the days of the voice of the seventh angel, when he shall begin to sound, the mystery of God shall be finished, as he hath declared to his servants the prophets," 10:7. This mystery Paul thus explains: "Now this I say, brethren, that flesh and blood cannot inherit the kingdom of God, neither doth corruption inherit incorruption. Behold, I show you a mystery: We shall not all sleep, but we shall all be changed, in a moment, in the twinkling of an eye, at the last trump: for the trumpet shall sound, and the dead shall be raised incorruptible, and we shall be changed," 1 Cor. 15:50-54. This "saying" was thus written by Isaiah,--"He will swallow up death in victory; and the Lord God will wipe away tears from off all faces; and the rebuke of his people shall he take away from off all the earth; for the Lord hath spoken it. And it shall be said in that day, Lo, this is our God; we have waited for him, and he will save us: this is the Lord; we have waited for him, we will be glad and rejoice in his salvation," Isa. 25:8, 9. It follows, then, that the voices heard in heaven, shouting "Alleluia," and ascribing "salvation, and glory, and honor, and power, unto the Lord our God" (v. 1), synchronize with those heard when "the seventh angel sounded: and there were great voices in heaven, saying, The kingdoms of this world are become the kingdoms of our Lord, and of his Christ; and he shall reign for ever and ever.--And the four and twenty elders, which sat before God on their seats, fell upon their faces and worshipped God, saying, We give thee thanks, O Lord God Almighty, which art, and wast, and art to come; because thou hast taken to thee thy great power, and hast reigned: And the nations were angry, and thy wrath is come, and the time of the dead, that they should be judged, and that thou shouldest give reward unto thy servants the prophets, and to the saints, and them that fear thy name, small and great; and shouldest destroy them which destroy the earth," Rev. 11:15-18.

The time of the dead being come that they should be judged, and the saints rewarded, is another evidence that this epoch is that of the second advent and kingdom of Christ, "who shall judge the quick and the dead at his appearing and kingdom," 2 Tim. 4:1. Consequently it must synchronize with that of:

The Marriage of the Lamb.

"And a voice came from the throne saying, Praise our God, all ye his servants, and ye that fear him, both the small and the great! And I heard a voice like that of a great crowd, and like the voice of many waters, and like the voice of mighty thunders, saying, Praise ye Jehovah! for the Lord God

Almighty reigneth. Let us rejoice and exult, and give glory up him: for the marriage of the Lamb hath come, and his wife hath prepared herself! And it was granted to her to be arrayed in fine linen, clean and white: (for the fine linen is the righteousness of the saints.) And he saith to me, Write, Happy are those called to the marriage-supper of the Lamb. And he saith to me, These are the true words of God. And I fell before his feet to worship him. And he saith to me, See thou do it not: I am thy fellow-servant and one of thy brethren, who have the testimony of Jesus: worship God: for the testimony of Jesus is the spirit of prophecy." Rev. 19:5-10.

The marriage of the Lamb is at the epoch when "the kingdoms of this world are to become our Lord's and his Christ's"--when the Lord God Almighty takes to himself his great power and reigns, 11:15, 17. Therefore, in connection, are heard the mighty thunderings, saying, "Alleluia; for the Lord God Omnipotent reigneth," 9:16. This scripture, then, corresponds with that in Matt. 24:30, 31, when "they shall see the Son of Man coming in the clouds of heaven with power and great glory; and he shall send his angels with a great sound of a trumpet, and they shall gather together his elect from the four winds, from one end of heaven to the other." For, "when the Son of Man shall come in his glory, and all the holy angels with him, then shall he sit upon the throne of his glory: and before him shall be gathered all nations: and he shall separate them one from another as a shepherd divideth his sheep from the goats--the one on his right hand and the other on his left," Matt. 25:31, 32. Those on his right, we learn from 1 Cor. 15:51, and 1 Thess. 4:16, 17, are the elect, gathered by the angels from all parts under heaven, who are caught up to meet the Lord in the air--and those on the left are consequently the living wicked, who are to be slain by the sword which proceedeth out of the mouth of the Lamb, 19:21.

The wife who "hath made herself ready," is shown by the foregoing scriptures to be, undoubtedly, the church triumphant--the redeemed, who have been raised out from among the dead, and the living saints, caught up together to meet the Lord in the air; to welcome him in his coming to reign. These constitute the bride, the Lamb's wife; for as "the husband is the head of the wife," even so "Christ is the head of the church," Eph. 5:23. He "loved the church, and gave himself for it, that he might sanctify and cleanse it with the washing of water by the word, that he might present it to himself a glorious church, not having spot or wrinkle, or any such thing; but that it should be holy and without blemish," Eph. 5:25-27. This accords with God's ancient promises to his people. Thus Isaiah saith: "Thy Maker is thy husband; the Lord of hosts is his name, and thy Redeemer the Holy One of Israel: the Lord of the whole earth shall he be called," Isa. 54:5. Also Hosea: "And it shall be at that day, saith the Lord, that thou shalt call me Ishi," my husband; "and shalt call me no more Baali," my Lord. "And I will betroth thee unto me in righteousness, and in judgment, and in loving kindness, and in mercies. I will even betroth thee unto me in faithfulness; and thou shalt know the Lord," Hos. 2:16, 19. Thus is the church "espoused to one husband," to be presented "as a chaste virgin to Christ," 2 Cor. 11:2.

The epoch of this presentation being here symbolized, it synchronizes with that part of the parable of the "ten virgins which took their lamps and went forth to meet the Bridegroom," when, the Bridegroom having come, "they that were ready went in with him to the marriage, and the door was shut"-- those left without, afterwards crying in vain for admittance, Matt. 25:10. The wife had been made ready by its having been "granted that she should be arrayed in fine linen, clean and white--[mar. 'bright']; for the fine linen is the righteousness of the saints," 19:8. Such were the "white robes" given to those who cried from under the altar (6:11), and who afterwards, at an epoch synchronizing with the marriage of the Lamb, appeared, "a great multitude which no man could number, of all nations, and kindreds, and people, and tongues," who "stood before the throne, and before the Lamb, clothed with white robes, and palms in their hands, and cried with a loud voice, saying, Salvation to our God which sitteth upon the throne, and unto the Lamb," 7:9, 10. These were they of whom one of the elders asked, saying, "What are these which are arrayed in white robes? and whence came they?" and who was answered: "These are they which came out of great tribulation, and have washed their robes and made them white in the blood of the Lamb. Therefore are they before the throne of God, and serve him day and night in his temple: and he that sitteth on the throne shall dwell among them. They shall hunger no more, neither thirst any more; neither shall the sun light on them, nor any heat. For the Lamb which is in the midst of the throne shall feed them, and shall lead them unto living fountains of waters; and God shall wipe away all tears from their eyes," 7:13-17. These had complied with the condition to the promise: "He that overcometh, the same shall be clothed in white raiment; and I will not blot out his name out of the book of life, but I will confess his name before the Father and before his holy angels," 3:5. "These are they which follow the Lamb whithersoever he goeth. These were redeemed from among men, being the first fruits unto God and to the Lamb," 14:4.

"Blessed are they which are called unto the marriage supper of the Lamb," 19:9. Truly are they blessed; for "they shall hunger no more, neither thirst any more; neither shall the sun light on them, nor any heat," 7:16. They attain the promised blessing: "Blessed and holy is he that hath part in the first resurrection," 20:6. "And God shall wipe away all tears from their eyes; and there shall be no more death, neither sorrow, nor crying, neither shall there be any more pain: for the former things are passed away," 21:4. So entranced was the apocalyptic seer at these symbols of the glorified redeemed, that he fell at his feet to worship the angel who showed him these things. But his fellow servant shrank back from the reception of homage, and pointed to God as the only object of adoration.

The union of the saints to Christ in the clouds of heaven being symbolized, they receive the gracious welcome: "Come, ye blessed of my Father, inherit the kingdom prepared for you from the foundation of the world," Matt. 25:34. But first it is necessary to redeem the "purchased possession" (Eph. 1:14), to reconquer the revolted province, which, since the fall, has been subject to "the god of this world" (2 Cor. 4:4), the "prince of the power of the air" (Eph. 2:2), to rescue it from the dominion of the usurper, and deliver it from its present mis-rule "up to God the Father" (1 Cor. 15:24), who will bestow it on One who is worthy to wear its crown. For when Daniel saw that "the judgment was set and the books were opened," he also "saw in the night visions, and, behold, one like the Son of man came in the clouds of heaven, and came to the Ancient of days, and they brought him near before him; and there was given him dominion, and glory, and a kingdom, that all people, nations and languages, should serve him: his dominion is an everlasting dominion, which shall not pass away, and his kingdom that which shall not be destroyed," Dan. 7:10, 13, 14. He comes, then, to dispossess the usurper, and to take possession of his kingdom. The next representation, then, symbolizes the coming of:

The King and his Armies.

"And I saw heaven opened, and behold, a white horse: and he who sat on him was called Faithful and True, and in righteousness he judgeth and maketh war. His eyes were like a flame of fire, and on his head were many diadems; and he had a name written which no one knew except himself. And he was clothed with a garment dipped in blood: and his name is called The Word of God. And the armies in heaven followed him on white horses, clothed in fine linen, white and clean. And from his mouth goeth forth a sharp sword, that he may smite the nations with it: and he will rule them with a rod of iron: and he treadeth the wine-press of the furious wrath of God, the Almighty. And he hath on his garment and on his thigh a name written, KING OF KINGS AND LORD OF LORDS." Rev. 19:11-16.

According to the significance of symbolic language, Christ is here represented as coming personally. The heavens open and he appears in resplendent majesty, in accordance with the predictions respecting his second advent. When the clouds of heaven had received the ascending Saviour, the shining ones who stood by said to the gazing disciples, "This same Jesus which is taken up from you into heaven, shall so come in like manner as ye have seen him go into heaven," Acts 1:11. "And they shall see the Son of man coming in the clouds of heaven with power and great glory," Matt. 24:30. "Behold, he cometh with clouds; and every eye shall see him, and they also which pierced him: and all kindreds of the earth shall wail because of him," Rev. 1:7.

The white horse of the King, and those of his armies, are symbols of the pomp and grandeur of their descent, and show that they will triumph in victory.

The names ascribed to the descending Monarch are applicable only to Christ. He was "the Faithful and True Witness" who commanded John to write "to the angel of the church of the Laodiceans," (3:14); for he who commanded John to "write in a book and send it unto the seven churches" of Asia (1:11), was the One whom John saw "in the midst of the seven candlesticks, like unto the Son of man" (1:13), and who announced himself as "the Alpha and Omega, the beginning and the ending, saith the Lord, which is, and which was, and which is to come--the Almighty," 1:8. "The Word of God," was the "Word" that was "in the beginning," that "was with God," and that "was God," the same that was "in the beginning with God," and which "was made flesh and dwelt among us, and we beheld his glory, the glory as of the only begotten of the Father, full of grace and truth," John 1:1-14. Jesus is "the Lamb of God which taketh away the sin of the world," (Ib., 29); and "the Lamb" "is Lord of lords and King of kings," 17:14. It is "Jesus Christ, who is the faithful witness, and the first begotten of the dead, and the Prince of the kings of the earth," (1:5); and he alone is possessed of that incomprehensible "Name" which no man knoweth, and which he hath promised to write on "him that overcometh," 3:12.

That the visible and personal coming of Christ, and not any providential interposition, is here symbolized, is self-evident. For, while no created object can adequately symbolize Him, it would derogate from the dignity of his character and position to be a symbol of some inferior object. In all mere providential interpositions, foreshown by symbolic imagery, the predicted events are represented by corresponding acts of symbolic agents. War between nations is symbolized by beasts, representatives of the nations, contending with each other. (See Dan. 8th chap.) Pestilence and famine are symbolized by analogous results, and not by Christ's appearing. When, therefore, he is seen coming in person, it must symbolize his personal advent.

His eyes "as a flame of fire," show his identity with the one "like unto the Son of man" in the "midst of the seven candlesticks" (1:13), the author of the message to "the church in Thyatira;" which "things saith the Son of God, who hath his eyes like unto a flame of fire, and his feet like unto fine brass," 2:18.

His "many crowns" are symbols of his sovereignty. Rome undivided and mistress of the world, when symbolized by the seven-headed and ten-horned dragon, is represented with the crowns on the heads, which were the seven successive kinds of government by which its sovereignty was enforced, 12:3, and 17:9, 10. But when its imperial had given place to its decem-regal form, and it is to be shown under the government of ten contemporaneous kingdoms, "the crowns," the symbols of sovereignty, are represented as encircling the "horns" of the beast, 13:1. So, when "the King of kings" cometh, to take to himself his great power, and to reign, and "the kingdoms of this world are become those of our Lord and of his Christ" (11:15, 17), He, "the head of all principality and power" (Col. 2:10), at whose name "every knee should bow" (Phil. 2:9), is shown the wearer of "many crowns."

"Come, then, and, added to thy many crowns, Receive yet one, the crown of all the Earth, Thou who alone art worthy! It was thine By ancient covenant, ere nature's birth; And thou hast made it thine by purchase since, And overpaid its value with thy blood." Cowper's Task.

His "vesture dipped in blood" is symbolic of his coming to tread "the wine-press of the fierceness and wrath of Almighty God" (19:15), when he shall "smite the nations," and "rule them with a rod of iron," (Ib.) Thus Isaiah prophesied: "Who is this that cometh from Edom, with dyed garments from Bozrah? this that is glorious in his apparel, travelling in the greatness of his strength? I that speak in righteousness, mighty to save. Wherefore art thou red in thine apparel, and thy garments like him that treadeth in the wine-fat? I have trodden the wine-press alone; and of the people there was none with me: for I will tread them in mine anger, and trample them in my fury; and their blood shall be sprinkled upon my garments, and I will stain all my raiment. For the day of vengeance is in my heart, and the year of my redeemed is come. And I looked, and there was none to help; and I wondered that there was none to uphold: therefore mine own arm brought salvation unto me; and my fury, it upheld me. And I will tread down the people in mine anger, and make them drunk in my fury, and I will bring down their strength to the earth," Isa. 63:1-6.

The "armies" which follow him, symbolize the attending saints and angels who will accompany his advent. They are all "clothed in fine linen, white and clean," which constituted the wedding garments of those who were called to the marriage-supper of the Lamb, and which was worn by those who had washed their robes, and made them white in his blood, (7:14); "for the fine linen is the righteousness of saints," 19:8. The righteous being caught up in the clouds to meet the Lord in the air (1 Thess. 4:17), "when Christ, who is our life shall appear," they will "appear with him in glory," (Col. 3:4); so that "the Lord my God shall come and all the saints with thee," Zech. 14:5. "Enoch also, the seventh from Adam, prophesied of these, saying, Behold, the Lord cometh with ten thousand of his saints, to execute judgment upon all, and to convince all that are ungodly among them of all their ungodly deeds which they have ungodly committed, and of all their hard speeches which ungodly sinners have spoken against him," Jude 14, 15.

Not only saints, but angels also, will attend his coming. For "when the Son of man shall come in his glory," there will be "all the holy angels with him," Matt. 25:31. "He cometh in the glory of his Father, with the holy angels," Mark 8:38. "The Lord Jesus shall be revealed from heaven with his mighty angels," 2 Thess. 1:7.

The "sharp sword," going out of his mouth, must be a symbol of his word. He speaks, and it is done, Psa. 33:9. "For the word of God is quick and powerful, and sharper than any two-edged sword, piercing even to the dividing asunder of soul and spirit, and of the joints and marrow, and is a discerner of the thoughts and intents of the heart," Heb. 4:12. As "he shall smite the earth with the rod of his mouth, and with the breath of his lips shall he slay the wicked," (Isa. 11:4); and as "the Lord shall consume" "that Wicked" one "with the spirit of his mouth" (2 Thess. 2:8), it follows that the sword proceeding out of his mouth is a symbol of the words he shall speak for their destruction; for with it he smites the nations, 19:15. And this he does when he comes to "rule them with a rod of iron" (Ib.) and tread them in "the wine-press" of the wrath of God. This brings us to the object of his coming, which is to "judge and make war," 19:11.

And first, "To judge." This proves, that Christ's second advent is here symbolized; for, as before quoted, he is to "judge the quick and the dead at his appearing and kingdom," 2 Tim. 4:1. This is at the sounding of the seventh trumpet, for then is "the time of the dead that they should be judged," 11:18. "With righteousness shall he judge the poor, and reprove with equity for the meek of the earth," when he "shall smite the earth with the rod of his mouth, and with the breath of his lips shall he slay the wicked," Isa. 11:4. "Let the heavens rejoice, and let the earth be glad; let the sea roar, and the fulness thereof. Let the field be joyful, and all that is therein: then shall all the trees of the wood rejoice before the Lord: for he cometh to judge the earth: he shall judge the world with righteousness, and the people with truth," Psa. 96:11-13. He cometh "to execute judgment upon all," Jude 15.

To "make war." That this is another object of his coming, is shown by:

The Final Conflict.

"And I saw an angel standing in the sun; and he cried with a loud voice, saying to all the birds flying in the midst of heaven, Come! gather yourselves to the great supper of God; that ye may eat the flesh of kings, and the flesh of commanders, and the flesh of the mighty, and the flesh of the horses, and of those who sit on them, and the flesh of all, both free and bond, both small and great. And I saw the wild beast, and the kings of the earth, and their armies, gathered to make war with him, who sat on the horse, and with his army. And the wild beast was taken, and with him the false prophet, who wrought signs in his sight, with which he had deceived those who received the mark of the wild beast, and those who worshipped his image. These two were cast alive into the lake of fire burning with brimstone. And the rest were slain with the sword of him who sat on the horse, which sword goeth forth from his mouth; and all the birds were filled with their flesh." Rev. 19:17-21.

The contest being between the Lord and his armies on the one part, and the wicked nations on the other, the angel seen standing in the sun and performing an important act in connection with the Lord's army, must represent one of his attending angels; for the acts to be performed are to be by their instrumentality: "In the end of this world, the Son of man shall send forth his angels, and they shall gather out of his kingdom all things that offend, and them which do iniquity; and shall cast them into a furnace of fire," Matt. 13:40-42.

His crying to the fowls of heaven to come and sup on the bodies of the slain, is indicative of the certainty of victory and of the entire overthrow of those who war against the Lamb. As birds gather on fields of slaughter to feast on the slain, so a cry to "all the fowls of heaven" is expressive of the extent and thoroughness of the destruction to be inflicted. It is the same cry which is made in Ezekiel, 39:17, when the armies of Gog are slain on the mountains of Israel. The beast and the kings of the earth symbolize the various governments in the world. The "beast" is that which had seven heads and ten horns (13:1, and 17:3), and was a symbol of Rome in its decem-regal form. It was said of this beast, it shall "go into perdition," (17:8); so that under some manifestation, it must continue till the end of the world: the earth being "reserved unto fire against the day of judgement, and perdition of ungodly men," 2 Pet. 3:7. As only in its divided form, the Roman empire continues till then, the beast is here significant of the divisions represented by its ten horns--the governments of modern Europe. "These shall war with the Lamb, and the Lamb shall overcome them: for he is Lord of lords and King of kings; and they that are with him are called and chosen and faithful," 17:14.

"The false prophet," which is taken with the beast, is described as the one "that wrought miracles before him, with which he deceived them that had received the mark of the beast and them that worshipped his image," v. 20. This identifies him as the two-horned beast of Rev. 13. (13:11-17). The two-horned beast being a representative of the Eastern Roman empire, when that was subverted by the Turks it became the seat of the false prophet,--the Mahometan hierarchy.

The kings of the earth must be the remaining governments which are not represented by those two. By their subsequently warring with the Lamb, it follows that the previous resurrection and translation of the saints does not produce a cessation of all government. Those events may not be apparent to all eyes; or they may serve only to madden the unbelieving, and to make them more desperate in their infidelity.

They gather their armies to war against the Lamb. They resist his authority. They will not have Him to reign over them. They are instigated to oppose him by "unclean spirits like frogs" (16:13), which are the spirits of devils [demons, understood by the Jews to be spirits of the wicked dead] working miracles, which go forth unto the kings of the earth and of the whole world, to gather them to the battle of that great day of God Almighty, Ib. v. 14. This is when Christ is to "come as a thief;" and they are to be gathered "into a place called in the Hebrew tongue Armageddon," 16:15, 16. This was the name of the valley at the foot of Mount Megiddo (Judg. 5:19), which was famous as a valley of slaughter. In it Jehu fought against Ahaziah and Joram, and slew both the kings of Israel and Judah, 2 Kings 9:27. It was afterwards memorable for the death of king Josiah, when Pharaoh-necho fought against him, (2 Kings 23:29); so that the mourning as "in the valley of Megiddon," became a proverbial expression in Israel for great mourning, Zech. 12:11,12. It is therefore significantly applied to the final battle.

Thus do "the kings of the earth set themselves, and the rulers take counsel together against the Lord, and against his Anointed;" but "He that sitteth in the heavens shall laugh; the Lord shall have them in derision." For the decree has gone forth: "I shall give thee the heathen for thine inheritance, and the uttermost parts of the earth for thy possession. Thou shalt break them with a rod of iron; thou shalt dash them in pieces like a potter's vessel," Ps. 2:2-9. In this victory the saints, also, have a part; for it is written: "He that overcometh, and keepeth my works unto the end, to him will I give power over the nations, and he shall rule them with a rod of iron; as the vessels of a potter shall they be broken to shivers: even as I received of my Father," 2:26, 27.

As thus predicted, in this final conflict the nations are smitten, 19:15. Those symbolized by the beast and false prophet are cast alive into the burning flame; i.e., the individuals constituting the bodies of those beasts are cast therein: their governments cease when taken by the Lamb and his armies. This is in accordance with what Daniel saw, who "beheld, even till the beast was slain, and his body destroyed and given to the burning flame," Dan. 7:11.

"The remnant" also are slain; so that there are none left alive on the earth of all the wicked. Thus Daniel interpreted to king Nebuchadnezzar his dream: "Thou sawest till that a stone was cut out without hands, which smote the image [representing the governments of earth] upon his feet, that were of iron and clay, and brake them to pieces. Then was the iron, the clay, the brass, the silver, and the gold broken to pieces together, and became like the chaff of the summer threshing-floors; and the wind carried them away, that no place was found for them," Dan. 2:34, 35. It will "break in pieces, and consume all these kingdoms" (Ib.), according to the prediction: "The nation and kingdom that will not serve thee shall perish; yea, those nations shall be utterly wasted," Isa. 60:12. "And this shall be the plague wherewith the Lord will smite all the people which have fought against Jerusalem: Their flesh shall consume away while they stand upon their feet, and their eyes shall consume away in their holes, and their tongues shall consume away in their mouth," Zech. 14:12. "For, behold, the day cometh, that shall burn as an oven; and all the proud, yea, and all that do wickedly shall be stubble, and the day that cometh shall burn them up, saith the Lord of hosts, that it shall leave them neither root nor branch," Mal. 4:1. "Behold, the day of the Lord cometh, cruel both with wrath and fierce anger, to lay the land desolate: and he shall destroy the sinners thereof out of it," Isa. 13:9. Thus will the Saviour come "in flaming fire, taking vengeance on them that know not God, and obey not the gospel of our Lord Jesus Christ; who shall be punished with everlasting destruction, from the presence of the Lord, and from the glory of his power, when he comes to be glorified in his saints, and to be admired in all them that believe in that day," (2 Thess. 1:8-10): saying to the nations on his left, "Depart from me ye cursed, into everlasting fire, prepared for the devil and his angels," Matt. 25:41. Thus will he "gather out of his kingdom all things that offend, and them which do iniquity, and shall cast them into a furnace of fire: there shall be wailing and gnashing of teeth," Ib., 13:41, 42. The destruction of all the wicked from the earth is followed by:

The Binding of Satan.

"And I saw an angel descending from heaven, having the key of the abyss and a great chain in his hand. And he seized the dragon, the old serpent, who is the Devil, and Satan, and bound him a thousand years, and cast him into the abyss, and shut him up, and set a seal over him, that he should deceive the nations no more, till the thousand years were completed; and after that, he must be loosed a short time." Rev. 20:1-3.

The angel descending from heaven, must be a representative of his own order; for at this epoch there are no other orders of beings for him to be a representative of. He therefore symbolizes the angels who are commissioned to "gather out of his kingdom all things that offend," Matt. 13:41.

The "key," "pit," and "chain," symbolize the instruments of restraint and confinement to which Satan is to be subjected; and his being bound and confined symbolize his restraint.

The "Dragon" is expressly called "that old serpent, which is the Devil and Satan." With the appendages of heads and horns--symbols of political sovereignty--he is used in Rev. 12:3, as a symbol of the Roman civil power, under Pagan rule; and in verse 7, when divested of political insignia, of the pagan hierarchy. But now, as the beast, another symbol of Roman civil rule, has been cast into "the lake of fire and brimstone," and the "remnant" are "slain with the sword" (19:21), there are no analogous powers remaining on earth for him to be a representative of, and consequently he is here represented as a symbol of himself.

Of his identity there can be no question: He is "that Old Serpent," who, being "more subtle than any beast of the field which the Lord God had made" (Gen. 3:1), "beguiled Eve through his subtlety," 2 Cor. 11:3. He is also the Devil, by whom our Saviour was tempted in the wilderness, (Matt. 4:1-12); and the Satan, whose working is "with all power and signs and lying wonders," 2 Thess. 2:9. He is our adversary the devil, who, "as a roaring lion, walketh about seeking whom he may devour," (1 Pet. 5:8); and against whom we are to guard continually, "lest Satan should get an advantage of us," 2 Cor. 2:11.

With the fall, the promise was given that his head should in due time be bruised, and he is not ignorant of his doom; for when the legion saw the Saviour about to dispossess them of the two men among the tombs, they recognized him as "the Son of God," and cried, "Art thou come hither to torment us before the time?" (Matt. 8:29); "and they besought him, that he would not command them to go out into the deep,"--the pit, or abyss, Luke 8:31. The epoch when he should be there confined, is also shown by Isaiah to be when "the Lord cometh out of his place to punish the inhabitants of the earth for their iniquity," when "the earth also shall disclose her blood, and no more cover her slain," Isa. 26:21. For "in that day the Lord with his sore and great and strong sword shall punish leviathan [the dragon], the piercing serpent, even leviathan that crooked serpent," Ib. 27:1. This synchronizes with the slaying of the remnant with the sword, when Satan is bound and cast into the abyss, to continue there a thousand years.

His being bound and confined must symbolize his dejection to a position where he can have no possible influence over the nations during the time he is bound. It can be no partial restraint, as some theologians hold; for that is contrary to the conditions of the symbolic representation. His restraint is full, complete, and entire. Consequently his influence, for the time being, will have entirely ceased. The period of his confinement, therefore, cannot be one of partial exemption from sin; but the living will be perfectly free from all its contagious influences. He is to deceive the nations no more, till the thousand years shall be fulfilled.

"The nations" who are freed from his influences, and also those whom he is subsequently to deceive, are not, necessarily, organized political bodies, under civil rulers, as they now exist. The original term, {~GREEK SMALL LETTER EPSILON~}{~GREEK SMALL LETTER THETA~}{~GREEK SMALL LETTER NU~}{~GREEK SMALL LETTER OMICRON~} {~GREEK SMALL LETTER FINAL SIGMA~}, is defined by Robinson to be "a multitude, people, race, belonging and living together." At this epoch, the national organizations having disappeared, and the people constituting them being translated or slain, the only nations remaining will be "the nations of them which are saved" (21:24), over whom the influence of Satan will have ceased forever; and those constituting "the rest of the dead" (20:5), who will not live again till the end of the thousand years--at the very time when Satan is to be loosed from his prison to go out to deceive them, 20:7, 8.

The Cleansing of the Earth.

There is, in the Apocalypse, no symbolic representation of the act of the cleansing of the earth, yet various scriptures show that it is at the epoch of the second advent, and of the establishment of the kingdom of God. If so, it follows the destruction of the wicked and the binding of Satan, while the raised and transfigured saints--constituting "the bride"--are still with the Lord in the clouds of heaven (19:7-9), where they were caught up to meet him in the air, 1 Thess. 4:17.

A restoration of the earth, in connection with the first resurrection, is in accordance with the testimony of scripture, and was the opinion of the ancients. We read in Isaiah: "Behold, I create new heavens and a new earth: and the former shall not be remembered, nor come into mind," Isa. 65:17.

"As for my opinion," saith R. Menasse, a Jewish Rabbi, "I think that after six thousand years, the world shall be destroyed, upon one certain day, or in one hour; that the arches of heaven shall make a stand as immovable; that there will be no more generation or corruption; and that all things by the resurrection shall be renovated, and return to a better condition." He also assures us that "this, without doubt, is the opinion of the most learned Aben Ezra," who looked for it in the new earth of Isa. 65:17.

"Man shall be restored in that time, namely, in the days of the Messiah, to that state in which he was before the first man sinned."--R. Moses Nachmanides in Duet. ?45.

"Although all things were created perfect, yet when the first man sinned, they were corrupted, and will not again return to their congruous state till PHEREZ (i.e., the MESSIAH) comes." "There are six things which shall be restored to their primitive state, viz.: the splendor of man, his life, the height of his stature, the fruits of the earth, the fruits of the trees, and the luminaries, (the sun, moon, and stars.)"--R. Berakyah, in the name of R.

Samuel--Bereshith Rabba, Fol. 11, Col. 3.

"In that time (i.e., of the Messiah) the whole work of creation shall be changed for the better, and shall return into its perfect and pure state, as it was in the time of the first man, before he had sinned."--R. Becai, in Shilcan Orba, Fol. 9, Col. 4, p. 360.

"Theopompus, who flourished three hundred and forty years B. C., relates that the Persian Magi taught that the present state of things would continue 6000 years; after which hades, or death, would be destroyed, and men would live happy," &c. "The opinion of the ancient Jews, on this head, may be gathered from the statement of one of their Rabbins, who said, 'The world endures 6000 years, and in the thousand, or millennium that follows, the enemies of God would be destroyed.' It was in like manner a tradition of the house of Elias, a holy man, who lived about B. C. 200, that the world was to endure 6000 years, and that the righteous, whom God should raise up, would not be turned again into dust. That, by this resurrection, he meant a resurrection prior to the millennium, is manifest from what follows.... It is worthy of remark, that the two ancient authors, whose words have just been quoted, speak of the seventh millennium as 'that day'--the day in which God will renew the world, and in which he alone shall be exalted."--Dis. on Mill. by Bishop Russell, Prof. Eccl. Hist. in the Scottish Epis. Ch.

"The Divine institution of a sabbatical, or seventh year's solemnity among the Jews, has a plain typical reference to the seventh chiliad, or millenary of the world, according to the well known tradition among the Jewish doctors, adopted by many in every age of the Christian Church, that this world will attain to its limit at the end of 6000 years."--Mede.

"The observance of the Sabbath is essential to the faith; for such only as observe the Sabbath confess that the earth will be renewed: because He who created it out of nothing will renew it."--David Kimchi, on Isa. 55:5, quoted by Mede.

"In as many days as this world was made, in so many thousand years it is perfected; for if the day of the Lord be as it were a 1000 years, and in six days those things that are made were finished, it is manifest that the perfecting of those things is in the 6000th year, when anti-Christ, reigning 1260 years, shall have wasted all things in the world, ... then shall the Lord come from heaven in the clouds, with the glory of his Father." Irenæus, Bish. of Lyons, A. D. 178.

"In six thousand years, the Lord will bring all things to an end, ... when iniquity shall be no more, all things being renewed by the Lord."--Epst. of Barnabas, sec. 14, 15.

"Let philosophers know, who number thousands of years, ages since the beginning of the world, that the 6000th year is not yet concluded or ended. But that number being fulfilled, of necessity there must be an end, and the state of human things must be transformed into that which is better."-- Lactantius, B. of Divine Inst., A. D. 310.

Thomas Burnet (Theory of Earth, Lon. 1697) states "that it was the received opinion of the primitive church from the days of the apostles to the council of Nice, that this earth would continue 6000 years, when the resurrection of the just, and conflagration of the earth, would usher in the millennium and reign of Christ on earth."

"God's blessing the Sabbath day, and resting on it from all his works, was a type of that glorious rest that the saints shall have when the six days of this world are fully ended.... He will finish the toil and travail of his saints, with the burden of the beasts and the curse of the ground, and bring all into rest for a thousand years.... None ever saw this world as it was in its first creation but Adam and his wife, neither will any see it until the manifestation of the children of God; i.e., until the redemption or resurrection of the saints."--John Bunyan's Works, vol. 6, pp. 301, 329.

"I expect with Paul a reparation of all the evils caused by sin, for which he represents the creatures as groaning and travailing."--John Calvin, in his "Institutes."

The reformation of the earth "never was, nor yet shall be, till the righteous

King and Judge appear for the restoration of all things."--John Knox.

"The groans of nature in this nether world, Which heaven has heard for ages, have an end. Foretold by prophets, and by poets sung, Whose fire was kindled at the prophet's lamp, The time of rest, the promised Sabbath, comes: Six thousand years of sorrow have well nigh Fulfilled their tardy and disastrous course Over a sinful world; and what remains Of this tempestuous state of human things, Is merely as the working of a sea Before a calm, that rocks itself to rest; For HE, whose car the winds are, and the clouds The dust that waits upon his sultry march, When sin hath moved him, and his wrath is hot, Shall visit earth in mercy; shall descend, Propitious, in his chariot paved with love; And what his storms have blasted and defaced For man's revolt, shall with a smile repair." Cowper's Task.

The above are only a few of many extracts which might be made, showing the faith of the church in past ages; but which are of no weight, only as they are in accordance with the harmony of scriptural testimony.

When man sinned, this earth was cursed for his sake. The Lord said to him, "Cursed is the ground for thy sake; in sorrow shalt thou eat of it all the days of thy life; thorns also and thistles shall it bring forth unto thee, and thou shalt eat the herb of the field; in the sweat of thy face shalt thou eat bread, till thou return unto the ground; for out of it wast thou taken: for dust thou art, and unto dust shalt thou return," Gen. 3:17-19.

Such was the curse to which the whole creation was subjected because man sinned. "For the creature was made subject to vanity, not willingly, but by reason of him who hath subjected the same in hope," Rom. 8:20. And this hope is for a removal of the curse thus inflicted, and a restoration of all things to their original condition.

As the earth was subjected to the curse at the time when man was made subject to death, the removal of the former would naturally be expected at the epoch of the fulfillment of the promise to the just: "I will ransom them from the power of the grave; I will redeem them from death: O death I will be thy plagues; O grave I will be thy destruction," Hos. 13:14. And thus

Paul testifies: "For the earnest expectation of the creature waiteth for the manifestation of the sons of God, ... Because the creature itself, also, shall be delivered from the bondage of corruption into the glorious liberty of the children of God. For we know that the whole creation groaneth and travaileth in pain together until now. And not only they, but ourselves also, which have the first fruits of the Spirit, even we ourselves groan within ourselves, waiting for the adoption, to wit, the redemption of our body," Rom. 8:19, 21-23.

The removal of the curse removes also its consequences. Thus it is promised: "Instead of the thorn shall come up the fir tree, and instead of the briar shall come up the myrtle tree," Isa. 55:13. "The inhabitant shall not say I am sick: the people that dwell therein shall be forgiven their iniquity," Isa. 33:24. "He will swallow up death in victory; and the Lord God will wipe away tears from off all faces; and the rebuke of his people will he take away from off all the earth; for the Lord hath spoken it," Isa. 25:8. "For behold, I create new heavens and a new earth," Isa. 65:17. "And there shall be no more curse," Rev. 22:3. "For the Lord shall comfort Zion: he will comfort all her waste places; and he will make her wilderness like Eden, and her desert like the garden of the Lord; joy and gladness shall be found therein, thanksgiving, and the voice of melody," Isa. 51:3.

The removal of the curse is called "the regeneration" (Matt. 19:28), "the times of refreshing," and of "restitution;" which Peter places at the advent of Christ: "whom the heavens must receive until the times of restitution(10) of all things, which God hath spoken by the mouth of all his holy prophets since the world began," Acts 3:21. He also places it at "the perdition of ungodly men," which must synchronize with the epoch when the beast "goeth into perdition" (17:11), and "the remnant" are "slain with the sword," (19:21); "when the Lord Jesus shall be revealed from heaven, with his mighty angels, in flaming fire taking vengeance on them that know not God, and that obey not the gospel of our Lord Jesus Christ," 2 Thess. 1:7, 8. Says Peter: "The heavens and the earth, which are now, by the same word ['whereby the world that then was, being overflowed with water, perished' v. 6] are kept in store, reserved unto fire, against the day of judgment, and perdition of ungodly men.... But the day of the Lord will come, as a thief in the night; in the which the heavens shall pass away with a great noise, and the elements shall melt with fervent heat, the earth also; and the works that are therein shall be burned up.... Nevertheless, we, according to his promise, look for new heavens and a new earth, wherein dwelleth righteousness," i.e., "righteous persons"--Horsely, 2 Pet. 3:7-13. This harmonizes with the day that "cometh that shall burn as an oven," when "all the proud, yea, and all that do wickedly" shall be burned up, and become "ashes under the soles" of those on whom "shall the Sun of righteousness arise," (Mal. 4:1-3); which must be the time intervening between the resurrection of the righteous and that of the wicked. This also harmonizes with the testimony of our Saviour, that when, "in the end of this world," He "shall send forth his angels and gather out of his kingdom all things that offend, and them which do iniquity, and shall cast them into a furnace of fire; ... then shall the righteous shine forth as the sun in the kingdom of their Father," Matt. 13:40-43.

The earth being cleansed, and all things made new, it will have been prepared for the "dwelling" of "righteous persons" (2 Pet. 3:13), who,-- having "put on incorruption" (1 Cor. 15:53), and been "caught up ... in the clouds to meet the Lord in the air" (1 Thess. 4:17), where, constituting "the bride," "the Lamb's wife," they were "called unto the marriage supper of the Lamb" (19:7-9),--will descend from heaven to take possession. Thus John writes, that one of the angels said to him: "Come hither, I will show thee the bride, the Lamb's wife. And he carried me away in the spirit to a great and high mountain, and he showed me that great city, the holy Jerusalem, descending out of heaven from God," 21:9, 10.

"Lo, what a glorious sight appears To our believing eyes: The earth and seas are passed away, And the old rolling skies!

From the third heaven where God resides, That holy, happy place, The New Jerusalem comes down Adorned with shining grace.

Attending angels shout for joy, And the bright armies sing, Mortals, behold the sacred seat Of your descending King."--Watts.

The Kingdom given to the Saints at the resurrection of the just.

"And I saw thrones, and they sat on them, and judgment was given for them: and I saw the persons of those beheaded for the testimony of Jesus, and for the word of God, and those, who had not worshipped the wild beast, nor his image, nor had received the mark on their forehead, or on their hand; and they lived and reigned with Christ the thousand years. But the rest of the dead lived not until the thousand years were completed. This is the first resurrection. Happy and holy is he, who bath part in the first resurrection: on such, the second death hath no power, but they will be priests of God and of Christ, and will reign with him a thousand years!" Rev. 20:4-6.

"Thrones" are symbols of power. As the saints are to reign with Christ on the renewed earth, in obedience to the invitation: "Come ye blessed of my Father, inherit the kingdom prepared for you from the foundation of the world," (Matt. 25:34); their being inducted into the kingdom is symbolized by their being seated on thrones. Thus they sing in the "new song," addressed to Christ: "Thou wast slain, and hast redeemed us to God by thy blood, out of every kindred, and tongue, and people, and nation, and hast made us unto our God kings and priests: and we shall reign on the earth," 5:9, 10. In the first chapter, also, all who ascribe praises to "Him that loved us, and washed us from our sins in his own blood," also add: "and hath made us kings and priests unto God, and his Father," 1:5, 6.

All the saints being thus exalted to kingly and priestly dignity, symbolizes the exalted rank they are to hold in the new creation--the symbols of their station being taken from the most exalted offices known on earth. Thus God said to ancient Israel: "Ye shall be unto me a kingdom of priests, and a holy nation," (Ex. 19:6); and the Christian church is addressed as "a chosen generation, a royal priesthood, a holy nation, a peculiar people," 1 Pet. 2:9.

The time when the saints shall reign on the earth is in connection with the destruction of the "little horn" of Daniel's "fourth beast," which, as he saw, "made war with the saints and prevailed against them, until the Ancient of days came, and judgment was given to the saints of the Most High, and the time came that the saints possessed the kingdom," Dan. 7:21, 22. "The saints of the Most High shall take the kingdom, and possess the kingdom forever, even forever and ever," Ib. v. 18. "And the kingdom and dominion and the greatness of the kingdom under the whole heaven, shall be given to the people of the saints of the Most High, whose kingdom is an everlasting kingdom, and all dominions shall serve and obey him," Ib. v. 27. "And they shall reign forever and ever," 22:5. Thus the Saviour said: "Fear not, little flock; for it is your Father's good pleasure to give you the kingdom," Luke 12:32.

Those who receive the kingdom are symbolized by the souls of martyrs, &c., living again and reigning with Christ. The symbol includes, with the martyred saints, those who had stood aloof from the worship of the beast and his image, and those who had not received his mark; who are shown by a parallel scripture to represent all who are redeemed to God "out of every kindred, and tongue, and people, and nation," 5:9, 10. Some of these were symbolized, under the fifth seal, as crying from under the altar in anticipation of this day, 6:9. Now, with "their fellow servants," they receive their reward.

The souls of the departed living again, can only symbolize those who have been subjected to death, and are again raised. Consequently they are the subjects of a real resurrection. And this is shown by the explanation of the symbol, which affirms that, "This is the first resurrection."

It is denied by many that a literal resurrection is here taught; but in so doing they deny the faith of the church in its best and purest ages. In the first two centuries after Christ, there was not an individual, who believed in any resurrection of the dead whose name or memory has survived to the present time, who denied that the resurrection of the just is here taught.

Eusebius, who opposed this view, quotes Papias, who he admits was a disciple of St. John and a companion of Polycarp, as saying that "after the resurrection of the dead the kingdom of Christ shall be established corporeally on this earth." And Jerome, another opposer, quotes from him that "he had the apostles for his authors; and that he considered what

Andrew, what Peter said, what Philip, what Thomas said, and other disciples of the Lord."

Polycarp was another of John's disciples; and Irenæus testifies in an epistle to Florinus, that he had seen Polycarp, "who related his conversation with John and others who had seen the Lord, and how he related their sayings, and the things he had heard of them concerning the Lord, both concerning his miracles and doctrine, as he had received them from the Lord of life; all of which Polycarp related agreeable to the scriptures." Following such a teacher, Irenæus taught that at the resurrection of the just, the meek should inherit the earth; and that then would be fulfilled the promise which God made to Abraham.

Justin Martyr, born A. D. 89, says that, "A certain man among us, whose name is John, being one of the twelve apostles of Christ, in that Revelation which was shown him, prophesied that those who believe in our Christ shall fulfil a thousand years at Jerusalem." He affirms that himself "and many others are of this mind"--"that Christ shall reign personally on earth;" and that "all who were accounted orthodox so believed."

Tertullian, about A. D. 180, says it was a custom for Christians to pray that they might have part in the first resurrection. And Cyprian, about 220, says that Christians "had a thirst for martyrdom that they might obtain a better resurrection."

Mosheim assures us that the opinion "that Christ was to come and reign 1000 years among men," had, before the time of Origen, about the middle of the 3d century, "met with no opposition." And it is the testimony of ecclesiastical historians, that the first who opposed it, seeing no way of avoiding the meaning of the words in Rev. 20th, denied the authenticity of the Apocalypse, and claimed that it was written by one Cerenthus, a heretic, for the very purpose of sustaining what they called "his fiction of the reign of Christ on earth." This doctrine is not now evaded in this way, but by spiritualizing the language of the Apocalypse, and thus finding a meaning in it which is not expressed by any of the admitted laws of language. Theologians who thus reason make the first resurrection the conversion of the world. But those who are affirmed to be raised, are persons who have lived and are dead. If the resurrection is a mere metaphor, then the martyrs must have metaphorically died, and must have comprised only those who had been previously converted and were fallen away. The rest of the dead must then be understood as persons morally dead, which would be inconsistent with the idea of a converted world. Those who were raised being those who were previously converted, they must have been literally dead, and the only resurrection predicable of such is a literal resurrection.

The Bible teaches such a resurrection of the righteous prior to that of the wicked. Thus the Psalmist says of them: "Like sheep they are laid in the grave; death shall feed on them, and the upright shall have dominion over them in the morning." But of himself he says: "But God will redeem my soul from the power of the grave," Psa. 49:14, 15. Of the wicked Isaiah testifies: "They are dead, they shall not live; they are deceased, they shall not rise," i.e. with the righteous; but to Zion he says: "Thy dead men shall live, together with my dead body shall they arise. Awake and sing, ye that dwell in the dust: for thy dew is as the dew of herbs, and the earth shall cast out her dead," Isa. 26:14, 19. To the same import is the prophecy of Daniel, respecting the time when Michael shall stand up, and "thy people shall be delivered, every one that shall be found written in the book. And many of them that sleep in the dust of the earth shall awake, some, [the awakened, shall be] to everlasting life, and some, [the unawakened, shall be] to shame and everlasting contempt," Dan. 12:1, 2. Such, according to Prof. Bush, is the precise rendering of the original.

The New Testament also teaches a resurrection of the just, in distinction from that of the wicked. Paul says, while all are to be made alive, that it will be "every man in his own order," or band--"Christ the first fruits; afterwards they that are Christ's at his coming," 1 Cor. 15:23. None others are spoken of as being raised at that epoch. When the Lord descends from heaven with a shout, at the trump of God, not the entire mass of the dead, but "the dead in Christ shall rise first," before the righteous living are changed, 1 Thess. 4:16. In accordance with this priority in the resurrection of the righteous, Paul teaches that the worthies who died in faith "accepted not deliverance, that they might obtain a better resurrection," (Heb. 11:13); and himself, he says, counted all things loss for Christ, "if by any means I might attain unto the resurrection of the dead," (Phil. 3:11); which is "the resurrection from among the dead"--it being a resurrection to which some will not attain. Thus also the Saviour taught: while "they that have done good shall come forth at [as it is literally] the resurrection of life, and they that have done evil at the resurrection of damnation" (John 5:29), the two are not co-etaneous; for the righteous shall be "recompensed at the resurrection of the just," Lu. 14:14. That must be the resurrection of which those are the subjects who receive the kingdom; for "flesh and blood cannot inherit the kingdom of God," 1 Cor. 15:50. While "the children of this world marry and are given in marriage," "they which shall be accounted worthy to obtain that world, and the resurrection from the dead, neither marry, nor are given in marriage; neither can they die any more: for they are equal unto the angels, and are the children of God, being the children of the resurrection," Lu. 20:34-36.

The children of the resurrection thus include all who attain unto that world, which, consequently, the wicked do not obtain, and of which the righteous dead and the living saints are made equal subjects, according to Paul's "mystery:" "We shall not all sleep, but we shall all be changed, in a moment, in the twinkling of an eye, at the last trump: for the trumpet shall sound, and the dead shall be raised incorruptible, and we shall be changed," i.e., to the same incorruptible state to which the dead are raised, (1 Cor. 15:50-54); so that all the righteous will alike "bear the image of the heavenly" (v. 49) when they "shall be caught up together" (1 Thess. 4:16) "to meet the Lord in the air."

The resurrection state is that to which the ancients looked for the restoration of Israel.

Rabbi Eliezer the great, supposed to have lived just after the second temple was built, applied Hosea 14:8 to the pious Jews, who seemed likely to die without seeing the glory of Israel, saying: "As I live, saith Jehovah, I will raise you up, in the resurrection of the dead; and I will gather you with all Israel."

The Sadducees are reported to have asked Rabbi Gamaliel, the preceptor of

Paul, whence he would prove that God would raise the dead, who quoted Deut. 9:21: "Which land the Lord sware that he would give to your fathers." He argued, as Abraham, Isaac and Jacob had it not, and as God cannot lie, that they must be raised from the dead to inherit it.

Rabbi Simai, though of later date, argues the same from Ex. 6:4, insisting that the law asserts in this place the resurrection from the dead, when it said: "And also I have established my covenant with them, to give them the Canaan;" for, he adds, "it is not said to you, but to them."

Mennasseh Ben Israel says: "It is plain that Abraham and the rest of the patriarchs did not possess that land; it follows, therefore, that they must be raised in order to enjoy the promised good, as otherwise the promises of God would be vain and false."--De Resurrec. Mort., L. i., c. 1. ?4.

Rabbi Saahias Gaion, commenting on Dan. 12:2, says: "This is the resuscitation of the dead Israel, whose lot is eternal life, and those who shall not awake are the forsakers of Jehovah."

"In the world to come," says the Sahar, fol. 81, "the blessed God will vivify the dead and raise them from their dust, so that they shall be no more an earthly structure."

Thus "Abraham, when he was called to go out into a place which he should after receive for an inheritance ... sojourned in the land of promise, as in a strange country, dwelling in tabernacles, with Isaac and Jacob, the heirs with him of the same promise; for he looked for a city which hath foundations, whose builder and maker is God," Heb. 11:8-10. While he dwelt in that land, God "gave him none inheritance in it, no, not so much as to set his foot on; yet he promised that he would give it to him for a possession, and to his seed after him," Acts 7:5. This was also true of all those "who died in faith, not having received the promises, but having seen them afar off, and were persuaded of them, and embraced them, and confessed that they were strangers and pilgrims on the earth,"--desiring "a better country, that is, a heavenly" (Heb. 11:13-16), "not accepting deliverance, that they might obtain a better resurrection" (v. 35), "God having provided some better thing for us, that they without us should not be made perfect," v. 40.

When the promises are thus made good to Israel, all who are of the faith of Abraham will participate in the same promises. For "Christ hath redeemed us from the curse of the law ... that the blessing of Abraham might come on the Gentiles through Jesus Christ." "And if ye be Christ's, then are ye Abraham's seed, and heirs according to the promise," Gal. 3:13, 14, 29. So the Saviour said to the Jews: "Many shall come from the east and west, and shall sit down with Abraham, and Isaac, and Jacob, in the kingdom of heaven; but the children of the kingdom [unregenerate Jews] shall be cast into outer darkness," Matt. 8:11, 12. And then, as the Saviour said to the twelve: "Ye which have followed me, in the regeneration when the Son of man shall sit in the throne of his glory, ye also shall sit upon twelve thrones, judging the twelve tribes of Israel," Matt. 19:28.

"The rest of the dead," who live not again till the thousand years are ended, must be the wicked dead; for, the righteous being raised, no other dead ones remain. They include all the wicked, who have died in all ages, and "the remnant" who "are slain with the sword" (19:21), when the kingdom is cleansed from all things that offend.

"The thousand years" to intervene between the two resurrections, are regarded by some as a symbol of 360,000 years. There seems to be no necessity for such an interpretation. When time is symbolized, it is always proportioned to the duration of the other symbols used. Thus, in Dan. 8th, when beasts symbolize kingdoms, it would have been incongruous to have specified the duration of the vision in literal years; for beasts do not continue during centuries, as the kingdoms symbolized by them have done. But days are proportioned to years, as beasts are to kingdoms; so that there is a fitness in symbolizing the years foreshadowed in that vision, by 2300 days; between which measure of time and the duration of the existence of beasts, there is a perfect congruity.

In the 4th of Daniel, where the cutting down of a tree is used to symbolize the loss of the king's reason, there is no such disproportion between the duration of man's existence and that of a tree, as there is between the life of a beast and that of an empire. And therefore there is no incongruity if the time specified is a symbol of literal time, i.e., if a time is used to symbolize a year. In this case, the seven years could not have been symbolized by seven days; for there is no marked disproportion between the duration of the other symbols in connection, and the things symbolized; and had days been used, days must have been understood in the fulfilment.

There might be either 1000 years, or 360,000, between the first and second resurrections, without conflicting with any other Scripture. But there is no disproportion between the other symbols and the things symbolized,--the living again of the martyrs in vision, and their actual resurrection; and therefore the 1000 years need not, by any parallel usage or law of language, be understood, to be other than a literal thousand.

The Wicked Raised, and Satan Loosed

"And when the thousand years are completed, Satan will be loosed out of his prison, and will go out to deceive the nations in the four corners of the earth, Gog and Magog, to gather them to battle: the number of whom is like the sand of the sea. And they ascended on the breadth of the earth, and encompassed the camp of the saints, and the beloved city: and fire descended from God out of heaven, and devoured them. And the devil, who deceived them, was cast into the lake of fire and brimstone, where both the wild beast and the false prophet are, and will be tormented day and night for ever and ever. And I saw a great white throne, and him who sat on it; from whose face the earth and the heaven fled away, and a place was not for them. And I saw the dead, the small and the great, standing before God; and the books were opened: and another book was opened, which is the book of life: and the dead were judged from the things written in the books, according to their works. And the sea gave up the dead in it; and death and the pit gave up the dead in them: and they were judged every one according to their works. And death and the pit were cast into the lake of fire. This is the second death, the lake of fire. And whoever was not found written in the book of life, was cast into the lake of fire." Rev. 20:7-15.

Verses 11-15 contain the record of the symbolization John saw, of what was to transpire at the end of the thousand years; while verses 7-10 appear to be explanatory of events which would then be fulfilled. This explanation, previous to the exhibition of the symbolization, is appropriate in the connection, and makes more forcible the fact that "the rest of the dead lived not again until the thousand years were finished."

As the rest of the dead live not till the end of the thousand years, they come forth at "the resurrection of damnation," at the end of a thousand years of the reign of the saints on the earth, and at the epoch when Satan was to be loosed from his prison. As all who had part in the first resurrection were to be exempted from the power of the second death, the nations who are then deceived by Satan, must be the nations composing the rest of the dead, who live again at that epoch.

Their number "as the sand of the sea," and their coming from "the four quarters of the earth," show that they are no obscure people, living unknown to the saints; and their existence can only be accounted for by the event of a resurrection of the wicked.

Their names, "Gog and Magog,"--those applied to the ancient enemies of Israel, (Ezek. 38:38),--are appropriate titles to designate the subjects of the second resurrection.

They encompass the camp of the saints, and the beloved city--showing that the city descends at the commencement of the thousand years--but there is no battle: before they are permitted to harm the saints, fire from heaven devours them; and the devil that thought to lead them against the holy city, is cast into the lake of fire, where the beast and false prophet were cast at the commencement of the millennium.

In connection with the resurrection of the wicked, is their judgment--not following necessarily in the precise order of the record. The "small and great" who stand before God, are not small and large persons, but those from all stations and ranks in society. The king and the beggar equally receive according to their deserts: They are the bond and the free, the high and the low, the rich and the poor, including those who fought against the Lamb, and were overcome by Him, 19:18.

The open books symbolize the record of their evil deeds, for which they are to be judged. And the "book of Life" is opened to symbolize that the names of those who are judged are not there recorded, and that consequently they are justly condemned. To "him that overcometh," the Saviour promised "I will not blot his name out of this book of life," 3:3.

The sea, death, and hell giving up their dead, indicates that all of the "rest of the dead" are here resurrected, and that none are left out from among whom these are raised, as these were, from whom came forth the subjects of the first resurrection.

The casting of death and hell into the lake of fire, symbolizes the casting in of those who were within their domains; and "the lake of fire," symbolizes the place into which--the impenitent are consigned--which is the "second death."

The New Creation.

"And I saw a new heaven and a new earth: for the first heaven and the first earth were passed away; and the sea was no more. And I saw the holy city, new Jerusalem, descending out of heaven, from God, prepared like a bride adorned for her husband." Rev. 21:1, 2.

The new heaven and new earth are symbols of the new order of things. The old heavens and earth having been dissolved, their elements melting with fervent heat (2 Pet. 3:12), the "new heavens and the new earth, wherein dwelleth righteousness," for which Peter looked, succeed to their place. So much more resplendent are these than the former, that those "shall not be remembered, nor come into mind," i.e., to be desired, Isa. 65:17. This is the eternal state in which we are commanded to be "glad and rejoice forever," when God shall "create Jerusalem a rejoicing, and her people a joy." Then "the voice of weeping shall be no more heard in her, nor the voice of crying." There "the elect shall long enjoy the work of their hands;" for "as the days of a tree, are the days of my people," saith the Lord; who has also declared that, "as the new heavens and the new earth, which I will make, shall remain before me, so shall your seed and your name remain," Isa. 66:22.

The sea is now "no more," in the same sense that the first heavens and earth are passed away--all having disappeared in the conflagration, and given place to the "restitution of all things spoken of by the mouth of all the holy prophets," Acts 3:21. Whether the new creation will comprise both sea and dry land, as was first created (Gen. 1:10), is not here decided; but there is no reason to suppose that this characteristic of the original creation will be forever obliterated.

The new Jerusalem descends, adorned as a bride for her husband. She is shown in the 19th chapter to be "arrayed in fine linen, clean and white"--a symbol of "the righteousness of the saints." As the corrupt Roman hierarchy was symbolized by an adulterous woman (17:3), and also by the corrupt city of Babylon (18:2), so symbols of an opposite character--a chaste bride, and the new Jerusalem--are chosen representatives of the church triumphant, whose Maker is her husband.

Mr. Lord very justly remarks: "The descent of the city is to take place at the commencement of the millennium, manifestly from the representation that the marriage of the Lamb was come, and that his wife had prepared herself, immediately after the destruction of great Babylon, (19:7, 8); from the exhibition of the risen and glorified saints, as seated on thrones, and reigning with Christ during the thousand years; and from the representation of the beloved city as on earth at the revolt of Gog and Magog, after the close of the thousand years."--"Ex. Apoc." p. 529.

"Jerusalem, my happy home, O how I long for thee; When shall my sorrows have an end? Thy joys when shall I see?

"When shall these eyes thy heaven-built walls And pearly gates behold! Thy bulwarks with salvation strong, And streets of shining gold?

"O when, thou city of my God, Shall I thy courts ascend, Where congregations ne'er break up, And Sabbaths have no end?"

The Tabernacle of God with Men.

"And I heard a loud voice out of heaven, saying, Behold, the tabernacle of God is with men, and he will dwell with them, and they will be his people, and God himself will be with them, even their God. And God will wipe away every tear from their eyes; and there will be no more death, nor mourning, nor crying out, nor will there be any more pain: for the former things are passed away. And he who sat on the throne said, Behold, I make all things new. And he said, Write, for these words are faithful and true. And he said to me, It is done. I am the Alpha and the Omega, the beginning and the end. I will give to him, who thirsteth, from the fountain of the water of life freely. He, who overcometh, will inherit these things; and I will be his God, and he will be my son. But the cowardly, and unbelieving, and abominable, and murderers, and fornicators, and sorcerers, and idolaters, and all liars, will have their part in the lake burning with fire and brimstone, which is the second death." Rev. 21:3-8.

The utterances of the "great voice out of heaven" are not what John saw, but are what he heard; and are therefore to be interpreted, not by the laws of symbols, but by those of tropes and literal language.

The "tabernacle of God with men" is explained in the same connection to be his "dwelling with them."

"When our Saviour was incarnate, and vouchsafed to dwell amongst the children of men, the same phrase is used by this same author, Eskeenoose (John 1:14), 'The Word was made flesh, and tabernacled amongst us: and we beheld his glory,' etc. We read it, he dwelt amongst us: but rendered more closely, it is, he set his tabernacle amongst us. And that which the Hebrews call the Shekinah, or divine presence (Maimon, Mor. Nev. par. 1, chap. 25), comes from a word of the like signification, and found with the Greek word here used. Therefore there will be a Shekinah in that kingdom of Christ."--Tho. Burnett.

When Israel first entered the wilderness, God entered into a covenant with them (Ex. 19:3-8), in consequence of which he said to Moses, "Let them make me a sanctuary, that I may dwell among them," (Ex. 25:8)--the pattern of which was shown Moses in the mount; and when completed "the glory of the Lord filled the tabernacle" (Ex. 40:34), and there "the Lord talked with Moses," Ex. 33:9. Thus did God dwell among them while they were in a probationary state; but he indicated a more intimate connection with them, by promising, if they were obedient to his statutes in all things, that "I will set my tabernacle among you: and my soul shall not abhor you. And I will walk among you, and will be your God, and ye shall be my people," Lev. 26:11, 12. This promise was not fulfilled to the Jews, because of their sins; but Paul quotes it (2 Cor. 6:16), and applies it as a promise still to be made good to the church of Christ. Thus, the "Word" that "was God," who was made flesh and tabernacled among us at his incarnation, is again to come and dwell with us in his human tabernacle, as at his first advent. Then will God enter into a new covenant with his people, as he has said: "Behold, the days come, saith the Lord, that I will make a new covenant with the house of Israel, and with the house of Judah; not according to the covenant that I made with their fathers, in the day that I took them by the hand, to bring them out of the land of Egypt, which my covenant they brake, although I was a husband unto them, saith the Lord; but this shall be the covenant that I will make with the house of Israel; After those days, saith the Lord, I will put my law in their inward parts, and write it in their hearts; and will be their God, and they shall be my people. And they shall teach no more every man his neighbor, and every man his brother, saying, Know the Lord: for they shall all know me, from the least of them unto the greatest of them, saith the Lord: for I will forgive their iniquity, and I will remember their sin no more," Jer. 31:31-34.

As the saints, before the resurrection of "the rest of the dead," "reign with Christ 1000 years," (20:4); it follows that during that period the tabernacle of God is with men, when he dwells among them, which is an additional evidence that "the restitution of all things" (Acts 3:21) is at the commencement of the millennium.

This is a tearless state--all tears being then wiped from every eye. Isaiah predicted, when "He will swallow up death in victory," that "the Lord God will wipe away tears from off all faces: and the rebuke of his people shall he take away from off all the earth: for the Lord hath spoken it. And it shall be said in that day, Lo, this is our God; we have waited for him, and he will save us: this is the Lord; we have waited for him, we will be glad and rejoice in his salvation," Isa. 25:8, 9. The commencement of the tearless state is thus placed by Isaiah at the resurrection, and at the appearance of Christ; which is confirmed by Paul, in his inspired commentary on the same, who affirms that at the last trump, "when this corruptible shall have put on incorruption, and this mortal shall have put on immortality, then shall be brought to pass the saying that is written, Death is swallowed up in victory," 1 Cor. 15:54. This state was also promised to the entire company "which came out of great tribulation, and have washed their robes, and made them white in the blood of the Lamb. Therefore are they before the throne of God, and serve him day and night in his temple: and he that sitteth on the throne shall dwell among them. They shall hunger no more, neither thirst any more; neither shall the sun light on them, nor any heat. For the Lamb, which is in the midst of the throne, shall feed them, and shall lead them unto living fountains of waters: and God shall wipe away all tears from their eyes," Rev. 7:14-17.

There shall then "be no more death"--for that "last enemy shall be destroyed" (1 Cor. 15:26), and there shall be nothing to "hurt nor destroy, in all my holy mountain, saith the Lord." Death will have been swallowed up in victory, (Isa. 25:8)--the redeemed having been ransomed "from the power of the grave," Hos. 13:14. "Neither can they die any more: for they are equal unto the angels; and are the children of God, being the children of the resurrection," Luke 20:36.

After the destruction of death, there shall be "neither sorrow, nor crying, neither shall there be any more pain." This was to be when "the ransomed of the Lord shall return, and come to Zion with songs and everlasting joy upon their heads: they shall obtain joy and gladness, and sorrow and sighing shall flee away," Isa. 35:10. And one of these songs was to be: "Thou wast slain, and hast redeemed us to God by thy blood out of every kindred and tongue, and people and nation; and hast made us unto our God kings and priests: and we shall reign on the earth," Rev. 5:9,10.

Then, everything which distinguishes the present world from that, will have passed away; for all things will be created anew. These words, uttered by Him who is the "Alpha and Omega," are no rhetorical flourishes, nor mere figures of speech, but contain the exact and literal truth, and are not to be set aside as unmeaning figures. For He who sat upon the throne has declared: "These words are true and faithful." Faithful is He who hath promised, and he will surely make good his words--bestowing on the righteous the inheritance of all things; and on the wicked, their fearful doom.

The New Jerusalem.

"And there came to me one of the seven angels, who had the seven bowls full of the seven last plagues, and talked with me, saying, Come, I will shew thee the bride, the wife of the Lamb. And he carried me away in spirit to a vast and high mountain, and shewed me the holy city Jerusalem, descending out of heaven from God, having the glory of God. Her light was like a most precious stone, like a jasper stone, clear as crystal; having a wall vast and high, and having twelve gates, and at the gates twelve angels, and names written on the gates, which are the names of the twelve tribes of the sons of Israel. On the east, three gates; on the north, three gates; on the south, three gates; and on the west, three gates. And the wall of the city had twelve foundations, and on them, the twelve names of the twelve apostles of the Lamb. And he, who talked with me, had a golden measuring-reed to measure the city, and its gates, and its wall. And the city lieth square, and the length is as much as the breadth: and he measured the city with the measuring-reed, twelve thousand furlongs. The length, and the breadth, and the height of it are equal. And he measured its wall, a hundred and forty-four cubits, according to the measure of a man, that is, of the angel. And the structure of its wall was jasper: and the city was pure gold, like clear glass. And the foundations of the wall of the city were adorned with every kind of precious stone. The first foundation was a jasper; the second, a sapphire; the third, a chalcedony; the fourth, an emerald; the fifth, a sardonyx; the sixth, a sardius; the seventh, a chrysolite; the eighth, a beryl; the ninth, a topaz; the tenth, a chrysoprasus; the eleventh, a jacinth; the twelfth, an amethyst. And the twelve gates were twelve pearls; each one of the gates was of one pearl; and the wide street of the city was pure gold, like transparent glass." Rev. 21:9-21.

"And he shewed me a pure river of water of life, clear as crystal, proceeding out of the throne of God and the Lamb. In the midst of its wide street, and on each side of the river, was the tree of life, bearing twelve kinds of fruit, yielding its fruit monthly, and the leaves of the tree were for the healing of the nations. And there will be no more curse: but the throne of God and of the Lamb will be in it; and his servants will serve him: and they will see his face; and his name will be on their foreheads. And there will be no night there; and they have no need of the light of a lamp, nor of the light of the sun; for the Lord God giveth them light: and they will reign forever and ever." Rev. 22:1-5.

Objects of great interest, of which only a passing glance was permitted in previous visions, are again and again presented, until their relative glory is sufficiently manifested. Thus the new earth was considered worthy of being the subject of a special vision; and now the Bride, the Lamb's wife, although before referred to, is again made the subject of a special vision, under the symbol of a city, explained to be the bride.

The descent of the city, to harmonize with corresponding scriptures, has been shown to be at the commencement of the millennium, when those who are called to the marriage supper of the Lamb descend from the clouds of heaven, to receive "an inheritance incorruptible, and undefiled, and that fadeth not away, reserved in heaven for you ... ready to be revealed in the last time," 1 Pet. 4:5.

"The glory of the Lord," which is the light of the city, is explained to be "the Lamb" (21:23), which "is the light thereof." "In him was life, and the life was the light of men." "That was the true light which lighteth every man that cometh into the world," John 1:4, 9. In Him dwelleth all the fulness of the Godhead bodily (Col. 2:9), so that as the Holy Shekineh illumined the pathway of ancient Israel, the nations of the redeemed will walk in the light of His glory.

The gates of the city correspond with the number of the tribes of Israel; and the "names of the apostles" are in its foundations. Thus Paul affirms that the "fellow citizens" of "the household of God" are built upon the foundation of the apostles and prophets, Jesus Christ himself being the chief corner-stone, Eph. 2:20.

The dimensions of the city are in length equal to the breadth--and 1500 miles in circumference, or 375 miles square. The length is in all parts equal; and so is the breadth, and the height,--the latter being 216 feet.

Its splendor is fully equal to all that inspiration has recorded respecting those on whom the Lord will have "everlasting kindness;" and to whom he saith: "O thou afflicted, tossed with the tempest, and not comforted! behold, I will lay thy stones with fair colors, and lay thy foundations with sapphires. And I will make thy windows of agates, and thy gates of carbuncles, and all thy borders of pleasant stones. And all thy children shall be taught of the Lord; and great shall be the peace of thy children. In righteousness shalt thou be established: thou shalt be far from oppression; for thou shalt not fear: and from terror; for it shall not come near thee," Isa. 54:11-14. "Therefore thy gates shall be open continually; they shall not be shut day nor night; that men may bring unto thee the forces of the Gentiles, and that their kings may be brought. For the nation and kingdom that will not serve thee shall perish; yea, those nations shall be utterly wasted. The glory of Lebanon shall come unto thee, the fir-tree, the pine-tree, and the box together, to beautify the place of my sanctuary; and I will make the place of my feet glorious. The sons also of them that afflicted thee shall come bending unto thee; and all they that despised thee shall bow themselves down at the soles of thy feet; and they shall call thee, The city of the Lord, The Zion of the Holy One of Israel. Whereas thou hast been forsaken and hated, so that no man went through thee, I will make thee an eternal excellency, a joy of many generations. Thou shalt also suck the milk of the Gentiles, and shalt suck the breast of kings: and thou shalt know that I the Lord am thy Saviour and thy Redeemer, the mighty One of Jacob. For brass I will bring gold, and for iron I will bring silver, and for wood brass, and for stones iron: I will also make thy officers peace, and thine exactors righteousness. Violence shall no more be heard in thy land, wasting nor destruction within thy borders; but thou shalt call thy walls Salvation, and thy gates Praise. The sun shall be no more thy light by day; neither for brightness shall the moon give light unto thee: but the Lord shall be unto thee an everlasting light, and thy God thy glory. Thy sun shall no more go down; neither shall thy moon withdraw itself: for the Lord shall be thine everlasting light, and the days of thy mourning shall be ended. Thy people also shall be all righteous: they shall inherit the land forever, the branch of my planting, the work of my hands, that I may be glorified. A little one shall become a thousand, and a small one a strong nation; I the Lord will hasten it in his time," Isa. 60:11-22.

O scenes surpassing fable, and yet true, Scenes of accomplish'd bliss! which who can see, Though but in distant prospect, and not feel His soul refresh'd with foretaste of the joy? Rivers of gladness water all the Earth, And clothe all climes with beauty. The reproach Of barrenness is past. The fruitful field Laughs with abundance; and the land, once lean, Or fertile only in its own disgrace, Exults to see its thistly curse repeal'd. The various seasons woven into one, And that one season an eternal spring, The garden fears no blight, and needs no fence; For there is none to covet: all are full. The lion, and the libbard, and the bear, Graze with the fearless flocks; all bask at noon Together, or all gambol in the shade Of the same grove, and drink one common stream. Antipathies are none. No foe to man Lurks in the serpent now: the mother sees, And smiles to see, her infant's playful hand Stretch'd forth to dally with the crested worm, To stroke his azure neck, or to receive The lambent homage of his arrowy tongue. All creatures worship man, and all mankind One Lord, one Father. Error has no place; That creeping pestilence is driv'n away: The breath of Heav'n has chas'd it. In the heart No passion touches a discordant string, But all is harmony and love. Disease Is not: the pure and uncontaminate blood Holds its due course, nor fears the frost of age. One song employs all nations; and all cry, "Worthy the Lamb, for he was slain for us!" The dwellers in the vales and on the rocks Shout to each other, and the mountain-tops From distant mountains catch the flying joy; Till, nation after nation taught the strain, Earth rolls the rapturous Hosanna round. Behold the measure of the promise fill'd! See Salem built, the labor of a God! Bright as a sun the sacred city shines: All kingdoms and all princes of the Earth Flock to that light; the glory of all lands Flows into her; unbounded is her joy, And endless her increase. Thy rams are there, Nebaioth, and the flocks of Kedar there: The looms of Ormus, and the mines of Ind, And Saba's spicy groves, pay tribute there. Praise is in all her gates; upon her walls, And in her streets, and in her spacious courts, Is heard salvation. Eastern Java there Kneels with the native of the farthest west; And Æthiopia spreads abroad the hand, And worships. Her report has travel'd forth Into all lands. From ev'ry clime they come To see thy beauty, and to share thy joy, O Sion! an assembly such as Earth Saw never, such as Heav'n stoops down to see. Thus Heav'nward all things tend. For all were once Perfect, and all must be at length restor'd, So God has greatly purpos'd: who would else In his dishonor'd works himself endure Dishonor, and be wrong'd without redress. Haste then, and wheel away a shatter'd world, Ye slow-revolving seasons! we would see (A sight to which our eyes are strangers yet) A world that does not dread and hate his laws, And suffer for its crime; would learn how fair The creature is, that God pronounces good, How pleasant in itself what pleases him.--Cowper.

Final Admonitions.

"And he said to me, These words are faithful and true. And the Lord, the God of the spirits of the prophets, sent his angel to shew his servants the things, which must shortly take place. And behold, I come quickly: happy is he, who keepeth the words of the prophecy of this book. And I John saw and heard these things. And when I had heard and seen, I fell down to worship before the feet of the angel who shewed me these things. And he saith to me, See thou do it not: I am thy fellow-servant, and one of thy brethren the prophets, and one of those, who keep the words of this book: worship God. And he saith to me, Seal not up the words of the prophecy of this book: for the season is near. He, who is unjust, let him be unjust still: and he, who is filthy, let him be filthy still: and he, who is righteous, let him perform righteousness still: and he, who is holy, let him be holy still. Behold, I come quickly; and my reward is with me, to give each one as his work shall be. I am the Alpha and the Omega, the first and the last, the beginning and the end. Happy are those, who do his commandments, that they may have the privilege of the tree of life, and may enter through the gates into the city. For without are the Sodomites, and the sorcerers, and the fornicators, and the murderers, and the idolaters, and whoever loveth and practiseth falsehood. I Jesus have sent mine angel to testify to you these things in the congregations. I am the root and the offspring of David, the bright morning-star. And the Spirit and the bride say, Come! And let him, who heareth, say, Come! And let him, who thirsteth, come. And whoever will, let him take the water of life freely.

"I testify to every one, who heareth the words of the prophecy of this book, If any one shall add to these things, God will add to him the plagues written in this book: and if any one shall take away from the words of the book of this prophecy, God will take away his part from the tree of life, and out of the holy city, and from the things written in this book. He, who testifieth these things, saith, Surely I come quickly. So be it, come, O Lord Jesus!

"The grace of our Lord Jesus Christ be with all the saints." Rev. 22:6-21.

With the representation of the city, the symbols of the Apocalypse are terminated. What follows are the words of Christ. The import of these is guarded by his declaration that they are "true and faithful." There is a reality and definiteness in them, which will not admit of their being added to, or taken from. So that any attempt to fritter away their meaning, will be followed by the curses written in the book, and a loss of the blessings therein promised.

The command not to seal this prophecy, is in contrast with the close of Daniel's prophecy, which was "closed up and sealed till the time of the end," Dan. 12:9. The Apocalypse, as its name imports, being an "unveiling" of the obscurities of Daniel, the seal from the former was removed--the time of the end, in that sense, being equivalent to the last days, or the gospel dispensation.

The time was "at hand," when the great series of predicted events was to commence. As he that was unjust was to be unjust still, and he that was righteous was thus to remain, it follows that the visions therein recorded, continue down to the close of probation; and that the new earth is one of everlasting reward, wherein is to be fulfilled the promise: "Blessed are the meek; for they shall inherit the earth," Matt. 5:3.

In this connection the Saviour answers the question, which so perplexed the Pharisees: If David then call him Lord, how is he his son? Matt. 22:45. Being the Root from whence David sprang, and in his humanity David's offspring, he was both his Lord and son.

The invitation appended is one of the most endearing that it is possible to conceive of, and the threats are the most terrific. These are given for the admonition of all; and yet how many will turn away from the study of the book, which commences with a blessing on him "that readeth, and they that hear the words of this prophecy, and keep those things which are written therein," (1:3); and closes with an invitation for all to come and "take of the water of life freely." It is no mystical record, and there is nothing equivocal in its predictions. Neither is it to be fulfilled in the distant future; for "He which testifieth these things saith: Surely I come quickly." And shall not every one who loves his Lord respond, "Even so; come, Lord Jesus."

"The Church has waited long Her absent Lord to see; And still in loneliness she waits, A friendless stranger she. Age after age has gone, Sun after sun has set, And still, in weeds of widowhood, She weeps, a mourner yet."

"The whole creation groans, And waits to hear that voice That shall restore her comeliness, And make her wastes rejoice. Come, Lord, and wipe away The curse, the sin, the stain, And make this blighted world of ours Thine own fair world again. Come, then, Lord Jesus, come!"

Rev. H. A. Bonar, (Eng.)

THE OLD EARTH.

Old Mother EARTH is wan and pale, Her face is wrinkled sore; Her locks are blanched, her heart is cold, Her garments stiff with gore; With furrowed brow and dim sad eyes, With trembling steps and slow, She marks the course that first she trod Six thousand years ago!

The Earth is old, the Earth is cold, She shivers and complains; How many Winters fierce and chill Have racked her limbs with pains! Drear tempests, lightning, flood and flame Have scarred her visage so, That scarce we deem she shone so fair, Six thousand years ago!

Yet comely was the youthful Earth, And lightly tripped along To music from a starry choir, Whose sweet celestial song Through Nature's temple echoed wild, And soft as streamlets flow, Where sister spheres replied with her, Six thousand years ago!

And many happy children there Upon her breast reclined, The young Earth smiled with aspect fair, The heavens were bright and kind; The azure cope above her head In love seemed bending low, O happy was the youthful Earth, Six thousand years ago!

Alas! those children of the Earth With hate began to burn, And Murder stained her beauteous robe, And bade the young Earth mourn. And ages, heavy ages, still Have bowed with gathering woe The form of her whose life was joy, Six thousand years ago!

Old Earth! drear Earth! thy tender heart Bewails thy chosen ones; Thou look'st upon the myriad graves That hide their gathered bones; For them, by day and night, thy tears Unceasingly must flow; Death chilled the fountain-head of life Six thousand years ago!

Old Earth! old Earth! above thy head The heavens are dark and chill, The sun looks coldly on thee now, The stars shine pale and still; No more the heavenly symphonies Through listening ether flow, Which swelled upon creation's ear, Six thousand years ago!

Weep not in bitter grief, O Earth! Weep not in hopelessness! From out the heavens "a still small voice" Whispers returning peace. Thy tears are precious in the sight Of ONE who marks their flow, Who purposes of mercy formed, Six thousand years ago!

Thy days of grief are numbered all, Their sum will soon be told: The joy of youth, the smile of God, Shall bless thee as of old; Shall shed a purer, holier light Upon thy peaceful brow, Than beamed upon thy morning hour Six thousand years ago!

Thy chosen ones shall live again, A countless, tearless throng, To wake creation's voice anew, And swell the choral song. Go, Earth! go wipe thy falling tears, Forget thy heavy woe: Hope died not with thy first-born sons, Six thousand years ago!

KNICKERBOCKER.

FOOTNOTES

1 The first Advent was, according to the best-settled chronological data, about four thousand one hundred and twenty years from creation.

2 See margin of Whiting's Testament. Lord has it, "when he can be ready to sound."

3 The constitutional language was, "By the authority of the senate, and consent of the soldiers."--Gibbon, vol. I., p. 44.

4 This is given on the authority of the London Quarterly Journal of Prophecy, for 1852, p. 330, which states that the edict will be found in the "Theodosian Code, XVII. to XX."

5 "Ubi cogniti fuerint illius hesis sectatores, ne receptaculum iis quisquam in terra sua prere prumat: sed nec in venditione aut emptione aliqua cum iis omnino commercium habeatur."--Hard., vi. ii. 1597.

6 The following philological law or canon of criticism is universally admitted, and all dictionaries, grammars, and translations, are formed in accordance with it:

"Every word not specially explained or defined in a particular sense, by any standard writer of any particular age and country, is to be taken and applied in the current or commonly received signification of that country and age in which the writer lived and wrote."--Campbell.

7 This possession by demons is similar to the mode by which pretended spirits claim that they communicate through mediums. One of them, purporting to be the spirit of a departed son of Adin Ballou, in answer to the question, by his father, "Can you describe how you are able to write through a medium?" says, "I feel as though I enter into her for the time being, or as if my spirit entered into her. I am disencumbered of my spiritual form, and take hers. More than one spirit can enter the medium at once. The mediums all go into the trance by means of several spirits entering the body at one time."--Spiritual Telegraph, May 8, 1852.

8 The word is demon or demons in all the instances referred to.

9 Necromancy is derived from the Greek words nekros, dead, and mantis, a diviner. The Greek, Necromantia, is defined: "The revealing future events by communication with the dead; necromancy." And Nekromantis: "One who reveals future events by communication with the dead; a necromancer."

10 This is in the Syriac, "Until the fulness of the time of all things." Irenes says, "Till the time of the exhibition or disposal of all things;" and OEcumenius, "Till the time of all things does come to an end;" and we have the suffrage of Thesychius and Phavorinus, that "{~GREEK SMALL LETTER ALPHA WITH PSILI~}{~GREEK SMALL LETTER PI~} {~GREEK SMALL LETTER OMICRON~}{~GREEK SMALL LETTER KAPPA~}{~GREEK SMALL LETTER ALPHA~}{~GREEK SMALL LETTER TAU~}{~GREEK SMALL LETTER ALPHA WITH OXIA~} {~GREEK SMALL LETTER SIGMA~}{~GREEK SMALL LETTER TAU~}{~GREEK SMALL LETTER ALPHA~}{~GREEK SMALL LETTER SIGMA~}{~GREEK SMALL LETTER IOTA~}{~GREEK SMALL LETTER FINAL SIGMA~} is {~GREEK SMALL LETTER TAU~}{~GREEK SMALL LETTER EPSILON~}{~GREEK SMALL LETTER LAMDA~}{~GREEK SMALL LETTER EPSILON~}{~GREEK SMALL LETTER IOTA~}{~GREEK SMALL LETTER OMEGA~} {~GREEK SMALL LETTER SIGMA~}{~GREEK SMALL LETTER IOTA~}{~GREEK SMALL LETTER FINAL SIGMA~}, 'the consummation' of a thing."--Whitby.